DEATH RIGHTS

DEATH RIGHTS

Romantic Suicide, Race, and the Bounds of Liberalism

DEANNA P. KORETSKY

Cover art: *The Suicide*, Alexandre-Gabriel Decamps (French, 1803–1860), ca. 1836. Oil on canvas. The Walters Art Museum, Creative Commons.

Published by State University of New York Press, Albany

© 2021 State University of New York Press

All rights reserved

Printed in the United States of America

No part of this book may be used or reproduced in any manner whatsoever without written permission. No part of this book may be stored in a retrieval system or transmitted in any form or by any means including electronic, electrostatic, magnetic tape, mechanical, photocopying, recording, or otherwise without the prior permission in writing of the publisher.

For information, contact State University of New York Press, Albany, NY
www.sunypress.edu

Library of Congress Cataloging-in-Publication Data

Names: Koretsky, Deanna P., author.
Title: Death rights : romantic suicide, race, and the bounds of liberalism / Deanna P. Koretsky.
Description: Albany : State University of New York Press, [2021] | Includes bibliographical references.
Identifiers: LCCN 2020028028 | ISBN 9781438482897 (hardcover) | ISBN 9781438482903 (ebook)| ISBN 9781438482880 (paperback)
Subjects: LCSH: Suicide in literature. | Literature and race. | Romanticism. | Liberalism in literature. | Suicide and literature.
Classification: LCC PN56.S744 K67 2021 | DDC 809/.933548--dc23
LC record available at https://lccn.loc.gov/2020028028

10 9 8 7 6 5 4 3 2 1

For Jay. Everlong.

Contents

	Acknowledgments	ix
	Introduction	1
Chapter 1	Liberty and Death	23
Chapter 2	Chained to Life and Misery	47
Chapter 3	Writ in Water	73
Chapter 4	In Sympathy	97
Chapter 5	Marvelous Boys	117
	Notes	129
	Bibliography	169
	Index	193

Acknowledgments

I am grateful, first and foremost, to Rebecca Colesworthy, the hardest-working editor in academic publishing, and to the entire team at SUNY Press for believing in this book. I can't thank the anonymous readers enough for their generous and thorough feedback. I owe more than I could possibly express here to the trusted friends, brilliant colleagues, and supportive mentors who patiently read and commented on parts of this project when it was in various states of nonsense. You know who you are, and I know that I couldn't have done this without you.

This book has been made possible in part by a major grant from the National Endowment for the Humanities. Any views, findings, conclusions, or recommendations expressed in this book do not necessarily reflect those of the National Endowment for the Humanities. This book was also supported by a UNCF-Mellon Faculty Development Award, without which I'd probably still be writing. An early version of chapter 1 appeared previously as "Habeas Corpus and the Politics of Freedom: Slavery and Romantic Suicide" in *Essays in Romanticism* 22, no. 1 (2015): 21–33, and parts of it are reproduced with permission of the licensor through PLSclear . An early version of chapter 4 appeared as "Unhallowed Arts: *Frankenstein* and the Poetics of Suicide," in *European Romantic Review* 26, no. 2 (February 2015): 241–260, and parts of it are reproduced by permission of Taylor & Francis, Ltd.

Introduction

Each suicide is a poem sublime in its melancholy.
—Honoré de Balzac, *Le Peau de Chagrin*

Darkling I listen; and, for many a time
  I have been half in love with easeful Death.
—John Keats, "Ode to a Nightingale"

The Mind, that broods o'er guilty woes
Is like the Scorpion girt by fire;
In circle narrowing as it glows,
The flame around their captive close,
Till inly searched by thousand throes,
And maddening in her ire,
One sad and sole relief she knows –
The sting she nourished for her foes,
Whose venom never yet was vain,
Gives but one pang, and cures all pain,
And darts into her desperate brain:
So do the dark in soul expire,
Or live like Scorpion girt by fire.
—Lord Byron, *The Giaour*

Suicide is a complicated response to a broken world. The factors that motivate someone's decision to die are personal and, to a large extent, fundamentally unknowable. But cultural narratives about suicide are ours to read and weigh; they show us what it is to live in this world. This book recalls a historical moment when stories of suicide were used to rouse the racial consciousness of a nation. It is a book about why those efforts failed and how they were eroded by a cultural narrative still in circulation today—one that idealizes certain suicides in service to ideologies of white male supremacy.

In the ubiquity of sentiments such as those expressed in the epigraphs from Balzac, Keats, and Byron, we are reminded that literary romanticism characterized itself by brooding sensuality and irremediable malaise and that these strong emotions often were understood to result in suicide. Nor was interest in suicide limited to "high" literatures during this era. Toward the end of the eighteenth century, English newspapers published suicide notes (some real, others made up for shock value), while politicians debated ancient laws dictating how people who died by suicide should be buried (at crossroads, with stakes driven through their hearts—a gruesome practice finally eliminated in 1822).[1] The subject of the last epigraph, Byron's "Scorpion girt by fire," led the British ethologist C. Lloyd Morgan to conduct a series of sadistic experiments on whether animals consciously kill themselves, using scorpions as his test subjects.[2] Suicide even helped to launch the modern fashion industry: the blue and gold suit worn by the title character of Johann Wolfgang von Goethe's *The Sorrows of Young Werther* inspired one of the first ready-to-wear styles produced for mass market consumption, and a popular perfume of the day was called *Eau de Werther*.[3] With suicide being such a prominent and profitable cultural phenomenon, it is surprising that, among a recent wave of scholarship on the cultural history of suicide, not a single monograph has focused on romanticism.[4]

One reason for this may be that romanticism's role in the history of suicide seems self-evident. There is little doubt as to the relationship between romantic literature and the myth of the tortured artist—implicitly white and almost exclusively male—who is tragically undone by his own brilliance.[5] This myth remains with us even today. One especially clear example is *Savage Beauty*, the retrospective of the work of British fashion designer Alexander McQueen that opened in 2011 at the Metropolitan Museum of Art. Among the show's most widely publicized pieces were McQueen's intricately constructed coats, many of which were styled for the exhibition so as to be instantly reminiscent of romantic figures like the subject of Caspar David Friedrich's painting *The Wanderer Above the Sea of Fog*.⁶ The show also included pieces influenced by the Flemish masters, the Scottish Highlands, the Tudors, Plato's Atlantis, and others.⁷ While McQueen cited inspiration from many historical periods and subjects, the show was organized into sections titled "The Romantic Mind," "Romantic Gothic and Cabinet of Curiosities," "Romantic Nationalism," "Romantic Exoticism," "Romantic Primitivism," and "Romantic Naturalism," effectively rendering McQueen's entire corpus in terms of the aesthetic arguably most explicit in the curation and presentation of his coats. When an expanded version of the show opened at the Victoria and Albert Museum in 2015, the association between McQueen and romanticism was scaled back in its promotion, suggesting that in 2011, the heavy emphasis on romanticism was at least partly reflective of McQueen's much-discussed 2010 suicide.⁸

There are good reasons for the myth's endurance. Rendering suicide an extension of someone's art dulls the unsettling violence of the act of ending one's own life. It circumscribes its finality and quiets (however temporarily) questions that can never be answered. This, of course, is precisely the function of myth and part of why this particular myth endures so strongly: it renders the complex and inexpressible somewhat easier to grasp, if not always to accept. Romantic narratives of suicide turn worlds of private pain into something beautiful, something the public can continue to love, or at least consume. In this sense, it's not hard to see why the myth of romantic suicide still remains with us, in every public reckoning with the artist who hanged himself at the height of his success or the rock star who shot up and then shot himself. But the story we keep recirculating about these deaths—the romantic trope of lonely, tragic genius—barely scratches the surface of the lived realities that actually lead people to kill themselves. By the same token, despite its apparent ubiquity at the turn of the nineteenth century, this trope was hardly the only way in which suicide was represented during the historical moment with which it is most associated.

The Argument

Moving beyond conceptions of suicide as an index of romanticism's fascination with tragic or mad genius, *Death Rights: Romantic Suicide, Race, and the Bounds of Liberalism* reads the trope of romantic suicide within preexisting political narratives that engage suicide to index the limits of liberal subjectivity. Suicide first appeared as an explicitly political (as opposed to a psychological or emotional) theme in British abolitionist writing. This was no mere coincidence. As the following chapters discuss, it is in the institution of racialized enslavement and its afterlives that liberalism most clearly reveals itself as a system that enables freedom for some people at the expense of others. The trope of suicide was widely engaged by different political and aesthetic projects at the turn of the nineteenth century. While this was often (albeit not always) aimed toward emancipatory ends, this book will argue that these well-meaning efforts more often reflected, and functionally served to maintain, liberalism's foundational inequities. Beginning with literary portrayals of enslaved people's suicides as exemplary assertions of self-ownership, *Death Rights* examines how canonical and lesser-known writers of African and European descent combined suicide with liberal rhetorics of individualism, sovereignty, and natural rights to interrogate notions of propertied self-possession, personhood, sympathy, and the human. The texts and authors brought forward in these pages used suicide to challenge racialized logics of exclusion within a social structure based on selective claims to social legibility. However, insofar as most of these engagements turned on liberal fantasies of integration, they could articulate only fundamentally irrational solutions whereby African-identified people could, theoretically, define themselves as liberal subjects but not as free and living subjects on their own terms.

More specifically, then, this book examines how eighteenth- and nineteenth-century authors in Britain and the Atlantic world engaged the trope of suicide in ways that buttress antiblackness. They did this by rehearsing, in texts espousing emancipatory aims, what Frank B. Wilderson III identifies as the "symbiosis between the political ontology of Humanity and the social death of Blacks."[9] For Wilderson, whose work is foundational for the cadre of Afropessimist and black optimist thinkers with whom this book is also in conversation, the relation between blackness and death is a structural one—not a matter of intercultural antipathies per se but of antagonisms that constitute the very groundwork of the modern world. Wilderson understands blackness as the "position against which Humanity [i.e., the western bourgeois subject] establishes, maintains, and renews its coherence, its corporeal integrity."[10] In other words, the existence and conceptual coherence of the subject of liberal modernity hinges on black death.

Given that the enslavement of Africans, and with it the construction of "blackness" through and as ontological negation, long predates the era with which I am concerned here, it is deeply telling that one of the most popular figures to emerge from British abolitionist discourse is that of the "suicidal slave."[11] This figure appears in texts now long forgotten, such as John Gorton's *Tubal to Seba: The Negro Suicide*, and in those that remain significant, such as Aphra Behn's *Oroonoko* and William Wells Brown's *Clotel; or, the President's Daughter* (the first known novel in English by an author of African descent). In British literary studies, representations of enslaved people making the choice to die rather than remain in bondage have been widely understood as efforts to establish African-identified people's capacity to reason and, thus, the capacity to become liberal subjects deserving of rights.[12] Complicating these readings, *Death Rights* argues that when the goal is merely to expand, not to explode, the bounds of liberalism, framing the choice to die as a path to freedom only reinforces the structural antagonism between blackness and the human at the core of liberal modernity. Furthermore, *Death Rights* reads romantic suicide—the literary and critical commonplace that extols the singularity of white male genius, even in death—in direct relation to these vexed efforts to expand liberalism's racial and gendered bounds. Even today, as this book will show, the myth of romantic suicide reifies white male individualism. Thus, it is no mere coincidence that it gained in popularity just as the assumed supremacy of the bourgeois subject of liberal modernity was being called into question by abolitionist, protofeminist, and other revolutionary discourses.

Contexts

To understand how a certain narrative of suicide became romantic, we need to understand the role played by suicide in literary and cultural discourses proximate to romanticism. For some readers, no two figures will loom larger here than Thomas Chatterton, the seventeen-year-old poet who died of an arsenic overdose when he failed to achieve literary fame, and Goethe's Werther. Situated squarely within the culture of sensibility (Chatterton died in 1770, *The Sorrows of Young Werther* was published in 1774), both figures exemplify the "man of feeling" trope taken to its most taboo extreme.[13] As this book's conclusion will discuss in greater detail, Chatterton in his own day was widely dismissed as a forger and a hack, only later to be revived as an early exemplar of romanticism's "vague malaise and turbid emotions concerning love, death, and the irremediable human inability to communicate."[14] Goethe's novella, however, had a much more immediate impact.

The fictional story of the lovelorn Werther famously fed real-life concerns over the capacity of literature to sway readers to end their lives. Shortly after the novel's publication, parts of England and North America saw widespread panics over just that possibility (an idea that social scientists still refer to as "the Werther effect").[15] Goethe himself argued that the supposed suicide craze was due not to his novel but to the "earnest melancholy" considered endemic to English culture—a view popularized by George Cheyne's 1733 medical treatise, *The English Malady*, which posited that "the suicidal tendencies of the English were tied, on the one hand, to the progress of atheism and the philosophic spirit . . . and on the other, to the melancholy temperament of an island people living in unfavorable geographical and climactic conditions."[16] Recently, Kelly McGuire has suggested that the *Werther* controversy was symptomatic of a different sort of crisis in English national identity. The true threat, McGuire posits, was not suicide as such but rather the "contagion" of foreign influences on an overly sensitive reading public.[17] Indeed, as this book will suggest, when British stories of suicide center an English man (e.g., Chatterton), the motif functions to close the social field not only to foreign influences abroad but also to those already marginalized within England's borders by (re)emphasizing notions of white male "greatness."

Even in the ostensibly apolitical hands of these sad white men, literary suicide is necessarily political insofar as it extends from earlier debates that framed self-killing in relation to individualism, property, and other core tenets of liberal modernity. Eighteenth-century debates about suicide drew heavily from the discourses of natural rights, freedoms, and entitlements that would also animate the French, American, and Haitian revolutions, the abolitionist movement, and early agitation for white women's rights.[18] Historians of suicide have long held to the general thesis that loosening religious strictures led to more open discussions about voluntary death in general, which in turn laid the groundwork for drawing on the idea of killing the self in more abstractly political arguments. Michael McDonald and Terrance R. Murphy neatly summarize this evolution of European thought on suicide:

> Ancient philosophies that condoned and in some circumstances celebrated suicide gave way in the Middle Ages to theological condemnations and folkloric abhorrence. The Reformation intensified religious hostility to self-murder in England and some other European countries. Finally, in the eighteenth century, Enlightenment philosophy and the secularization of the world-view of European elites prompted writers to depict suicide as the consequence of mental illness or of rational choice, and these concepts still dominate discussions of self-destruction today.[19]

Prosuicide arguments emphasized the idea that people are born free and have the right to live and die as they choose. While nearly every major European thinker of the eighteenth and nineteenth centuries weighed in on the suicide debates, David Hume's essay "On Suicide" tends to be singled out by scholars today as the text that made the subject of suicide modern—that is, "secularized, decriminalized, medicalized."[20]

"On Suicide" was published and almost immediately pulled in 1756, not to be made available again until 1777, a year after the author's death. In that brief essay, Hume connects suicide to liberalism's pillars of reason, free will, and individual rights—that is, an individual's right to choose when and how he dies. First, Hume posits that every man possesses "the free disposal of his own life" and may "lawfully employ that power" because "Providence" or "the Almighty" designed it that way.[21] Flying in the face of centuries of religious dogma, Hume effectively suggests that suicide is divinely sanctioned: if "nothing happens in the universe without its consent and cooperation . . . then neither does my death, however voluntary."[22] Next, Hume considers whether suicide adversely impacts society and determines that it does not because "a man who retires from life does no harm to society: he only ceases to do good."[23] Likewise, when he becomes a drain on society, his "resignation of life must not only be innocent, but laudable."[24] Hume reckons that people who consider or complete suicide must fall into one of these categories because "those who have health, or power, or authority, have commonly better reason to be in humor with the world."[25] Finally, Hume posits that suicide can, in some cases, fulfill one's duty to oneself: "age, sickness, or misfortune, may render life a burden, and make it worse even than annihilation. I believe that no man ever threw away life while it was worth keeping."[26] What prevents people from killing themselves, Hume concludes, is the fear of death itself, and when someone takes it upon himself to conquer that fear, he is entitled to noninterference. And others have a duty to get out of his way.

Within the liberal framework in which he meant it, Hume's oft-quoted assertion that "no man ever threw away life while it was worth keeping" affirms the power of the individual will over state (if not also divine) sovereignty. Certainly, this is the sense in which abolitionist, protofeminist, and other "radical" liberal thinkers would engage the idea of suicide later in the eighteenth century. Implicitly left out of Hume's framework, however, are those people denied full ownership over their lives by the social structures of liberal modernity, including enslaved Africans, dispossessed indigenes, non-Christians, white women, the poor, and the list goes on. In different ways, these and other groups stand in opposition to "Man," the representative subject of liberal modernity that, as Sylvia Wynter puts it, "overrepresents itself as if it were the human itself."[27]

For Hume, as for many European thinkers credited with shaping the modern world, enslaved Africans represent the absolute limit point against which "Man" defines itself. Hume makes this apparent in the infamously racist footnote he added to his essay "Of National Characters" in 1753. In the first iteration of the footnote, Hume claims that "the negroes and in general all other species of men (for there are four or five different kinds) to be naturally inferior to whites. There never was a civilized nation of any other complexion than white, nor even any individual eminent either in action or speculation." Though he begins by measuring whiteness against all nonwhite people, the remainder of the statement clarifies his specific target:

> Not to mention our colonies, there are NEGROE slaves dispersed all over EUROPE, of which none ever discovered any symptoms of ingenuity; tho' low people, without education, will start up amongst us, and distinguish themselves in every profession. In JAMAICA, indeed, they talk of one negroe man of parts and learning; but 'tis likely he is admired for very slender accomplishments, like a parrot, who speaks a few words plainly.[28]

John Immerwahr has underscored the significance of Hume's sustained attention to the footnote, noting that the revisions he made to it while preparing the final edition of his works (the same 1777 edition in which "On Suicide" would reappear) indicate "that Hume's racism was deliberate rather than casual."[29] Namely, Hume "changed the target of his attack; the revised argument is directed only at blacks, rather than against all non-whites."[30] Challenging some scholars' efforts to dismiss these comments as incidental, Immerwahr rightly maintains that Hume's revision process shows that he "did seriously consider objections to his racist position. His response, however, was to sharpen his attack on blacks further. His racism should thus be read as something he was willing to defend, rather than an offhand remark."[31] And, as Henry Louis Gates Jr. reminds us, this matters a great deal for our understanding of the foundations of the modern world because "Hume's opinion on the subject ... became prescriptive."[32]

Understood in tandem with his antiblackness, Hume's essay on suicide highlights how liberal modernity constitutes itself through exclusion. More precisely, it demonstrates how black being and social standing in the world is positioned as the negative to the liberal subject's positive claims to the same. In this frame, Hume's pronouncement that "no man ever threw away life while it was worth keeping" contains within it an unheard question about whose life is worth keeping, and moreover, what it means to "keep" life in the first place—one's own life or someone else's. Here, the philosophical gambit that the decision to die represents the apotheosis of individual liberty reveals its limits. That logic presumes an autonomous subject whose coherence as such is marked against those classified as nonsubjects. In contradistinction to that subject's presumed entitlement to keep or destroy his life, the nonsubject's political, social, and physical existence is indexed as not her own, a kind of non- or not-quite life—"worth keeping," perhaps, but only as determined by someone else. Thus, Hume's essay implicitly forecloses the very liberation efforts to which its central idea would later be applied.

This proviso, implied in "On Suicide," is more apparent in Hume's footnote, which clearly reveals how liberal modernity fixes the racialization of black people in terms of nonbeing, even in relation to other minoritized groups. As an analytical framework, Afropessimism helps us to understand how "Black death is subtended by the psychic integration of everyone who is not Black."[33] It also exposes what Wilderson calls the ruse of analogy: the fiction that black suffering can be analogized to other structures of violent exclusion and oppression. Thus, as he explains in his foundational work, *Red, White and Black*, the racialization of people of African descent and of indigenous peoples in North America are variously underwritten by literal and metaphysical relations to death. Europeans rendered Africans "black" through ontological negation for the purpose of extrapolating the labor power of their bodies. Indigenous peoples in North America were made "red" through genocides that facilitated Europeans' expropriation of their lands. However, without denying the historical events of genocide and dispossession, Wilderson maintains that as a structuring modality, the "red" position remains "ontologically possible... half-alive" through, among other things, the discourse of sovereignty.[34] By contrast, the nonontology of blackness is absolute:

> Chattel slavery did not simply reterritorialize the ontology of the African. It also created the Human out of culturally disparate entities from Europe and the East.... The race of Humanism (White, Asian, South Asian, and Arab) could not have produced itself without the simultaneous production of that walking destruction which became

known as the Black. Put another way, through chattel slavery the world gave birth and coherence to both its joys of domesticity and to its struggles of political discontent; and with these joys and struggles, the Human was born, but not before it murdered the Black, forging a symbiosis between the political ontology of Humanity and the social death of Blacks.[35]

It is worth pausing here to acknowledge that this framework has serious limits. Iyko Day stresses that Afropessimist accounts put forward by Wilderson and Jared Sexton lean too heavily on notions of indigenous sovereignty that turn on recognition by the liberal state.[36] Along similar lines, Mark Rifkin contends that the two positions belong to fundamentally "disparate political imaginaries and trajectories," not least because the varied, culturally specific models of indigenous sovereignty are often at odds with the emphasis on (social) death and/ as political nonbeing in black radical discourses like Afropessimism.[37] Afropessimism's insistence on social death as the condition of possibility for black life has also been notably recalibrated by Fred Moten, whose answer to Afropessimism, black optimism, emphasizes the deathliness of liberal modernity itself. Discussed more fully in this book's third chapter, Moten posits that social death is "the field of the political . . . the fundamentally and essentially antisocial nursery for a necessarily necropolitical imitation of life."[38] In response to Moten, Sexton insists that "nothing in afro-pessimism suggests that there is no black (social) life, only that black life is not social life in the universe formed by the codes of state and civil society, of citizen and subject, of nation and culture, of people and place, of history and heritage . . . Black life is not lived in the world that the world lives in."[39] Likewise, Christina Sharpe, whose *In the Wake* resonates, in certain ways, with both Afropessimism and black optimism, demonstrates how "Black life [is] lived in, as, under, despite Black death" in multivalent ways that are irreducible to Eurocentric frameworks of sociality.[40]

That irreducibility is precisely what makes Afropessimism, black optimism, and related discourses that variously seek to demystify liberal modernity's dependence on black (social) death relevant to this study. If black life turns on what Moten calls "an always already imposed and interdicted 'right to death,'" it does so in ways that are thoroughly at odds with—and thus reveal the limits of—Hume's assertion of that right for "Man" and subsequent liberal revolutionaries' appropriations of that right for those excluded from that category, including enslaved Africans.[41] In this frame, to posit enslaved Africans' suicides as emancipatory is oxymoronic. The dead don't get free by dying. Rather, as Saidiya Hartman contends, what may appear to be an act of self-destruction is, in fact, "a radical refusal of the terms of the social order," an embrace of forms of life that can only be lived in spaces of death, inaccessible through (or, indeed, to) the liberal imaginary.[42] As a result, attempts by well-meaning liberals to appropriate Hume's formulation in order to highlight the wrongs of enslaving people of African descent presents a classic case—which is to say, an inevitable failure—of using the master's tools to dismantle his house.[43] The liberal trope of the "suicidal slave" forecloses the possibility of black life within and beyond the bounds of liberalism, rendering the suicidal figure really a murdered one.

And while historical cases of African-identified people choosing death over bondage certainly underline the brutality of enslavement, so too do the actions of those maintaining and profiting from the institution, and these are often obscured in literary efforts to build a case for abolition through the liberal argument for suicide. Sentimental depictions of black people dying by suicide diminish white culpability. In most cases, they write white people out of the picture completely (except, as we'll see, those who can be made into sympathetic avatars for white readers). Such representations feed the delusion that what's at stake is, in Wilderson's terms, conflictual rather than structural—that antiblackness can be overcome by facilitating African-identified people's entry into liberal society. But the point is that antiblackness is not an event that can be overcome. It is a structural foundation of the modern world. Thus, as Wilderson puts it, "The imaginary of the state and civil society is parasitic on the Middle Passage."[44] Extending the scope of the metaphor, Sharpe reminds us that "we are all positioned by the wake [of the slave ship], but positioned differently."[45] What is needed, then, is the wholesale destruction of "Man"—not the self-destruction of individual women or men—to move toward anything that might approximate liberation.

Methods

It is worth pausing here to explain my methodological foundation, with which readers situated in eighteenth- and nineteenth-century British literary studies may be unfamiliar. With some recent exceptions, these fields have historically authorized and have been authorized by epistemic and institutional structures grounded in liberal humanism, including the liberal arts and the neoliberal university.[46] These are some of the givens through and toward which Eurocentric humanistic knowledges continue to be produced. Discussions of race in these fields, especially in romantic literary studies (where I am primarily situated), have tended to be subordinated to or subsumed by discussions of enslavement or colonialism. As a result, much of the work on romanticism's relationship to the subject—and subjects—of African enslavement reads black histories and black lives through white critical lenses. In Marlon Ross's assessment, this is because to substantively foreground race in historically white fields requires confronting certain discomfiting truths: "No one wants to seem so vulgar as to call romantic writers racists."[47] Ross notes that much of the work on "race" (i.e., enslavement and/or colonialism) in romantic literary studies has avoided implicating romanticism as such, except where canonical writers can be praised for antislavery sentiments or abolitionist efforts. Thus, even as the field's interest in the historical construction of modern racial categories has grown in recent years, in its critical practices, it has largely avoided or actively precluded the necessary methodological transformations that must attend rigorous engagement with antiracist thought and action.

Notably, this is not the case in all areas of literary studies.[48] In romanticism, this discrepancy can be understood, at least in part, as a function of the field's peculiar relationship to western academia relative to other areas of literary and cultural studies. As Manu Samriti Chander has keenly observed, "Romanticism survived the culture wars unscathed."[49] This is not to say, as Chander acknowledges, that the social upheavals at the end of the last century had no effect on the study of romanticism. Without a doubt, one of the most profound and significant interventions in the history of romanticist scholarship was the expansion of the field to include (white) women writers. But attending to gender is not the same as attending to race, not least because evidence of "gender," however one defines or engages that concept, can be recovered in ways that evidence of "race" cannot. And thus Chander, like Ross, registers a largely unexamined privilege that runs through much scholarly work in the field—the luxury not to see race and the choice, conscious or unconscious, not to address it.

Indeed, as Bakary Diaby reminds us, efforts to bring race to the forefront of romantic literary studies have a long—and long-forgotten—history. In 1942, Eva Beatrice Dykes, the first African American woman to complete the requirements for a doctoral degree in the United States, published *The Negro in British Romantic Thought*. Written well before the interventions of feminist, postcolonial, or critical race theory, Dykes's work situates canonical romantic writers' engagements with the topic of African enslavement against texts by lesser-known British writers, including many white women whose "recovery" in the field is credited to white feminist scholars working later in the twentieth century. In so doing, Dykes highlights a related problem in historically white fields such as ours: the tendency to assume that "race" signals only nonwhiteness. We don't just encounter "race" because, for example, the subjects of antislavery texts are black; we also encounter "race" when the writers we study are white. In their efforts to represent blackness, white writers tell us a lot about the privileges and blind spots of whiteness—blind spots too often reproduced or insufficiently interrogated in our scholarship. Dykes's work underscores the urgency of recognizing and naming these forms of discursive violence, even as she decries the fact that romanticism's investment in antislavery efforts (which, she emphasizes, cannot be divorced from its antiblackness) is not more widely discussed: "Almost all the well-known writers of the eighteenth and early nineteenth centuries wrote against slavery; yet they are remembered by the general student of English literature not for their anti-slavery utterances but for their conforming more or less to those principles of writing which make their works take place among the classics of English literature."[50] Ultimately, as Diaby points out, Dykes recenters the canon, "ask[ing] us to believe that Romanticism can revolve around the lowly and the oppressed; that, at its best, Romanticism is a field of study intimately tied to the vulnerable."[51] Even so, in her insistence that "many of these writers were not prompted by any consideration of social equality for the Negro," Dykes challenges us to read against the grain of the self-professed emancipatory aims of many of the era's best-known texts and authors.[52] As this book will highlight, many of these texts exemplify how racism reproduces itself in discourses where we might expect to see it challenged.

Nearly a century since Dykes's groundbreaking work, and more than a generation after critical race, ethnic, and feminist studies were institutionalized in university curricula, it should go without saying that romanticism as a field of knowledge organized within the broader disciplinary construction of English literature is deeply rooted in racism in its most fundamental sense: "When a racial group's collective prejudice is backed by the power of . . . institutional control, it is transformed into racism, a far-reaching system that functions independently of the intentions or self-images of institutional actors."[53] In the imperial mission to "civilize" the world through domination and exploitation, British colonizers and enslavers enabled a knowledge economy that continues to reproduce ideologies of whiteness as the universal ideal and transparent default by way of (among other tools) literary education.

Gauri Viswanathan has shown that "as early as the 1820s, when the classical curriculum still reigned supreme in England... English as the study of culture and not just language had already found a secure place in the British Indian curriculum."[54] Building on this work, Chander has demonstrated how, in negotiating their relationship to colonial curricula, Indian intellectuals effectively consolidated one of the first canons of what we now recognize to be British romanticism.[55] When versions of this canon moved to England later in the nineteenth century, they came first, as Terry Eagleton has shown, to Mechanics' Institutes as a way of "providing a cheapish 'liberal' education for those beyond the charmed circles of public school and Oxbridge."[56] Long before romanticism was emblematic of bourgeois sophistication, it was "literally the poor man's Classics."[57] And while it has evolved, in some ways, beyond these roots in ideological apparatuses used to educate but not to equalize, the study of romanticism remains, as Paul Youngquist puts it, "oblivious to its whiteness."[58]

A word about my usage of the term "romanticism." I engage "romantic" and "romanticism" here in the most conventional sense, referring to the cadre of European poets and artists who turned against empiricism toward the epistemological efficacies of emotion, saw in the volatility of the natural world an answer to what they considered restrictive within their highly ordered societies, and took seriously the possibilities opened by idealism to counteract absolutism. While I can appreciate the intent of recent efforts to claim these characteristics toward more "inclusive" narratives of the historical era against which it developed, I maintain that the term itself is inextricable from the bourgeois white male individualism with which it has been most closely associated.[59] When speaking of the era in and against which romanticism developed, this book aims to highlight the period's cacophony of political, moral, and aesthetic ideologies—conflicts and antagonisms too often flattened by framing the period through romanticism (i.e., "the romantic era") because of that term's loaded relationship to bourgeois white male individualism. Romanticism, then, is treated here not as the defining discourse of an age but as one of many interconnected responses to social transformations that occurred between the rise of the abolition debates in the 1770s and the emancipation of enslaved people of African descent in Britain's colonies in the 1830s.

A word, too, about the term "whiteness," which refers not to ethnic or cultural identity but to the dominant institutions that socialize all of us into habits, attitudes, and value systems that enable the unequal distribution of cultural and financial capital and power. Whiteness, in this sense, is not reducible to skin color, even as the privileges associated with being read as white stem from racial hierarchies developed, in no small part, during the era many of us associate with romanticism. Because it is socially constructed, whiteness is fluid (who and what gets considered white changes over time), relational (it cannot exist without those against whom it defines itself), and turns on invisibility (those who benefit most from it usually do not see it).[60] Moreover, whiteness cannot be disarticulated from other instruments of oppression, including patriarchy.[61] In this sense, whiteness is really "white manness," or what Sara Ahmed discusses using the shorthand "white men": "When we talk of white men, we are describing an institution . . . a persistent structure or mechanism of social order governing the behavior of a set of individuals within a given community." This encompasses not only "what has already been instituted or built but the mechanisms that ensure the persistence of that structure."[62] Regardless of who we are or understand ourselves to be as individuals, scholars of romanticism in its current configuration are all white men, which is to say, we work in a field that was not only built around white bodies and sustained through white critical perspectives but that has explicitly and deliberately been used to maintain fictions of whiteness as transparent and thus universal ever since romantic literatures were introduced into school and university curricula. We cannot begin to think seriously about "race" in this field without naming whiteness as part of that discussion. However, it must be said that making whiteness visible as a category of analysis within the larger purview of "race" in romantic studies is only a small step toward unsettling "the production and perpetuation of [romanticism's] blank authority."[63]

That authority, I will argue here, is closely bound up with the myth of romantic suicide. Even as the canon as such was established around them, British romantic writers were intentional about how future generations would receive them. Instrumental to their efforts was the idea of creative genius that so thoroughly underpins the myth of romantic suicide. Andrew Bennett has shown how the romantic authors we inherit as canonical actively constructed their literary reputations in order to make themselves indispensable to their own and future generations. By making the white male "genius" into an aesthetic ideal, they effectively created the criteria through which they would achieve literary immortality. Their attention to posterity, according to Bennett, was intimately tied to "the crucial possibility that the death of the writer will, in itself, produce an effect on the survivors."[64] This was achieved, in part, by seizing on the idea of Chatterton. Through effusive affirmations of Chatterton's poetry, coupled with public self-identifications with the poet, many of our most canonical romantic writers elevated a now-familiar set of ideas about the relationship between genius and suicide as part of a strategy to fix their own posthumous fame.[65] In so doing, they also ensured the canon's epistemic homogeneity, creating inherently ethnocentric standards of supposedly universal taste.

Romantic suicide, then, is necessarily implicated in modernity's racial consciousness, even as it presents itself as apolitical and thus unrelated. Romantic suicide purports to turn our gaze to private suffering, but in highlighting the "genius" of representative white men, it reveals itself to be essentially political. In 1830, Victor Hugo celebrated romanticism as "liberalism in literature."[66] To a certain sensibility, liberalism held—and still does hold—the promise that all those whom it acknowledges as worthy can freely pursue individualistic goals. The primary texts and authors discussed in this book sought to call attention to liberalism's racial exclusions in order to reimagine and expand its boundaries. However, despite some recent arguments to the contrary, this book maintains that liberalism cannot be transformed to meaningfully serve the interests of those it holds as its "others."[67] Thus, *Death Rights* is oriented beyond it.

I am guided in this orientation by the work of, among others, Fran Botkin, Bakary Diaby, Jared Hickman, Atesede Makonnen, Patricia A. Matthew, Joel Pace, Marlon Ross, Matt Sandler, Rebecca Schneider, and Paul Youngquist. Each of these thinkers, in their own uniquely different ways, engages with critical modalities developed by scholars in black studies to read romanticism. Black studies and romantic literary studies are relevant to one another insofar as both fields are centrally concerned with many of the same historical events (e.g., the revolutions in America, France, and Haiti) and theorize many of the same issues (e.g., social transformation, freedom, human dignity). Dwight McBride has suggested that conversations between these fields should be undertaken in the interest of foregrounding the relationship between literary romanticism and the development of modern racial politics in the historical backdrop against which it unfolded. McBride asserts that such a practice of reading across academic disciplines and cultures would require scholars of romanticism to substantially expand how we understand the relevance of blackness to our knowledge of the early nineteenth century—that is, to move beyond noting "the appearance of traditional Romantic tropes in Black-authored texts."[68] Nor should such a practice be seen as purely in the service of contextualizing texts written by black authors. Rather, it can enable scholars across subdisciplines of literary and cultural studies to understand romanticism not only as an artistic watershed in European cultural history but as a set of discourses that have substantially shaped (and been shaped by) modern racial thinking. Moreover, it can enable romanticists to move beyond historicizing enslavement and colonialism toward rigorous interrogations of romanticism's role in producing—not merely reflecting—the antiblack logics of liberal modernity.

While many of the critical frameworks I engage in this book emerge from the study of enslavement and racialization in the United States, their theoretical elucidations of "blackness" and "the west" as complex transnational phenomena offer indispensable counternarratives to how scholars of, for example, eighteenth- and nineteenth-century Britain have understood modernity's discourses of death, freedom, and the particular relevance of suicide to both. As Moten reminds us, "what is called Western civilization is the object of black studies" just as surely as "blackness . . . is not but nothing other than Western civilization."[69] However, though romanticism and black studies can both be said to originate, in some way, in the eighteenth century, their epistemic orientations are fundamentally different and those differences should not be elided. Black studies, as Alexander Weheliye explains, "works toward the abolition of Man, and advocates the radical reconstruction and decolonization of what it means to be human . . . [thereby pursuing] a politics of global liberation beyond the genocidal shackles of Man."[70] By contrast, "Man" is the condition of possibility for the study of romanticism and, as I will show, romantic ideas continue to circulate in service to its attendant ideologies. In bringing romanticism into conversation with black studies, my goal is not to locate points of commonality but rather to attend rigorously and ethically to their frictions.[71]

Nowhere are these frictions more pronounced than in each field's relationship to liberalism. On one hand, even as individual romantic writers varied in their views on liberal politics and institutions, as a field of study, romanticism's epistemic grounding in liberal principles is often taken for granted as part of its engagement with the era's revolutionary ideologies.[72] Where scholarship on gender, class, disability, enslavement, and empire has brought much-needed nuance to the study of romanticism, as I note above, much less has been made of the role played by race, both within and beyond the black/nonblack binary. Black studies, by contrast, has been at the forefront of ongoing reassessments of liberalism. As Hartman elucidates in *Scenes of Subjection*,

> Liberalism, in general, and rights discourse, in particular, assure entitlements and privileges as they enable and efface elemental forms of domination primarily because of the atomistic portrayal

of social relations, the inability to address collective interests and needs, and the sanctioning of subordination and the free reign of prejudice in the construction of the social or the private. Moreover, the universality or unencumbered individuality of liberalism relies on tacit exclusions and norms that preclude substantive equality; all do not equally partake of the resplendent, plenipotent, indivisible, and steely singularity that it proffers. Abstract universality presumes particular forms of embodiment and excludes or marginalizes others. Rather, the excluded, marginalized, and devalued subjects that it engenders, variously contained, trapped, and imprisoned by nature's whimsical appointments, in fact, enable the production of universality, for the denigrated and deprecated, those castigated and saddled by varied corporeal maledictions, are the fleshy substance that enable the universal to achieve its ethereal splendor.[73]

Along similar lines, Charles W. Mills has shown how liberalism turns on a "racial contract" whereby the political ontology of the rights-bearing subject is buttressed by the state-sanctioned exclusion of racialized nonsubjects. While this is theoretically also true of those excluded through social logics other than racialization (e.g., white women), in practice, whiteness offers proximity to hegemonic power structures that remain inaccessible to racialized peoples. As a result, liberalism "has historically been predominantly a racial liberalism, in which conceptions of personhood and resulting schedules of rights, duties, and government responsibilities have all been racialized. And the [social] contract, correspondingly, has really been a racial one, an agreement among white contractors to subordinate and exploit nonwhite noncontractors for white benefit."[74] Thus, if literary romanticism developed at least partly as a set of engagements with liberal discourses of universal rights and freedoms, then taking seriously liberalism's foundational exclusions should fundamentally alter our understanding of and approaches to those engagements. By overlooking or minimizing the relevance of these exclusions, the study of romanticism effectively reproduces them.

Death Rights reads romanticism as part and parcel of the legal and philosophical discourses that underwrite liberal modernity's antiblack foundations. In this frame, I argue that the trope of romantic suicide (re)inscribes the rights, entitlements, and freedoms promised by liberalism as the exclusive province of white men. In romantic suicide, the choice to die represents neither a critique of an unlivable society nor even a sign of mental illness but instead suggests that a particular sort of "genius" transcends the material conditions and political ontologies that variously delimit everyone else's lived realities. Romantic suicide obscures structural inequities that can render some realities unlivable. Moreover, it stymies our capacity to recognize forms of social life that exist outside of hegemonic conceptions of "human being." Addressing this requires an epistemic reorientation, accessed here through careful engagements with critical modalities developed in black studies including, but not limited to, Afropessimism and black optimism. Ultimately, this book endeavors to ask what the study of romanticism stands to gain from embracing intellectual traditions that challenge epistemologies rooted in liberalism—and whether it offers them anything in return. But let me be clear: this is not about "solidarity" nor about opening the field to be more "inclusive." Opening historically Eurocentric fields to perspectives they have implicitly or explicitly marginalized does not address the underlying assumptions driving those fields' disciplinary formations. Consequently, this book is about complicity. It is about what, if anything, remains ethically possible.

Death Rights joins a growing movement to reorient romanticism's conventional self-definitions and confront structural racism in British literature and literary studies more broadly.[75] Making every effort not to elide foundational differences, I have tried to make connections while attending carefully to my positionality and speaking *with* and *to*—not *as* or *for*—positionalities that are not my own. The questions I raise in these pages are, I believe, the questions that will define the next generation of romanticist scholarship: On what foundations has our field been built? Toward what ends does it currently exist? How can we read these literatures ethically, attending honestly and rigorously to their internal contradictions rather than relegating those contradictions to the margins or worse, never becoming aware of them at all? If these questions unsettle some readers, that is testament to how urgently they need to be asked.

Chapters

The chapters that follow underline the absurdity of using the self-destruction of black bodies to advocate for the liberation of black people. This is not to minimize the important social transformations achieved by abolitionist and women's rights campaigns at the turn of the nineteenth century but to highlight the limitations of revising, rather than eradicating, the antiblack logics embedded in the structures those movements ostensibly sought to dismantle. The first three chapters examine how white abolitionists, early liberal feminists, and Afrodiasporic writers engaged the trope of suicide in different ways to negotiate liberal discourses of rights and freedoms. Chapters 4 and 5 are more speculative explorations of these ideas in practice, both historically and in the present day.

"Liberty and Death" traces how the idea of suicide enters liberal political discourses in England within broader discussions of the relationship between property, legal personhood, and individual freedom. This chapter reads Thomas Day and John Bicknell's 1773 abolitionist poem, *The Dying Negro*, as a reimagining of the 1772 ruling in *Somerset v. Stewart*, a decision that freed one man but did not extend to all enslaved people. Day and Bicknell replace the promise that some saw in that legal victory with an act of suicide, thus highlighting a fundamental aporia in the logic of classical liberalism found explicitly in John Locke's inability to reconcile enslavement with suicide in his *Second Treatise of Government*. Reading Locke alongside and against the legal principle on which Somerset was actually freed, the writ of habeas corpus, the chapter shows that *The Dying Negro* is not finally committed to the freedom or personhood of enslaved Africans at all. Rather, the poem capitalizes on its readers' interests in more general questions about the nature of Britons' freedoms, brought forward in public responses to the Somerset trial.

"Chained to Life and Misery" extends the scope of the inquiry to white women's negotiations of liberalism's racial logics for their own emancipatory ends. This chapter considers white women's racialized representations of suicide in early calls for (white) women's rights. In contradistinction to abolitionist representations of black, typically male figures choosing death to "prove" African-identified people's capacity to reason, in the hands of white women writers, nonwhite women's self-annihilation is tied to excessive emotionality and the inability to reason. Foregrounding the racism characteristic of the era's gendered discourses of feeling, this chapter observes how suicide operates to sublimate white supremacist logics in works by Mary Wollstonecraft, Mary Robinson, Claire de Duras, and Felicia Hemans. The chapter concludes with a reading of *The Story of Mattie J. Jackson*, an autobiography by a formerly enslaved woman that registers and challenges, at the level of form, the long reach of these discursive patterns of liberal feminist antiblackness.

"Writ in Water" extends the discussion of black life writing by considering how *The Interesting Narrative of the Life of Olaudah Equiano* likewise challenges European tropes associated with enslaved Africans' suicides. Calling into question the era's social and scientific theories of race as they undergirded liberal definitions of personhood and, more broadly, the human, Equiano uses suicide to develop an alternative imaginative space for black social existence. His radical (re)vision of black life is precisely not beholden to the bounds of liberalism, relying on a relational rather than an individualistic frame. This chapter concludes by reading the trope of tragic romantic genius, as developed in the poetry of John Keats, through the understanding of suicide put forth by Equiano.

"In Sympathy" considers how the treatments of suicide discussed in the first three chapters are synthesized and mobilized in Mary Shelley's *Frankenstein*. Incorporating philosophical essays on sympathy by Percy Shelley, Wollstonecraft's framing of suicide as a form of feminist protest, and Mary Shelley's personal experiences with suicide, this chapter argues that *Frankenstein* works to grapple with how liberalism frames suicide in two competing ways: on the one hand, Shelley treats suicide as the apotheosis of liberal subjecthood and on the other, marks self-destruction as the logical end to which nonsubjects like the creature are driven. The chapter concludes by reading Victor LaValle's *Destroyer*, a modern-day sequel of sorts to *Frankenstein*, as reflective of the limitations of engaging liberalism to imagine black freedom.

Finally, "Marvelous Boys" returns to where this book began: the popular and critical commonplace of romantic suicide. Theorizing its mythic structure and ideological function, this chapter demonstrates how romantic suicide reproduces fantasies of the posterity and invulnerability, even in death, of bourgeois white masculinity. Moreover, it argues that the deification of white male solipsism has served to reproduce an isolationist and exclusionary status quo. Through broad readings ranging from the Victorian afterlife of Thomas Chatterton to Kurt Cobain's resurgence in hip-hop, this chapter argues that the singular genius implied in the myth of romantic suicide has really been a representative man—an ideological symbol through which liberalism's social, epistemic, and ontological frameworks are reaffirmed, and threats to their cohesion are evacuated.

Though *Death Rights* happens to be the first book-length study of suicide during the period traditionally associated with British romanticism, this is not a comprehensive study of romantic representations of self-destruction. It is, rather, a work of cultural criticism that traces how ideas about suicide were mobilized to challenge liberal modernity's organizing structures of antiblackness even as they reinscribed them. While the authors discussed in these pages devote a great deal of narrative energy to death, most express a desire to change the world, not to leave it. There is no transcendental embrace of the sublime melancholy of oblivion and no fetishistic attraction to suicide as a means of securing literary immortality. These authors look outward and confront a broken world. And while I argue that suicide was always an ironic, failed cipher of liberalism's (im)possibilities of inclusion, I insist that there is value in understanding the nature of these failures. That they have been overwritten in our collective memory by a reverential ideal of bourgeois masculinity exemplifies how white supremacist logics reproduce themselves by seizing on the very discourses meant to challenge them.

chapter 1

Liberty and Death

> Go pine in want and anguish and despair,
> There is no mercy found in human-kind—
> Go Widow to thy grave and rest thee there!
> But may the God of Justice bid the wind
> Whelm that curst bark beneath the mountain wave,
> And bless with Liberty and Death the Slave!
> —Robert Southey, from *Poems Concerning the Slave Trade*

Before Werther was Europe's most fashionable ideal and Chatterton was immortalized as the romantic suicide par excellence, British society was captivated by another suicide—that of "a black [man] who shot himself on board a vessel in the river Thames," the protagonist and speaker of Thomas Day and John Bicknell's abolitionist poem, *The Dying Negro*.[1] First published in 1773 and revised five times over the course of the next two decades, *The Dying Negro* was among England's best-known abolitionist poems. According to the authors' prefatory note, the poem was "occasioned by an article of news" that discussed an enslaved man who left his captors and was baptized in preparation for marrying a white woman. Before the wedding could take place, he was kidnapped and detained aboard a docked slave ship set to sail for the Americas. Refusing to be forced back into bondage, he "took an opportunity of shooting himself through the head."[2] This framing narrative closely recalls the circumstances that led to the 1772 trial of *Somerset v. Stewart*, a landmark case in the history of human rights law, which Day and Bicknell evoke with one key difference: James Somerset obtained freedom through legal maneuvering, while the speaker of *The Dying Negro* chose to die for it.

This chapter reads Day and Bicknell's poem as a reassessment of the legal grounds on which the Somerset trial was decided—specifically, Somerset's successful appeal for a writ of habeas corpus. Habeas corpus, an injunction that protects against illegal detainment, gained special status in the eighteenth century as a legislative tool central to protecting the rights and freedoms of liberal subjects. Perhaps more than any other legal construct, habeas corpus turns on the interdependence of liberal modernity's pillars of personhood, property, and freedom: as Paul Halliday writes, "Ideas about liberties running through the writ of habeas corpus marked out an astonishingly vast subjecthood [such that] liberties came from subject status and thus from those parts of law that defined who were subjects."[3] By replacing the victory that granted Somerset some degree of legal standing with an act of self-destruction, Day and Bicknell introduce an important and far-reaching idea into eighteenth-century suicide debates, framing the choice to die not in terms of insanity or criminality but as a sign of one's capacity to reason—and with it, one's suitability for inclusion in liberal society. More specifically, Day and Bicknell present the speaker's capacity to reason as evidence of African-identified people's suitability for inclusion in liberal modernity's covenant of personhood. But, crucially, they are only able to argue this by turning the ontological relation between blackness and death into an occasion for bolstering the social structures that compel that relation in the first place.

The politics of hyperliteralizing black death—of responding to it only at the level of individual events rather than as a structure—has been undertheorized in studies of British abolitionist literatures. Part of the reason for this stems from the liberal grounding of scholarly pursuits, especially as undertaken in this and other historically white fields. As Frank Wilderson suggests, "If the Black is death personified, the White is the personification of ... life itself ... White academics' disavowal of Black death as modernity's condition of possibility [bespeaks] their inability to imagine their productive subjectivity as an effect of the Negro."[4] This chapter situates Day and Bicknell's intervention in the habeas corpus debates of the late eighteenth century within critical frameworks that center blackness, namely Alexander Weheliye's concept of *habeas viscus*. Weheliye invents the term *habeas viscus* to disarticulate liberal politico-ontological categories from both the specific problem of establishing black social legibility within restrictive notions of "social life" in western modernity and the much more expansive project of acknowledging and accommodating all forms of human being.

The sections that follow establish the historical relation between habeas corpus and liberal subjectivity and then turn to how Day and Bicknell engage suicide to draw attention to paradoxes at the core of liberalism, which are traced here to John Locke's inability to reconcile slavery with suicide in his *Second Treatise of Government*. Through this reading of Locke, coupled with an analysis of Day and Bicknell's formal innovation of the suicide note in verse, this chapter argues that *The Dying Negro* is not finally committed to the freedom or personhood of African-identified people but to defining and maintaining white Britons' freedoms. Ultimately, then, *The Dying Negro* is an exemplar of how emancipatory arguments rooted in liberal notions of integration tacitly reproduce exclusionary logics. This book's larger argument concerning the relation of literary romanticism to racialized representations of suicide begins with *The Dying Negro* for two reasons. While it was not the first text to depict a black person dying by suicide, its immense popularity at the inception of a range of revolutionary eruptions in Europe (Britain's abolitionist movement chief among them) established a distinctively racialized dimension to popular discourses about rights, personhood, and voluntary death against which the trope of romantic suicide would subsequently develop.[5] Emerging as it does from this uniquely charged moment, *The Dying Negro* is thus also a paradigmatic example of how racialization often escapes scrutiny in well-intentioned texts and movements grounded in liberal epistemologies.

As defined by Weheliye, "racialization" refers here "not [to] a biological or cultural descriptor but [to] a conglomerate of sociopolitical relations that discipline humanity into full humans, not-quite-humans, and nonhumans."[6] In liberal modernity, this process has been underwritten by a vexed relation to property as a prerequisite for personhood. The legal framework of personhood adjudicates which humans are free based on evidence of self-ownership, usually expressed through rationality and self-consciousness. Because legal personhood is strongly predicated on an ontological relation to the body, the protection against unlawful detainment granted by the writ of habeas corpus has been central to establishing personhood by authorizing a claim of ownership of one's own body. But personhood is not necessarily restricted to people, which is to say, to human beings—corporations were granted personhood long before people of color and white women; and legal arguments for the personhood of nonhuman animals also gained traction in the nineteenth century.[7] Personhood grants those rights that liberal societies reserve for free individuals, but it does not speak to the more fundamental question of who or what is seen as worthy of those rights. The liberal logics of *The Dying Negro* appeal to and operate within the rule of law, seeking to redress wrongs done to enslaved Africans by demonstrating the speaker's capacity to be recognized as a person. But if personhood is not tantamount to humanity, then appealing to the former will only ever modify (without really confronting or moving to eradicate) those social logics that keep human beings defined against each other through largely nonsensical relations to property. A truly universal project of liberation would begin with the abolition of notions of self-definition through property—with the abolition, that is, of the construct of "Man." Though it draws attention to cracks in that construct's foundations, *The Dying Negro* ultimately does little to challenge them.

John Locke, Property, and Self-Destruction

Less than a year before *The Dying Negro* was published, the Somerset ruling declared illegal precisely the kind of scenario the poem opens with: the detainment of a person of African descent on a ship set to sail for the Americas. That the poem is based on an actual event demonstrates that the Somerset ruling, widely considered to have been a monumental step toward abolition, was in fact less effective than many believed. As Brycchan Carey has suggested, for Day and Bicknell, two London lawyers, to write a poem about "the extent to which the law could be flouted" indicates that the poem "must therefore be seen first as a commentary on the ineffectiveness of the law."[8] Indeed, *The Dying Negro* lays bare fundamental problems not only with the laws as they stood but also with their philosophical foundations.

In 1769, James Somerset was brought to England by the enslaver Charles Stewart. Because the legality of slavery in England was never codified, Somerset remained with Stewart as a servant until 1771, when he decided to leave. Though there was precedent for this, Stewart retaliated by having Somerset captured and held on board the *Ann and Mary* with the aim of reenslaving him once the ship set sail for Jamaica. With support from Granville Sharp, three abolitionists claiming to be Somerset's godparents from his baptism in England brought the case to court by appealing for a writ of habeas corpus. The ship's captain, John Knowles, was ordered to bring Somerset before the Court of King's Bench, which would determine whether his imprisonment aboard the ship had been legal. After six months of proceedings, on June 22, 1772, William Murray,

First Earl of Mansfield declared that the air in England was "too pure" to suffer the "odious" institution of slavery.[9] With these strong words, Somerset was pronounced legally free.[10]

For over two centuries, Mansfield's decision has been celebrated as a key precedent to the 1807 abolition of the trade in enslaved Africans and their 1834 emancipation in England's colonies. By extension, it is also considered an important precedent for emancipation in the United States. The Somerset case continues to be cited in everything from international human rights law to debates on the rights of nonhuman animals.[11] But despite Mansfield's vehement antislavery language, *Somerset v. Stewart* was not technically about the institution of slavery. It was, instead, a strong defense of habeas corpus. As Mansfield reminds us no fewer than four times in the decision, the ruling is not about the legality, nor even the morality, of enslavement. In fact, it is precisely because the case was about his seizure and detainment on English soil that Somerset was freed at all. Nevertheless, the case continues to be extolled as everything from "a major weapon in the arsenal of abolitionism" to "co-equal with the Declaration of Independence" in establishing and maintaining individual freedoms.[12]

Beyond exaggerated claims of its bearing on the institutions of slavery in England and the United States, *Somerset v. Stewart* also opened the door for an important reassessment of habeas corpus. Indeed, the widespread notion that habeas corpus is a fundamental safeguard of personal liberty is an eighteenth-century invention. Emerging largely from public responses to the Somerset trial, this reassessment gained traction again in response to Pitt's suspension of habeas corpus during the Treason Trials of 1794, and reemerged overseas during the uproar over Lincoln's suspension of habeas corpus in 1861.[13] In this sense, Mansfield's ruling in 1772 inaugurated what we might call the "habeas corpus century," wherein the relationship between the individual and the state grew increasingly embattled, even as that relationship became central to a range of policies and theoretical debates about the liberal subject. I emphasize that this particular shift occurred during the eighteenth century, although the idea of habeas corpus is ancient, traceable at least as far back as the Norman Conquest; some scholars have located its roots in ancient Greece.[14] All agree, however, that it was codified in its modern form in Britain on the eve of "enlightenment."

In 1679, Parliament passed 31 Cha. 2 c. 2, better known as the Habeas Corpus Act. Although there had been an earlier Habeas Corpus Act in 1641 and others subsequently passed in 1803, 1804, 1816, and 1862, the

Act of 1679 remains one of the most important events in modern legal history because of how substantially it limited the power of the state over the individual.[15] Specifically, the act laid out for the first time explicit procedures and timelines for carrying out the writ: it mandated near-immediate issue and return within three days, and it enabled those detained to appeal for a writ of habeas corpus even when courts were not in session. The act also established penalties for delaying trials and introduced fines for judges who refused to grant the writ, thereby incentivizing its strict enforcement. Prior to 1679, habeas corpus had been widely abused by agents of the state. For example, it was not unusual for members of the Privy Council to move detainees to secret prisons without due process; and while a number of measures were introduced to limit these abuses, most went unenforced.[16] The 1641 Habeas Corpus Act—the first explicitly named for the writ—stripped the Privy Council of its jurisdiction over civil matters and abolished the Star Chamber, which was "a notorious tribunal used by the Crown to circumvent judicial scrutiny over detainments."[17] When Charles I was dethroned, Parliament suspended habeas corpus for his supporters, and this fueled Charles II's attacks on Parliament when the monarchy was restored in the 1660s. Exactly why it was revisited in 1679 remains unclear due to a lack of documentation on the matter.[18] However, as summarized by nineteenth-century constitutional theorist A. V. Dicey, the 1679 Act and the revisions that followed "declare no principle and define no rights, but they are for practical purposes worth a hundred constitutional articles guaranteeing individual liberty."[19] More than a century later, in 2013, legal scholar Kevin Gutzman echoed Dicey's sentiment, calling the Habeas Corpus Act of 1679 "the chief reason that Anglophones have long been free."[20]

A decade after the 1679 Act was passed, John Locke published his *Two Treatises of Government*. In the oft-discussed section of the *Second Treatise*, "Of Property" (chap. 5), Locke famously declares that "every man has a property in his own person."[21] This claim is advanced as part of Locke's theoretical reconstruction of how "Man" emerged from the state of nature to civil society, the philosophical blueprint for the modern liberal state. To briefly summarize, for Locke, asserting ownership over parts of the commons begins with individuals exerting physical labor over entities in nature, thereby claiming the right to call those entities their own: "The labour that was mine, removing them [objects in nature, e.g. acorns and berries] out of that common state they were in, hath fixed my property in them."[22] He emphasizes here that one can only own as much property as one can reasonably use.

Moving from the advent of private property in a hunting and gathering society to one based on agriculture and land ownership, the labor imposed on the land delineates what land can be enclosed. The next stage involves the introduction of money. Before money, Locke imagines a degree of economic equality because exchange was largely confined to the satisfaction of needs, and most necessities were perishable—berries, meat, and so forth.[23] The introduction of money, however, leads to differential increases in private property ownership, resulting in economic inequality that results in contentions and increased violations of the laws of nature. This, then, leads to the formation of civil government. At this point, any limits on property ownership are set aside, and the system that develops allows for unlimited acquisition. In this system, possession of property is the precondition of legibility and political representation in society.[24]

Within such a context, it is not hard to see why the writ of habeas corpus emerges as central to establishing personhood by authorizing a claim of ownership over one's own body. In fact, both the notion that property ownership can be established through the use of one's body and that personhood is asserted through the possession of property are etymologically embedded. From the Latin *habeas* (second-person singular present subjunctive active of *habere*—to have, to hold) and *corpus* (accusative singular of *corpus*—body), habeas corpus literally means "you shall have the body." In delineating the terms by which one can challenge the state's claim to possess their body, the Habeas Corpus Act of 1679 effectively anticipates a common, if not altogether accurate, reading of Locke's *Second Treatise* that emerged in the late eighteenth century—a popular conflation that cemented habeas corpus as a defining marker of personhood.

Isaac Kramnick has shown the extensive influence of Locke's philosophy on reform movements of that era, even going so far as to call late eighteenth-century England "Locke's country."[25] According to Kramnick, late eighteenth-century reformers "made a clear link from Locke to British reform and socioeconomic change" by emphasizing natural rights over historical entitlements.[26] Where property was at the core of many other conceptions of freedom in civil society, Lockean liberalism was particularly embraced because it asserted that all people could, at least in theory, define and distinguish themselves through their work. Pointing to the wide circulation of pamphlets and treatises extolling Lockean ideas, Kramnick notes that "Of Property," the fifth chapter of the *Second Treatise*, "became the received wisdom in advanced radical circles in the late eighteenth century."[27]

Debates about habeas corpus, in turn, offered commentators an apt field within which to consider the vicissitudes of these Lockean principles. For instance, Thomas Hallie Delamayne, a barrister and author of the pamphlet *The Rise and Practice of Imprisonment in Personal Actions, Examined*, makes explicit the link between habeas corpus and Lockean principles of property. According to Delamayne, English courts had always been organized around three kinds of property, "body, land, and goods," and changing relationships among these three kinds of property shaped the course of English legal history.[28] Writing in 1772, the year of the Somerset trial, Delamayne notes that in his contemporary moment, this relationship was strongly influenced by the 1679 Habeas Corpus Act: "Here indeed the people rejoiced—they had much reason for so doing—and seemed satisfied in the acquisition of so great a second charter of their liberty" (the first being the Magna Carta).[29] Delamayne argues that throughout most of England's history, the laws had been determined by "the prerogative of the crown over the body" and that the 1679 Act's limitation of the Crown's claims of ownership over individual bodies set the course for a new epoch, one where the individual could be constituted through his own claims of ownership, either to external property or to his own body.[30]

Direct responses to *Somerset v. Stewart* exemplify further how strongly habeas corpus spoke to eighteenth-century notions of property as a precondition for personhood. In a 1773 pamphlet protesting the Mansfield decision, Samuel Estwick argues that the outcome of the case created what he considers an illogical shift in the relationship of property and personhood. Charles Stewart's case, as Estwick summarizes it, had rested on a legal claim to Somerset as an object of property. Estwick, in turn, is unable to understand "by what new law or magic [formerly enslaved people like Somerset] are now become the subjects of the Crown of England, and intitled [sic] to the benefit of Habeas Corpus."[31] In other words, Estwick maintains that Somerset was, in a purely legal sense, property—a shaky claim given that England's laws did not define the status of people enslaved elsewhere when they stepped on English soil—and that to assert otherwise would be to set a precedent that effectively entitles property (the capacity for ownership, including self-ownership, and the rights that accompany it) to property (enslaved people). Estwick maintains that Mansfield's decision did not adequately address the constitutional principles by which Somerset had been constituted as property via enslavement; thus, the protections granted to him through the writ of habeas corpus, which effectively established his personhood, should be treated as an undue exception to the laws of England rather than their full and just exercise.[32]

To make this argument, Estwick takes for granted a clear distinction between the constitution of an individual *through* property, as in Locke, and the notion of human beings *as* property under slavery. That is, in theory, the notion of an enslaved person as property differs categorically from the notion that liberal subjects are also constituted through a relationship to property. However, this distinction has never really been clear, not least because Locke's commitment to liberty is severely undermined by his own active participation in the institution of slavery.[33] Jennifer Rae Greeson has argued persuasively that Locke's core theory of personhood as constituted through property is predicated on an economic history in which people were already viewed and treated as property, thus the two ideas are necessarily linked.[34] Moreover, even if it were reasonable to except the realities of African enslavement for the sake of argument, the Lockean doctrine of self-ownership remains explicitly predicated on preventing the hypothetical enslavement of Britons and thus cannot be disarticulated from the idea that any and all human beings are, or can become, objects of property.

The *Two Treatises* are expressly framed as a challenge to Sir Robert Filmer's 1680 *Patriarcha*. Locke's counterpoint to Filmer's veneration of the divine right of kings is grounded in the assertion that a theory of government founded on the original sovereignty of one man over another is, in fact, an attempt to justify a form of slavery. Locke's *Second Treatise* asserts that a society based on the constitution of personhood through property is necessary specifically in order to curtail the possibility of free people—that is, Britons—becoming enslaved to their own government. The alternative to government as slavery, then, is government as contract. But as Fred Moten suggests below, the law of contract grants only a limited fantasy of freedom, one that turns on the exercise of the "free" individual's sovereignty over those excluded from the contract. This relationship between enslavement and freedom manifests itself in (among other places) how liberal society negotiates its relationship to death:

> What if slavery and freedom are each other's condition of possibility? What if the distinction between life and death is just a way of naming the distinction between life and lives? What if the irreducible mutuality of slavery and freedom occurs in the realm of lives, which is the zone in which life and death are made to (seem to) negotiate? What if the right of death and power over life that is given in and as

sovereignty . . . is given and held in the fantastic domain of individuated lives. . . . If individuation is the regulation of social life, then the law of contract is one of its most essential formal mechanisms.[35]

This aporia—the inability to fully reconcile the dependence of (social) life and freedom on (social) death—asserts itself elsewhere in the *Second Treatise*.

In his explication of the limits of individual liberty in a contractarian system of government, Locke has severe difficulties in dealing with two seemingly unrelated kinds of actions: owning another person (i.e., actual practices of enslavement) and suicide. In order to explain why suicide cannot be classified as an assertion of individual liberty, Locke reverts to the very schema of sovereignty he had argued against in the *First Treatise*. To make suicide the exception to self-determining individualism, Locke insists that free individuals are still subject to a more powerful entity, God, and thus "though man . . . have an uncontrollable liberty to dispose of his person or possessions, yet he has not liberty to destroy himself."[36] Elsewhere in the *Second Treatise*, he also claims that the voluntary death of an enslaved person isn't really suicide. For Locke, enslavement is acceptable as a form of punishment: when a man has committed an act for which he deserves to have his liberty taken away, he may justly lose his legal standing as a person and be enslaved to another. And thus, "having, by his fault [effectively] forfeited his own life, by some act that deserves death . . . whenever he finds the hardship of his slavery outweigh the value of his life, 'tis in his power, by resisting the will of his master, to draw on himself the death he desires."[37] Because the enslaved person no longer belongs to himself, if he ends his life it is not a self-determining act but rather the logical extension of his punishment. The voluntary death of an enslaved person thus does not "count" as suicide because to lack freedom is to be, in some sense, already dead. It follows, then, that to commit suicide, one must first be free; and yet, Locke insists that free individuals are not actually free to kill themselves.

These stipulations are fundamentally irreconcilable with one another, as well as with Locke's larger notion of a society governed by self-determining individuals who are constituted as such through property. Even as Locke claimed to be opposed to the condition of slavery in general, his theory is troubled from within at two levels. Firstly, Locke's theory is unable to distance itself from the theory of sovereignty he claims makes slaves of free individuals. Secondly, Locke has difficulty allowing for what most readers would consider as obvious—that the voluntary death of an enslaved person is, indeed, an act of suicide. It is this tension between sovereignty and individualism—which, in Locke, exists in both the question of suicide and that of enslavement—that comes to the fore in *The Dying Negro*, as separate debates over suicide and racialized enslavement converge around the limits of freedom and the exclusionary logics that underwrite legal personhood.

The Dying Negro and the Politics of Freedom

Understood in the context of *Somerset v. Stewart* and the debates it engendered among eighteenth-century Britons, *The Dying Negro* calls attention to the precarious grounds on which the category of personhood determines and underwrites the condition of freedom, broadly defined. Written in heroic couplets sustained over nineteen pages (in its original 1773 printing), *The Dying Negro* is presented as the final words of an unnamed African man aboard a slave ship bound for the Americas. The poem primarily addresses the white woman he left behind in England, though it also periodically appeals to the enslavers holding him captive. *The Dying Negro* is, at bottom, a defense of the speaker's decision to kill himself. The poem begins with a series of assertions about why suicide is his only recourse and then alternates between sentimental addresses to his lover and vengeful rage over his captivity. It concludes with his thoughts of the guilt and shame his enslavers will feel when they witness his death. The implication, then, is that once the poem is complete, he shoots himself in the head.[38]

The Dying Negro opens by complicating a seemingly straightforward category, the language of secular freedoms that we might expect from a late eighteenth-century poem about suicide. In its opening lines, Day and Bicknell set the language of individual rights against that of religion:

> Blest with thy last sad gift—the power to dye,
> At length, thy shafts, stern fortune, I defy;
> Welcome, kind pass-port to an unknown shore!—
> The world and I are enemies no more.
> This weapon ev'n in chains the brave can wield,
> And vanquish'd, quit triumphantly the field.[39]

By opening with the word "blest," the poem suggests that the decision to kill himself, as the rest of the stanza contends, is not only the speaker's natural right—a "weapon" he will "wield" against the structures that keep him enslaved—but also providential, a divine "gift." It is worth underscoring here that liberalism holds natural rights to be, indeed, those "gifts" with which each person enters life. However, it is unclear from whom or what this "gift" (the right to suicide) is bestowed: whether "the power to dye [*sic*]" is given by nature, by those who oppose enslavement, or by God. As Marcus Wood has demonstrated, the idea that freedom can be given or "gifted" is deeply problematic because freedom, in this scenario, must first be taken away:

> *Gift* is a key word—but a very slippery word . . . *Gift* might not seem to be a very hard word to define; in *Chambers Dictionary* it has two primary meanings as a noun, and they are short and sharp: 'A thing given; a quality bestowed by nature.' But certain things, freedom being one of them, cannot be given, and freedom in the context of slavery and emancipation consequently has a difficult, maybe impossible relation to these two definitions of *gift*. The impossibility is exposed in the following question: How can freedom be given, either individually or collectively, if it already exists as nature's gift to all?[40]

This question conjures a long history of racial oppression written through "a series of justificatory, indeed self-serving, rhetorics that take liberty and dress it up as a gift."[41] Freedom, Wood argues, is a mythology created by self-professed liberators to obscure wrongdoings that made liberation necessary in the first place. Thus, the opening lines of *The Dying Negro* obscure—perhaps intentionally, or perhaps simply because it has never really been clear within a liberal framework—the question of whether freedom is an entitlement of nature, a blessing bestowed by some higher power, or a social state that can be fought for and won. Compounded by the poem's historical situatedness in the immediate aftermath of the Somerset trial, it is not entirely clear which of these options (if any) the final act of suicide is meant to evoke or suggest. Arguably, the condition the poem purports to be aimed at—freedom—is itself the condition in question.

For Locke, freedom can be taken away but not given. The controversial fourth chapter of the *Second Treatise*, "Of Slavery," posits that enslavement is justifiable when one deserves to have his freedom taken away. Locke does not indicate whether or how it can ever be attained again. Enslavement as a form of retributive punishment suggests that the removal of one's freedom (which everyone implicitly has in the state of nature) creates a permanent condition of living death. And it is only here, as we have seen, that Locke condones suicide, reasoning that although the free individual does not possess the right to take his own life, an enslaved person may choose to do so. But if enslavement suggests that the lack of freedom is tantamount to a kind of death, how do we categorize the actual death of someone who is considered, in this society, already dead? More precisely, as Sharon Patricia Holland asks, "When 'living' is something to be *achieved* and not *experienced*, and figurative and literal death are very much a part of the social landscape, how do people of color gain a sense of empowerment?"[42] In *The Dying Negro*, an enslaved African must kill himself to claim a form of power. By replacing Somerset's release (what, in Wood's terms, can be understood as a bestowal of the "horrible gift of freedom"[43]) with the narrator's decision to demonstrate self-ownership by dying, the poem raises a question it is not equipped to answer: what or who gets to define the interrelated conditions of life and/as freedom?

Although it opens on an ostensibly Christian note, by immediately turning to the paradoxical condition of freedom, *The Dying Negro* divorces from the issue of suicide its Christian prohibitions and instead turns suicide into a tool that may be used even by Christians to combat social evils far greater than the spiritual evil of self-murder. Later, this becomes the poem's explicit argument. In this sense, the poem follows a long tradition of drawing on rhetoric associated with Christianity to argue against institutions of enslavement. Seymour Drescher locates this strategy in European thought going as far back as the Middle Ages, when rural peasants "grounded their claims to liberation in Christian teachings and general assertions of human dignity, liberty, and equality . . . Christ's sacrifice did not just free humanity from original sin but restored it to its original liberty."[44] In a similar vein, the poem concludes with an extensive indictment of the hypocrisy of Christian "morality" in perpetuating institutionalized enslavement. The long final stanza begins:

> Thou Christian God, to whom so late I bow'd,
> To whom my soul its fond allegiance vow'd,
> When crimes like these thy injur'd pow'r prophane,
> O God of Nature! Art thou sall'd in vain?[45]

The speaker appeals directly to Christ, asking, "Did'st thou for this sustain a mortal wound?"[46] In the background here there is perhaps some parallel between the speaker and Christ, who, in early Christianity, was sometimes considered a suicide.[47] Day and Bicknell do not go so far as to make this parallel explicit, though their poem does hearken back to eighteenth-century conventions of black martyrdom.

In her expansive work on the subject, Celeste-Marie Bernier has demonstrated how African and Afrodiasporic peoples "have been conceptualized solely as either barbaric fiends in an array of pro-slavery atrocity literatures or as sacrificial martyrs in didactic, seemingly redemptive antislavery tracts."[48] *The Dying Negro* propagates both stereotypes. By disseminating antiblack stereotypes, even from within a framework ostensibly interested in challenging them, the poem assumes the paternalistic position of "proving" or "redeeming" Africans' humanity. Yet where it moves to humanize the speaker, the poem cannot help but reduce him to a less-civilized counterpart to "Man." For example, much of the middle of the poem depicts the original enslavement of West Africans. The authors' footnotes tell us that these depictions are based on a European travelogue: Michel Adanson's *A Voyage to Senegal* (1759). The speaker recalls how his people (who may or may not have been Senegalese) bestowed "gifts" on the colonizers, rendering the "last, sad gift" of the opening especially poignant by recalling the paradox of the "gift of freedom" in the last place where he was physically free. He then describes how European traders tricked his people onto slave ships, foreclosing further consideration of African agency. The language of detainment here hearkens to the Somerset trial, which was likewise only superficially invested in the personhood and humanity of the black subject at its center. In the absence of human recourse or agency, the speaker turns to the divine. Prefiguring the manner in which he will rebuff Christianity later in the poem, in an anticlimactic narrative of becoming, the speaker denounces African deities who did not come to save him: "No power descended to assist the brave, / No lightning flashed, and I became a slave."[49]

Shortly thereafter, Day and Bicknell divorce the speaker from any claims to martyrdom in the Christian sense. *The Dying Negro* calls up Christianity in order to emphasize its ethical incoherence in a society that profits from enslaving others. Thus, even as the speaker's regular reminders that he, too, is a Christian may be strategic moves toward establishing common ground with the poem's intended readers, they simultaneously serve the opposite function of distinguishing him from his audience and calling the entire institution of Christianity into question:[50]

> On thee I call'd with reverential awe,
> Ador'd thy wisdom, and embrac'd thy law;
> Yet mark thy destin'd convert as he lies,
> His groans of anguish, and his livid eyes,
> These galling chains, polluted with his blood,
> Then bid his tongue proclaim thee just and good![51]

God's power, he argues here, is either "too weak"[52] to spare him the sufferings of enslavement, or this God simply doesn't care. Relinquishing the possibility of Christian salvation, the speaker turns, finally, to revenge—if not against Christianity itself, then at least against its adherents, the perpetrators of his suffering. The speaker's revenge will come through the power of sympathy to affect Christian readers, in whom he expects suicide will elicit intense moral outrage:

> And may these fiends, who now exulting view
> The horrors of my fortune, feel them too!
> Be theirs the torment of a ling'ring fate,
> Slow as thy justice, dreadful as my hate,
> Condemn'd to grasp the riven plank in vain,
> And chac'd by all the monsters of the main,
> And while they spread their sinking arms to thee,
> Then let their fainting souls remember me![53]

As he moves toward his conclusion, it is clear that this poem is less interested in sympathy than it is in guilt and shame—emotions commonly associated with suicide but that are here linked to those upholding the system of enslavement. In his final plea that his death be remembered, readers are made to focus not on his suicide but on the conditions that drove him to it and to find those conditions, rather than the act of suicide, deplorable and outrageous.

The moral strategy here is convoluted at best. Having rejected Christianity because of its inability to recognize the suffering of enslaved people, the speaker nevertheless imagines that his captors and implied readers will be moved to sympathy by his death and that the negative emotions elicited by his suicide will be his revenge. But why should the speaker believe that his captors will care about his suicide? Here, the poem reveals itself to be primarily interested in the social conditions that define its intended Anglo-European readership rather than the freedom of enslaved Africans. By beginning and ending with the Christian prohibition against suicide, Day and Bicknell emphasize that this is a poem about subverting rhetorical and conceptual norms, including those on which readers assume their society is built. Where Christianity is expected to be opposed to suicide, within the logic of the poem, suicide emerges as the only reasonable option. And as the poem moves away from religious restrictions against voluntary death, it makes apparent deeper paradoxes at the core of liberal modernity. Thus, beyond circumventing Christian stigma in drawing a parallel between suicide and habeas corpus (and with it, liberal political categories and ideologies more broadly), *The Dying Negro* makes an important political intervention: by alternately referring to the decision to die as a blessing, a gift, a power, and a weapon, the poem suggests an inherent tension in western conceptions of freedom. As Wood has asked, once freedom is taken away, who gets to restore it? Or, who finally "owns" freedom?

Though Day and Bicknell claim an antislavery ethos, *The Dying Negro* cannot get past paradoxes laden within the liberal principles it engages to bolster its cause. The trope of the "suicidal slave" raises far more questions than the poem can reasonably answer about the foundations of modern political and legal institutions. And precisely because of its ubiquity in European and American discourses of abolition, it behooves us to remember that this trope has never been a beacon of black liberation.[54] As Wilderson rightly explains, "the circulation of Blackness as metaphor and image at the most politically volatile and progressive moments in history (e.g., the French, English, and American revolutions) produces dreams of liberation which are more inessential to and more parasitic on the Black, and more emphatic in their guarantee of Black suffering, than any dream of human liberation in any era heretofore."[55] In *The Dying Negro*, the parasitism of white freedom dreams at the expense of black liberation is particularly visible at the level of form: the relatively obscure form of the suicide note in verse. Juxtaposing the legal and philosophical foundations of habeas corpus with the idea of suicide, Day and Bicknell call into question the right to own one's body, the right to own and sell other people's bodies, and whether self-possession constitutes the right to do what one pleases with either. By engaging a literary form that presupposes the speaker's death, Day and Bicknell circumvent the black subject ostensibly at the center of their interrogation.

The Suicide Note and the Poetics of Personhood

The issue of personhood emerges not only in the poem's abolitionist politics and engagement with contemporary legal questions but also at the level of form. It is important, first of all, to acknowledge the rhetorical distinctiveness of the suicide note as an anticipatory account of one's own death. In terms of genre, it exists at the intersection of, at least, autobiography, epistle, confession, and apologia. It also draws on a then-popular print form. In the mid-eighteenth century, newspapers began to publish suicide notes—first real ones and, when these proved to be popular reading, fictional ones sometimes presented as real. Public consumption of the suicide note reached its peak in the 1770s, the same decade as the first three printings of *The Dying Negro* (1773–1775) and declined sharply after 1779. Michael MacDonald has posited that this fad was reflective of a larger cultural shift toward increasingly tolerant, secular attitudes toward suicide.[56] Eric Parisot has gone a step further, suggesting that the publication of suicide notes also made visible the limits of morality in literary sensibility and sentimentalism. Parisot argues that the suffering suggested by suicide notes gave readers the occasion to "test their own capacity to feel and ... to provoke substantive moral response" and that in so doing, suicide notes "reinforce[d] patterns of social dysfunction."[57] Insofar as the culture of sensibility enabled readers' self-congratulatory postures of sympathy toward evils of their own making, Parisot understands published suicide notes as "uncomfortably public notices where the failures of society are writ large."[58]

In this sense, Day and Bicknell's choice of form buttresses the tenuousness of their political strategy. Among the first explicitly abolitionist poems in English, *The Dying Negro* is widely considered to be a prototypical example of the problem of engaging sentimental strategies for political ends. As Parisot argues, political sentimentalism encourages readers to assert themselves as moral individuals without effecting any real ethic of care toward others. Thus, sentimental texts can, and often do, enable a self-involved myopia that masquerades as outward-looking concern for others while excusing a culture of unexamined bigotry.[59] Saidiya Hartman offers arguably the definitive explication of how sentimental strategies in abolitionist writing subsume the agency of the person or group positioned as the object of the sentimental stance. Recalling the white abolitionist John Rankin's attempts to express the atrocities of the institution by imaginatively describing himself in the position of enslaved people being whipped, Hartman contends that Rankin does more to reveal his own ideas about torture than he does to enable readers to understand those who actually are tortured: "by virtue of this substitution the object of identification threatens to disappear.... [I]n making the other's suffering one's own, this suffering is occluded by the other's obliteration."[60] This projection of the self onto the other "fails to expand the space of the other but merely places the self in its stead."[61] By writing in the voice of an enslaved person, Day and Bicknell likewise assume that their subject's suffering can be "known" through the imaginations of free white men and women. Without denying that the effort to voice others can be understood as a complex and daring act toward knowing, in this context, that act renders dispensable the lives, experiences, and voices of the very people it ostensibly means to liberate.

Much has been made of the interracial love story as the rhetorical vehicle for the poem's intended sentimental effect on its implicitly white readership. If the speaker's bride is understood to function as a proxy for English readers, the speaker's declarations of love for her, as well as his memory of her love for him, are meant to engender some degree of sympathy for the speaker among Day and Bicknell's readers. Lynn Festa argues that the speaker's appeals to his white lover's compassion "reanimate the speaker from the social death of slavery" in the minds of English readers who, in consuming his final words, issue him a kind of "afterlife."[62] Such a reading captures the rhetorical function of racialized sentimentalism in the era's abolitionist discourses. However, centering the interracial love story deflects from the poem's engagement of the cultural and religious politics of suicide. Indeed, the suggestion that the speaker is given an "afterlife" in readers' minds effectively undermines the impact of his final act, thereby leaving his blackness, rather than his death, as the apparent object of readers' sympathies. In this way, too, his "afterlife" circumvents the ethnoreligious politics that the poem brings forward. As we have already seen, the speaker argues that the horrors of enslavement are so un-Christian that suicide is a more forgivable sin than the ones perpetrated by those who profit from slavery. By aligning the reader with the position either of the speaker or his bride (in the absence of whose voice we assume her agreement), the poem seems to argue the same thing.[63]

What goes largely unaccounted for are the diverse religious and cultural beliefs that actually informed many enslaved African-identified people's decisions to kill themselves. Even accepting that the discourse of Christianity is part of the poem's political appeal to white readers, in its overwhelming emphasis on the speaker's relationship to Christianity (both in positive and negative terms), *The Dying Negro* reveals its inability to fully imagine the subject it wants to represent. Terri L. Snyder has shown that attitudes toward suicide differed substantially among West African peoples. The Yoruba and Ashanti saw it as acceptable and even commendable in certain circumstances, while other nations condemned or weaponized it as a form of punishment. Snyder theorizes that the brutal realities of enslavement "may have rendered suicide both more easily imaginable and more acceptable for forcibly transported Africans regardless of their origins."[64] Europeans, however, saw African peoples' suicides within a homogenizing framework of "racial character," as we see in the following firsthand account by a crew member on a slave ship:[65] "In the barracoons, it was known that if a Negro was not amused and kept in motion, he would mope, squat down with his chin on his knees and arms clasped about his legs and in a very short time, die. Among the civilized races it is thought impossible to hold one's breath until death follows. It is thought that the African can do so."[66] The speaker of this passage claims that Africans kill themselves through a method that seems impossible or inaccessible to Europeans. This sailor's sense of distance from the method he is describing underscores the vast cultural and conceptual distance between how acts of suicide were understood by enslaved peoples and how they were represented by European observers.

One widely circulated explanation for why enslaved people killed themselves was the idea of transmigration, or the notion that the soul or spirit of the dead would be returned to the community into which the person had been born—a belief held by some African cultures. A 1791 British House of Commons report notes that enslaved Africans felt "such an aversion to leaving their native places that they threw themselves overboard, on an idea that they should go back to their own country."[67] Snyder suggests that transmigration took hold among Europeans as a popular explanation for voluntary death among enslaved Africans because it rendered the act of suicide a function of cultural or racial difference rather than unlivable conditions of Europeans' making. With the publication of *The Dying Negro*, Day and Bicknell further transformed an already whitewashed set of ideas about African peoples' relationship to suicide by reframing it in political terms. While *The Dying Negro* was not the first text to misapprehend and misrepresent enslaved people's cultures and experiences, in popularizing the sentimental trope of the "suicidal slave" and couching it in explicitly antislavery terms (which earlier texts, such as Behn's *Oroonoko*, did not do), the poem was instrumental in popularizing a particular trope of black suffering ameliorated by freedom in death. This trope compromises, even as it appears to facilitate, the capacity of well-meaning white people to recognize the prospect of black freedom as on par with their own.[68] In this way, it also maintains blackness as a politico-ontological impossibility within the world it claims to want to bring into being, perhaps illuminating but never challenging liberal modernity's inability to make space for black life on its own terms.

That inability becomes acutely visible in Day and Bicknell's choice of form. That *The Dying Negro* is written as a suicide note aligns it with the aesthetic and political work of another kind of death note popular in the eighteenth century: the epitaph.[69] Like the suicide note, the epitaph reflects a culture's understanding of its ideological assumptions, interests, and commitments. Barbara Johnson has suggested that key rhetorical features of poetic epitaphs—anthropomorphism/personification (the act of conferring human attributes onto a nonhuman entity) and prosopopoeia/apostrophe (an address to an absent or dead person)—also inform the legal construction of personhood. In positing a relationship between a lyric person ("emotive, subjective, individual") and a legal person ("rational, rights-bearing, institutional"), Johnson argues that the two illuminate each other such that these seemingly unrelated categories are, in fact, complementary structures through which personhood is negotiated and understood.[70] If we take seriously Johnson's claim that "lyric and law are the fault lines along which 'personhood' is structured," then Day and Bicknell's suicide note in verse can be read as a formal interrogation of the racialized limitations of legal personhood within the bounds of liberal modernity's general enterprise of freedom.[71]

The Dying Negro answers in the affirmative Johnson's question of "whether there is a relation between the 'first person' (the grammatical 'I') and the 'constitutional person' (the subject of rights)."[72] However, unlike the epitaph, through which Johnson draws her analysis, the suicide note in verse reverses the ontological position implied by legal and literary logics wherein personhood is negotiated on the related sites of anthropomorphism and apostrophe. That is, both anthropomorphism and apostrophe—and by extension, the epitaph—rely on positive relations to aspects of personhood (and it is worth emphasizing that these aspects are implicitly forged in positive relation to whiteness). Anthropomorphism calls up or imposes "humanness" onto something nonhuman, while apostrophe makes live and implicitly present something or someone otherwise absent or dead. Both shift absence into presence, death into life, nonbeing into being. Suicide does precisely the opposite. The suicide note in verse, then, poses a special kind of interpretive challenge. What are we to make of the subjectivity and temporality of a lyric "I" whose very purpose in coming into being is to herald its self-destruction? Moreover, how do we read a poem that announces itself as an affirmation of black life but can only see itself as achieving that affirmation by ventriloquizing (and thus whitewashing) an African-identified person's decision to die? These questions can only be addressed by reading against the grain of liberalism's relation to whiteness and social "life."

Life After (Social) Death

The Dying Negro epitomizes what Moten calls the "elaboration of blackness as death-bound emanation," which is "determined by incapacity or refusal to think blackness as if it were neither bound by nor originated in the white/nonwhite binary."[73] This association—between blackness as "other" to whiteness, inhabiting a structural position of "death" to whiteness as "life"—has strongly informed the study of transatlantic slavery since (at least) Orlando Patterson's 1982 study, *Slavery and Social Death*, which names the condition of enslavement as fundamentally and unchangeably exterior to those forms of social life that civil society affords its subjects. Recently, social death has been criticized as an overly simplistic abstraction that ignores the inner and interpersonal lives of enslaved people and precludes considerations of black agency. As Vincent Brown puts it, "Social death, so well suited to the tragic perspective, stands in for the experience of enslavement."[74] While Brown and others mean this critique in terms of how some contemporary scholars treat the subject (and subjects) of transatlantic slavery, the same associations are to be found in centuries of well-intentioned antislavery arguments. *The Dying Negro* is one such text. Capitalizing as it does on the romance of the speaker's tragedy, it cannot see beyond its antiblack foundations.

Cleaved of personhood, separated from his love, and trafficked as a commodity, the poem's speaker is, in Patterson's terms, socially dead. The fact that the poem takes the form of a suicide note compounds this point by indicating to readers that by the time they read his words, he is also literally dead. Moreover, by choosing to kill himself, the speaker marks himself as a particular kind of social outcast. In life, he is forbidden "the rights of man to claim," but one right remains inalienable to him, "The gloomy privilege to die," because, as he reminds his captors, "Not beyond the grave, / Thy power extends."[75] As he looks at the ocean that will be his final resting place, the speaker notes a "vast watry barrier, 'twixt thy world and me."[76] He sees death as a way to freedom because it is the only way he can remove himself—that singular "me" whose assonance rings out into the emptiness at the end of the line—from a society that renders him "a thing without a name."[77] But the act of suicide doesn't just take him out of society; it erases his whole existence, ensuring that "no pageant wreaths [will] deck an outcast's tomb" and no epitaph will "mark the friendless victim of despair."[78] Thus, although the poem presents the speaker as freed from bondage, it leaves an uneasy reconciliation between the struggle for freedom and the implications of achieving it by dying.[79]

If the speaker's suicide signifies his capacity to reason through a kind of self-ownership, the poem serves as a plea for the recognition of these capacities in all enslaved people of African descent. A key question raised by the poem, then, is how to bring an entire group of people to (social) life from (social) death. There is no space here to consider that the question itself is part of the system that condemns African-identified people to death, social and otherwise, in the first place. Moreover—or perhaps as a result of this first evasion—*The Dying*

Negro cannot conceive of the possibility that social death within the terms of liberal modernity does not preclude other forms of social life. As Jared Sexton puts it, "Black social life does not negate black social death by vitalizing it. A living death is a much a death as it is a living."[80] Day and Bicknell assume that social life—those forms of legibility established by liberalism's schedules of rights and liberties—is the categorical opposite of social death and, moreover, that social life so defined must be everyone's goal. And yet, per Sexton, "Black life is not lived in the world that the world lives in ... black life is not social ... black life is *lived* in social *death*."[81]

Weheliye comes to this point another way. In contradistinction to habeas corpus and its attendant implications about personhood, property, and the body, Weheliye invents the term *habeas viscus* to account for "the existence of alternative modes of life alongside the violence, subjection, exploitation, and racialization" that underwrite liberal modernity.[82] Moving from "you shall have the body" to "you shall have the flesh," habeas viscus draws on Hortense Spillers's foundational argument that the systematic denial of the black body in (the afterlife of) the era of transatlantic slavery produces a distinct ontological category, the flesh.[83] The abolitionist trope of the "suicidal slave" assumes a desire to be recognized as a liberal subject—to be transformed from flesh to body. But the flesh offers alternative modalities of thinking and being. Habeas viscus exemplifies how those excluded from liberal modernity's sociopolitical constructs find modes of asserting themselves and acknowledging one another as full human beings. Crucially, this occurs independently of liberalism's social logics, and it always has: as Holland has suggested, "Spillers's idea of the flesh as 'primary narrative' places 'the body' in the context of captive ... and leaves 'the flesh' in the place where 'self' resides."[84] To acknowledge the primacy of the flesh is, for Weheliye, to authorize an epistemology that "sets the stage for a general theory of humanity, and not its particular exception."[85] *The Dying Negro* offers no such alternatives, just as it cannot conceive of the possibility that some people might not want to participate in those systems that liberal modernity delimits and upholds as part of social life. *The Dying Negro* turns on a belief that liberalism can be a route to freedom. And thus, it exemplifies how liberal modernity's hostility toward blackness is maintained, in part, through the belief and expectation that the state can be reformed to make room for those it has historically excluded.

Following *The Dying Negro*, a staggering number of texts engaged suicide to signal rational self-assertion through a kind of ownership of one's body: its self-imposed destruction. Suicide—particularly the suicide of an enslaved person—was widely engaged in efforts to disrupt hegemonic notions of the relationship between self-ownership, the body, and personhood. However, as the remainder of this book will show, even as it calls on the logic of liberal individualism to demonstrate enslaved people's capacity to reason, the ennobled figure of the "suicidal slave" utterly fails at creating for African-identified people a framework in which to actually live as free subjects. Moreover, recognizing that this trope emerged in the same decade as Chatterton's death and the publication of *The Sorrows of Young Werther* calls on us to ask whether romanticism's interests in suicide can be divorced from contemporaneous (re)considerations of liberalism through suicide. By recasting *The Dying Negro* as a poem about paradoxes inherent in the political structures and social logics of liberal modernity, Day and Bicknell use the story of one enslaved man's suicide to interrogate the more general enterprise of freedom as predicated on legal definitions and recognitions of personhood. If romantic literatures did not simply forget the political questions associated with suicide, then what are we to make of the continued distinction of white male suicides like Werther and Chatterton and not their racialized counterparts? One option is to recognize the romantic fetishization of suicide as an obfuscation of social realities that political narratives about suicide help to reveal but that liberalism is fundamentally unequipped to address.

chapter 2

Chained to Life and Misery

I cannot tell why, but death, under every form, appears to me like something getting free to expand in I know not what element.... My thoughts darted from earth to heaven, and I asked myself why I was chained to life and its misery.
  —Mary Wollstonecraft, *Letters Written during a Short Residence in Sweden, Norway and Denmark*

My heart throbbed with grief and terror so violently, that I pressed my hands quite tightly across my breast, but I could not keep it still, and it continued to leap as though it would burst out of my body. But who cared for that? Did one of the many by-standers, who were looking at us so carelessly, think of the pain that wrung the hearts of the negro woman and her young ones? No, no! They were not all bad, I dare say, but slavery hardens white people's hearts towards the blacks.
  —Mary Prince, *The History of Mary Prince, A West Indian Slave*

In the preceding chapter, we saw the black male body imaginatively sacrificed to a tenuous ideal of freedom. This chapter traces the even more troubling fates of black women's bodies in the liberal imagination. Where *The Dying Negro* presents suicide as a path (albeit a paradoxical one) toward legibility for black men, the texts examined here suggest that when black women kill themselves, they remain illegible as candidates for inclusion in liberal society. Stories of suicidal black women abound at the turn of the nineteenth century, particularly in literary works by white women writers. Where these have sometimes been read as signaling white women's recognition of collective struggle "as women," in point of fact, the trope of suicide as a path to freedom for black women is incompatible with white women's efforts to establish their own politico-ontological being in the world of "Man." Whether intentionally or as a function of liberalism's grounding in ideologies of dialectical differentiation, white women's representations of black women who kill themselves reveal not what women share across racial divides but what white women share with those already recognized as bearers of liberal rights and freedoms: whiteness. While this chapter will emphasize representations of suicidal black women, as I indicate toward the end, the same logic is also applied to women of other origins, effectively creating distance between all nonwhite women and the rights and freedoms sought by white women at the turn of the nineteenth century. Building on a robust body of feminist scholarship on romanticism's suicidal women, this chapter foregrounds the largely overlooked role of race in the era's gendered discourses of feeling.

Most scholarship on suicide in nineteenth-century British literature has focused on gender politics.[1] As Margaret Higonnet first noted, women writers drew from the era's liberal political discourses to raise questions about rational self-destruction and self-assertion, democracy, and a woman's right to own and control her body through the trope of suicide. Drawing on the popularity of abolitionist texts like *The Dying Negro*, white women writers drew comparisons between enslavement and marriage as, legally speaking, comparable forms of oppression. In so doing, they put pressure on the laws of coverture under which, in the words of William Blackstone, "husband and wife are one person in law: that is, the very being or legal existence of the woman is suspended during the marriage, or at least incorporated and consolidated into that of the husband."[2] In these terms, Kelly McGuire has shown how the suicides of white women were read as tantamount to destruction of property, while Michelle Faubert has discussed the ubiquity of the marriage-enslavement analogy as part of liberal feminism's intellectual debt to writing by formerly enslaved people.[3] Yet even where these and other scholars acknowledge that white women conjured narratives of enslaved and dispossessed people as proxies for discussing their own oppressions, race remains subordinate to gender as a category of analysis in the literary history of suicide at the turn of the nineteenth century. Racist tropes are overlooked in favor of reading death as a democratic equalizer, or they are brushed aside as presentist concerns that are irrelevant to the study of eighteenth- and nineteenth-century texts. Only Tricia Lootens has seriously addressed these elisions, and she rightly notes that the conversation about white women's discursive appropriations of other forms and experiences of oppression is old hat in disciplines with which nineteenth-century British literary studies has not historically engaged. Where "the convergence of African American literary studies with studies of nineteenth-century British literature may feel like the overcoming of reticence maintained over generations," this is really only true from a British literary studies perspective. African American literary studies has grappled for decades with the role played by Anglo-European texts and contexts in the racialized construction of modern gender categories.[4] British literary studies is thus long overdue for an honest reckoning such as the one begun in Lootens's *The Political Poetess* and, I hope, continued here.

Taking as central the ethical and political implications of white women's engagement with discourses of enslavement and dispossession in early feminist writing about suicide, this chapter considers how liberal calls for gender parity were also, in many cases, arguments *against* racial parity. White women writers from across the political spectrum drew on racialized discourses associated with suicide in service to fantasies of gender parity grounded not only in white supremacy but also, paradoxically, in patriarchy. In texts by Mary Robinson and Claire de Duras, sentimental depictions of black women who choose to die bring the already fraught politics of what we might today call postures of cross-racial solidarity to bear on liberal debates about the rights of white women. Felicia Hemans extends this to nonblack women of color. Drawing on Mary Wollstonecraft's foundational critique of sensibility—which was, for many years after her death, inextricable from her own vexed association with the topic of suicide—the writers discussed here align nonwhite women with excess feelings that lead to suicide, even as they work to distance their own political interests from those same emotions. The chapter concludes with a reading of the autobiography of a formerly enslaved woman, Mattie J. Jackson, whose extraordinary narrative was published in the United States in 1866. *The Story of Mattie J. Jackson* unequivocally refuses these tropes and works to define womanhood beyond the bounds of whiteness. The spatiotemporal leap from early nineteenth-century Britain to the postbellum United States underscores the transatlantic reach of these tropes, while the chapter as a whole endeavors to confront their continued manifestation in some feminist discourses even today.

Foundations: Mary Wollstonecraft, Suicide, and the Critique of Sensibility

Mary Wollstonecraft is easily one of the most important figures in the literary history of suicide. The tension in her legacy between suicide (as, alternately, an act of passion or one of rational resistance to patriarchal oppression) and sensibility (as a tool of that oppression) established the terms by which many subsequent thinkers would write about both suicide and gender liberation. In her writing, suicide functioned "to protest women's lack of control over their own destinies."[5] Her emphasis on suicide as a trope of rational feminist protest was sharply undercut by William Godwin's 1798 *Memoirs of the Author of A Vindication of the Rights of Woman*, which revealed details of Wollstonecraft's love affairs and actual suicide attempts. Godwin's misguided representation of Wollstonecraft as a "female Werther" called into question her efforts to liberate middle-class white women from what she saw as their indoctrination by the culture of sensibility, and this negatively impacted her reputation until well into the twentieth century.[6] Even so, Wollstonecraft had firmly established both suicide and sensibility as key sites through which others would continue to negotiate modernity's social hierarchies. Building on her work, subsequent thinkers drew clear divisions between arguments for gender, class, and racial parity. Reading the relationship between suicide and sensibility through later nineteenth-century writers thus exposes cracks in liberal feminism's foundations that are considerably harder to reconcile than the revelation that its "founding mother" was a complex woman.

In Wollstonecraft's writing, "sensibility" signifies "cultivated emotion or the capacity for it."[7] The culture of sensibility, she argues, teaches middle-class white women to nurture their emotions at the expense of their capacity to reason in order to mold them into frivolous beings and sexual objects. One of her chief aims in *A Vindication of the Rights of Woman* is "to convince [women] that the soft phrases, susceptibility of heart, delicacy of sentiment, and refinement of taste, are almost synonymous with epithets of weakness, and that those beings who are only the objects of pity and that kind of love ... will soon become objects of contempt."[8] She advocates transforming these women's educations to cultivate reason as a counterpoint to sensibility, which she argues traps women in states of "perpetual childhood" and "slavish dependence" on men.[9]

Wollstonecraft's unfinished final novel, *The Wrongs of Woman, or Maria*, stages a confrontation between sensibility and rationality in the figures of its eponymous protagonist—a bourgeois white woman who embodies what Wollstonecraft, in the *Vindication*, describes as "unnatural delicacy of feeling"—and Jemima, a working-class woman who offsets Maria's unhinged sensibility with what the narrative presents as a near-excess of reason.[10] Jemima undergirds Wollstonecraft's central point that sensibility is not the natural state of all women but a tool used to control middle-class white women. Jemima lacks access to the education that conditions Maria to indulge "that fire of the imagination, which produces *active* sensibility."[11] Instead, Jemima is aligned with rationality, although as Janet Todd observes, her behavior does not necessarily indicate that as a favorable alternative: "If excessive sensibility without reason makes people romantic and vulnerable, excessive reason without sensibility makes them coldly selfish."[12] The dynamic between the two women rehearses Wollstonecraft's call, in the *Vindication*, for equilibrium as a step toward equality: "Let us endeavor to strengthen our minds by reflection, till our heads become a balance for our hearts."[13]

Maria is also significant in Wollstonecraft's political thinking about suicide. Although she died before she could finish the novel, Wollstonecraft drafted five possible endings, two of which frame suicide as a reasonable response to the treatment of white women as property in England's social and legal codes. The most fully developed of the five endings suggests that Wollstonecraft understood the importance of attending to the intersection of gender and class, if not also race, in her political vision. In this version, Maria, pregnant and abandoned by her lover, swallows laudanum to end a lifetime of suffering at the hands of men. Jemima finds her just in time and "restore[s her] to life." The draft concludes with Maria declaring, "The conflict is over! I will live for my child!"[14] This is the only ending in which Jemima, rather than Maria's erstwhile lover, Darnford, is central to the story's resolution, and it is also the only one that offers even a hint of future happiness. Wollstonecraft emphasizes throughout the *Vindication* that her argument for educational reform is intended only for women of Maria's social station. She champions bourgeois white women's rights in terms of the nation's (and, by extension, the empire's) expectations that they will nurture the future citizenry: "If children are to be educated to understand the true principle of patriotism, their mother must be a patriot."[15] Jemima's central role in *Maria*, however, suggests a nascent critique of the class structures that keep women in different social positions from relating to one another.

In the *Vindication*, Wollstonecraft casually brushes off the lower classes: "though I consider that women in the common walks of life are called to fulfil the duties of wives and mothers... I cannot help lamenting that women of a superior cast have not a road open by which they can pursue more extensive plans of usefulness and independence."[16] The argument for representation here is unambiguously an argument for the representation of a larger portion of the middle class. In the hands of Wollstonecraft's "superior cast" of women, the call to "independence" is as much a call for gender parity as it is an avowal of the consolidation of power in bourgeois hands. Yet in the most complete version of *Maria*, the survival of the title figure and her unborn child—and with them, England's future—depends on a servant. Following the *Vindication*'s logic that gender hierarchies are constructed and thus open to interrogation, Jemima's presence in *Maria* suggests that ideologies naturalizing class difference may be challenged as well. Todd ascribes Jemima's extreme rationality to her class background, positing that because she was forced to survive on her own from an early age, she never had a chance to develop the capacity for sensibility.[17] In this way, the novel appears to suggest that social conditions, not nature, are at the root of both men's oppression of women and the class strata that socially alienate women from one another.

While it is impossible to say definitively whether Wollstonecraft would have pursued this nascent critique to its logical ends, or whether she might have extended it to challenge other forms of inequality, I am inclined to agree with Moira Ferguson's assessment that it seems unlikely. Even as Wollstonecraft was, according to Ferguson, "the first writer to raise issues of colonial and gender relations so tellingly in tandem" by making analogies between enslavement and white women's oppressions, any potential ethic of cross-racial sympathy is undercut by a "sociocultural myopia" that flattens difference and subordinates all considerations of gender to an implicitly white universal standard.[18] This is on full display in the following passage from the *Vindication*, in which Wollstonecraft excoriates a passage from James Fordyce's 1766 conduct book, *Sermons to Young Women*:

> Is not the following portrait—the portrait of a house slave? "I am astonished at the folly of many women, who are still reproaching their husbands for leaving them alone, for preferring this or that company to theirs, for treating them with this and the other mark of disregard or indifference; when, to speak the truth, they have themselves in a great measure to blame. Not that I would justify the men in any thing wrong on their part. But had you behaved to them with more respectful observance, and a more equal tenderness; studying their humours, overlooking their mistakes, submitting to their opinions in

matters indifferent, passing by little instances of unevenness, caprice, or passion, giving soft answers to hasty words, complaining as seldom as possible, and making it your daily care to relieve their anxieties and prevent their wishes, to enliven the hour of dulness, and call up the ideas of felicity: had you pursued this conduct, I doubt not but you would have maintained and even increased their esteem, so far as to have secured every degree of influence that could conduce to their virtue, or your mutual satisfaction; and your house might at this day have been the abode of domestic bliss." Such a woman ought to be an angel—or she is an ass—for I discern not a trace of the human character, neither reason nor passion in this domestic drudge, whose being is absorbed in that of a tyrant's.[19]

The rhetorical leap from domestic angel to "house slave" is a classic example of what Lootens, extending the work of Elizabeth Spelman, calls "'changing the subject' with a vengeance"—that is, invoking "terms like freedom or slavery as if these could be fully detachable from historical corporeal referents."[20] By engaging rhetoric associated with racial enslavement to describe paternalistic social expectations placed on bourgeois white women, Wollstonecraft engenders a mode of forgetting about the experiences of enslaved black women. Moreover, in framing the scene of gendered frivolity within a comparison to an enslaved person, her concluding judgment that the woman Fordyce describes has "not a trace of the human character" takes on a distinctly racist overtone: the "house slave" to whom this white woman is being pejoratively compared is already assumed to be less than human.

The problem with such analogies, as Hazel V. Carby explains, is that "the experience of black women does not enter the parameters of parallelism. The fact that black women are subject to the simultaneous oppression of patriarchy, class and 'race' is the prime reason for not employing parallels that render their position and experience not only marginal but also invisible."[21] That Carby's analysis is addressed to contemporary readers highlights the endurance of these early patterns and indicates the damage they continue to do to all women and to all iterations of "feminism." And while it's true, as Faubert notes, that progressive thinkers of Wollstonecraft's era "did not have the benefit of centuries of critical thinking based on rights-advocacy to gird their discussions as we do today," as scholars who choose the responsibility of interpreting these figures now, we do have that benefit.[22] Given the ever-expanding breadth of womanist and feminist-of-color contributions to our knowledge of the British Empire, transatlantic enslavement, and the social scripts of western modernity, it should no longer suffice to suggest that scholars can look past racist logics because the authors we write about were of a different time.[23] Sara Ahmed reminds us that "sexism and racism are reproduced by the techniques that justify the reproduction. When [they] are dismissed, we are witnessing the defense of the status quo: it is a way of saying, there is nothing wrong with this; what is wrong is the judgment that there is something wrong."[24] Turning, then, to the racialized legacy of Wollstonecraft's critique of sensibility, the sections that follow demonstrate that it is both possible and necessary to attend to the interlocking relations between patriarchy and white supremacy even though—or rather, precisely because—many of the texts and authors we inherit from the past did not.

Racial Sensibility and the Bounds of "Woman" in Mary Robinson and Claire de Duras

Mary Robinson's 1799 *Letter to the Women of England on the Injustice of Mental Subordination* echoes Wollstonecraft's arguments against sensibility. Referencing Wollstonecraft throughout, Robinson urges women to "read, and profit, by the admonition of Reason . . . Be less the slaves of vanity, and more the converts of Reflection."[25] Through interpretations of well-known historical figures and Robinson's own incisive reasoning, the *Letter* unpacks the logical leaps and double standards that support the idea that women are inferior to men. For example, Robinson lays bare the absurdity in the notion that men, ostensibly "stronger-minded creatures," are said to "*yield*" to drunkenness while "woman *resists* its power . . . because she is the *weaker*."[26] In similar fashion, she excoriates the idea that women are inferior because they are physically weaker against the expectation of physical labor in many aspects of domestic work: "Why are women, in many parts of the kingdom, permitted to follow the plough; to perform the laborious business of the dairy; to work in our manufactories; to wash, to brew, and to bake . . . Are women thus compelled to labour because they are of the weaker sex?"[27]

Moving beyond Wollstonecraft's emphasis on the middle class, Robinson appeals to women across class positions. However, as her title indicates, she is only speaking to English women. Thus, even as she raises the question of women's labor, she does not consider those women forced to do the most grueling physical work for the British Empire: the enslaved. The text's exclusionary racial politics are sometimes made plain, as in Robinson's comparison of the situation of English women to "those beyond the Ganges [where] wives are to be purchased like slaves, and every man has as many as he pleases."[28] More often, however, they emerge in her reliance on the twin discourses of liberalism and colonialism, as in the following: "They [white women] will not be your slaves; they will be your associates, your equals in the extensive scale of civilized society; and in the indisputable rights of nature."[29] Robinson hinges white women's liberation on racial "others" against whom the suitability to possess "the indisputable rights of nature" can be measured.[30] This comparison, then, advances white women's—and only white women's—eligibility to be treated equally to those men already empowered "in the extensive scale of civilized society."[31] In this way, her appeal for equality between English men and women turns on maintaining white supremacist racial hierarchies.

This logic is made even more explicit in Robinson's revision of an early periodical poem called "The Storm" into her better-known poem, "The Negro Girl." Both "The Storm," published in London's *Morning Post and Fashionable World* in 1796, and "The Negro Girl," which first appeared in Robinson's 1800 collection, *Lyrical Tales*, are sentimental narrative poems about lovers torn apart as a direct result of Britain's involvement in the transatlantic trade in enslaved Africans. In "The Storm," the lovers are William, a working-class crewmember on a slave ship wrecked by a storm, and Nancy, who witnesses the disaster from the English coast and decides to join the drowned William "in a WATRY GRAVE."[32] While the trade in human beings is condemned, the focus of the condemnation is its negative impact on the British working class. Robinson devotes two of the poem's ten stanzas to abolitionist-style expressions of sympathy for enslaved Africans, and the storm is presented as cosmic retribution for Britain's participation in "the barb'rous toil." However, the poem is mainly interested in the trade's fatal consequence for William and Nancy. Nancy denounces the economic conditions that led to William's employment on the ship; notably, however, she does not consider his agency in accepting that work. She emphasizes distinctions between those "nurs'd in lux'ry" who "sleep on beds of State" (i.e., those of the ruling class who advocate for and control the laws governing the trade) from those living in "Poverty and Woe" (i.e., those of the working class who carry out the practices underwritten by those laws). When she does attend to the fates of enslaved people, she does so only in the broadest terms: she denounces the fate of "The SABLE Race" and "the ETHIOP" but makes no mention of the actual people she presumably sees drowning alongside William. The institution of slavery, then, is the backdrop against which Nancy's personal loss occurs. The target of the poem's political scorn is its function as a source of conflict between the ruling class, which reaps its rewards, and the working class that performs the tasks required to maintain its daily operations. Thus, when the poem rails against the trade, it is unclear—perhaps deliberately so—whether this is done in support of the abolitionist cause as such or because, in a roundabout way, Britain's involvement with the institution of slavery endangers English lives (signaled here by William's death at sea and Nancy's decision to kill herself as a result).

In its later iteration as "The Negro Girl," the poem more directly condemns the institution of slavery. Between 1796 and 1800, Robinson more than doubled the length of the poem and made several key alterations to stanzas reproduced from "The Storm." Chief among these revisions, Robinson moves the setting to the African coast and rewrites the lovers as Draco, an enslaved man on a ship bound for the Americas, and Zelma, his lover who is left behind to serve a white man in Africa. The main story elements—the storm that claims the lives of all on the ship and the lover who sees it happen and decides to kill herself—remain the same. Shelley Jones considers Robinson's revision an act of "equalizing her characters" and "an indictment of imperialism" that underscores "the commonality of the experience between the colonizer and the colonized: that the slave trade is fatal for Britain as well as Africa."[33] Along similar lines, Margaret Higonnet reads "the mutual figuration of race and gender" as part of the poem's utopian erasure of difference in the "democratic" state of death.[34] Perhaps. But considered within the terms established by Robinson's *Letter*, Zelma is aligned with precisely those qualities that Robinson seeks to denaturalize in cultural attitudes toward white women. While both versions of the poem present sentimental stories of women who lose their lovers and choose death over life without them, the way Robinson treats each woman's capacity to reason accentuates the differences between them.

Among Robinson's major additions to "The Negro Girl" are several stanzas in which Zelma recalls the education she received from her enslaver. While an enslaved woman receiving a western education was not completely unheard of in 1800—perhaps most famously, Phillis Wheatley was taught to read and write by her enslavers and went on to publish a popular volume of poems in England in 1773—on the whole, enslaved people's access to education was strictly policed. That Zelma is taught not only to read but to *reason* is significant because this renders her education in line with the sort advocated by Wollstonecraft. Yet the poem curtails the possibility of reading this as a victory by emphasizing that Zelma is not its appropriate recipient. Beginning as follows, the stanzas on Zelma's education qualify her capacity to tell her own story by throwing the strong emotions she displays throughout the poem into relief against Nancy's:

> The Tyrant WHITE MAN taught my mind
> The letter'd page to trace;
> He taught me in the Soul to find
> No tint, as in the face:
> He bade my reason blossom like the tree—
> But fond affection gave the ripen'd fruits to thee.[35]

In "The Storm," Nancy similarly remarks, "Whate'er our Tints may be, our SOULS are still the same."[36] Significantly, her ability to make such a statement is never called into question. But Zelma's ability to see shared humanity beyond skin color is attributed to knowledges imparted to her by her enslaver. At its most extreme, this might be taken to suggest that Africans—not Europeans—adhere to and perpetuate the racist logics invented by Europeans to justify their enslavement. At the very least, it illuminates problems with liberal humanism's tendency to erase difference. Those working to critique "race" in humanist terms, however well intentioned, were doomed from the start.

Even as Robinson establishes Zelma's ability to reason as a product of her European education, in the last two lines quoted above, she implies that the exercise of reason is less comfortable for Zelma than subservience to her lover. That is, though she is freely (if improbably) given the tools so eagerly sought by liberal white women, she wields them in ways that undermine the liberating effects English feminists like Wollstonecraft and Robinson had envisioned. Exemplifying the dangers of romantic attachment, Zelma abandons reason to be subsumed—and ultimately submerged—by love:

> Swift, o'er the plain of burning Sand
> My course I bent to thee;
> And soon I reach'd the billowy strand
> Which bounds the stormy Sea.
> DRACO! My Love! Oh yet thy ZELMA's soul
> Springs ardently to thee; impatient of control.[37]

In view of the poem's abolitionist politics, the phrase "impatient of control" calls for both a literal and a figurative reading. Describing Zelma's physical escape from "the Tyrant WHITE MAN," it also anticipates her departure from life by way of her suicide.[38] At the same time, it signals her abandonment of control over her emotions, and with it, her abandonment of both sensibility *and* reason. Wollstonecraft and Robinson both contend that it is incumbent on women to develop their rational faculties to regulate and balance the "feminine" behaviors they are trained for. The scenario presented in "The Negro Girl" underscores that this argument is directed only to white women. Having been taught to develop her rational faculties, Zelma makes what the poem frames as an irrational choice to indulge her emotions without even the inhibitions of cultivated sensibility, and this leads directly to her death.

Crucially, Zelma's decision to die does not signify rational choice in the way that suicide in Day and Bicknell's *The Dying Negro* had done. In that poem, the speaker's decision to kill himself is offered as "proof" of his ability to reason. The undeniable judiciousness of that choice functions to highlight the pain that renders death preferable to life as an enslaved person and thus the moral indefensibility of those who enable that institution. Zelma's suicide, on the other hand, is marked by its fundamental irrationality. In this way, "The Negro Girl" makes visible a core impasse of liberal feminism. The poem can only envisage one form of freedom for black women: either from physical bondage or from the patriarchal control that some white women called "mental enslavement" but not both. In curtailing the sense of agency then associated with the suicides of enslaved male figures, Robinson's poem forecloses the possibility of freedom from bondage for Zelma. And in denouncing Zelma's decision to die for love in terms strongly associated with liberal debates about the rights of white women, the poem ensures that Zelma is ineligible for those rights as well.

Of course, Nancy is also the kind of woman against whom Robinson protests in the *Letter*. Defining herself solely as a lover, she chooses to die because she can see no existence for herself without William. Not one line after she witnesses his death, she is dead herself: "Poor NANCY saw him buried by the wave, / And, with her heart's true love, plung'd in a WATRY GRAVE!"[39] These lines remain virtually unchanged in "The Negro Girl" except for the fact that the last two words are not capitalized (signaling, perhaps, that Zelma's final resting place is less noteworthy than Nancy's). The main difference between these women's decisions to follow their lovers to the grave is that Nancy, as far as we know, is never taught to think otherwise. In reality, of course, neither the working-class Nancy nor the enslaved Zelma is likely to have had access to education. But the fact that Robinson chooses to emphasize Zelma as the exception fundamentally changes the meaning of her decision to choose love and, ultimately, death. The emotional excesses that lead Nancy to suicide can be explained in social terms as a sign of women's indoctrination by the patriarchy. Zelma's rejection of reason, however—a tool meant to resist such indoctrination—is, at best, an indicator of personal failing; at worst, it plays into racist stereotypes about African women's emotional volatility and unruly sexuality.

In either scenario, Robinson's revision marks a clear distinction between white and black women. While "The Negro Girl" critiques the institution of slavery, Zelma's inability or unwillingness to exercise the faculty of reason ultimately presents black women as unfit to possess the rights that Robinson and Wollstonecraft sought for white women. By transferring the negative association between sensibility and white womanhood to a black woman Robinson echoes the patriarchal arguments that hold such forms and expressions of femininity to be at odds with access to the rights of "Man." In this way, Robinson reproduces the same oppressive logics she decries in the *Letter*.

Claire de Duras's 1823 novella, *Ourika*, one of the first European novels to feature a black woman as the central protagonist, similarly emphasizes the rationality of white women by displacing qualities traditionally associated with white femininity onto a suicidal black woman. However, it does so in a political context that is less committed to rights advocacy drawn from liberalism. Written by an aristocrat forced to emigrate to England during the French Revolution, *Ourika* is loosely inspired by the true story of an African child who was purchased by the governor of Senegal and given to his uncle, M. de Beauvau, in 1788. Baptized Charlotte Catherine Benezet Ourika, she died in 1800, aged between sixteen and twenty. Little is known about her actual life. However, the popular fictionalization by Duras inspired plays, poetry, and artwork that revised and reimagined the aristocratic black heroine.[40]

In Duras's text, as in Robinson's, a white woman writes a black woman whose emotional excess leads to a tragic end. Like Zelma, Ourika is educated according to western epistemologies; however, unlike Zelma, Ourika is reared by European nobility. The figure of the black aristocratic heroine reflects, as Robin Mitchell has argued, ongoing anxieties about national identity. As "the 'other' side of what it meant to partake in French identity," Ourika's blackness and femaleness function to "[shore] up Frenchness" by way of antithesis. Per Mitchell, "Ourika encapsulated the problem of a woman educated out of race and class, with no real place or space to call her own."[41] Thus, Ourika's voice is doubly couched in whiteness: before we hear her story in the first person, we meet her through the frame narrative of a white male doctor summoned to the convent where she is, at the end of her short life, a nun. As Mitchell points out, this structure is reminiscent of frameworks used to "validate [the] authenticity" of enslaved people's autobiographies.[42] Ourika tells the doctor that she wants to be cured of a "prolonged and acute melancholia" that had made her suicidal.[43] To help him understand its causes, she shares her life story, which makes up the majority of the text.

The novella follows Ourika as she comes of age and struggles to negotiate her marriage prospects against European racism. She tells the doctor that as a child she never saw her blackness in negative terms: "I didn't regret being black. I was told I was an angel. There was nothing to warn me that the color of my skin might be a disadvantage."[44] This changes when, at age fifteen, she overhears a conversation between her benefactress, Mme. de B., and an unnamed marquise about Ourika's dim prospects for integrating into French high society: "I see the poor girl alone, always alone in the world."[45] Ourika internalizes this statement, and her self-perception changes instantly: "Lightning does not strike more swiftly. I comprehended all. I was black. Dependent, despised, without fortune, without resource, without a single other being of my kind to help me through life."[46] Her despondency grows over the course of the novel, and she learns to associate her blackness with alienation. This has been read as anticipating Frantz Fanon's discussion of traumas that undergird racial formation in colonized peoples.[47] However, a closer reading of the text reveals that Ourika's suicidal depression stems less from her budding racial consciousness than from her forbidden love for her adoptive brother, Charles. Indeed, Ourika's negotiation of her racial identity is framed in terms that closely align her with rationality, even as that faculty is gradually undercut by her secret desire for Charles.

Upon first overhearing the exchange between Mme. de B and the Marquise, Ourika is overcome by strong emotions that she immediately converts into reasoned self-reflection: "But now my mind stood back from these instinctive reactions . . . I became exacting. I analyzed and criticized almost all that had previously satisfied me."[48] Yet over the course of the text, Ourika's rationality is eroded and blurred with her despondency at the impossibility of her love. For instance, after Charles marries a white woman, and Ourika takes the veil, Duras emphasizes that the nun's habit—a loaded signifier of her marital and sexual status—became a comfort to Ourika. This was not, as we might expect, because wearing the habit helped her to move past her heartbreak but because it covered more of her skin than any of her other clothes had done. As Adeline Koh has suggested, the novel's pointed disavowal of marriage as an option for Ourika signals its ambivalence toward seeing black women as equal to white women: "If Ourika were to marry, she would become 'white': she would assimilate into French society." Thus, Koh argues, citing the fact that the overhead conversation follows closely after a scene in which Ourika dances publicly with a white man, it is by no coincidence that "Ourika's first hints of her marriage potential coincide with her racial trauma."[49] Though Duras sets up Ourika's race consciousness as the text's driving conflict, her prohibited desire for Charles quickly emerges as its actual focal point. By raising the possibility of miscegenation and summarily shutting it down, Duras reinforces the idea that Ourika's blackness precludes her from full assimilation. Thus, as Pratima Prasad puts it, the unrequited love story "evacuate[s] the core question of racial identity while simultaneously foregrounding it."[50] This is underwritten by Ourika's transformation from a thoughtful, rational woman to one who becomes hopelessly lost in her sadness.

Duras contrasts Ourika's increasingly volatile emotions against her white women characters' carefully curated performances of sensibility. In so doing, she echoes liberal feminist arguments about the necessity of balancing feeling with reason. As Wollstonecraft warns in *Maria*, "Indulged sorrow" will "blunt or sharpen the faculties to the two opposite extremes; producing stupidity, the moping melancholy of indolence; or the restless activity of a disturbed imagination."[51] Ourika exhibits both extremes and never finds a way to overcome them on her own. Though she eventually enlists the doctor's help, he cannot cure her either, and she dies while in his care. The only character the text suggests who might have been able to curtail what Wollstonecraft calls the "unnatural delicacy of feeling" is a white woman: the marquise whose insistence on the inevitability of Ourika's future isolation prompted her distress in the first place.[52] Reentering the novel's orbit when Ourika is at her most despondent—as she makes a "suicidal request" to God—the marquise chastises Ourika for failing to "find a brighter side to things," to which Ourika responds, "intelligence only makes real misfortunes seem worse."[53] Ourika reiterates what by this point she sees as an absolute correlation between her blackness and her misery: "You know very well what my problems are. My social situation. And the color of my skin."[54] The marquise reads her situation differently: "if you weren't madly in love with [Charles], you could come perfectly well to terms with being black."[55] Ourika cedes to the marquise's judgment without hesitation: "she is right, I am guilty."[56]

There are several problems with both the marquise's diagnosis and the ease with which Ourika accepts it. The marquise's patronizing directive to "find a brighter side to things" ignores the realities of racial prejudice that structure their society. Even if Ourika were to "come to terms" with her blackness (whatever that might mean in the context of this novel), the white supremacist culture she longs to have a place in would not. While a suggestion is raised that she might be allowed to marry someone below her station, she is categorically precluded from marrying a member of the aristocracy and thus attaining equal status with white women of her own class. The marquise's flippant response further betrays the extent to which her understanding of Ourika's situation is based on an implicitly white concept of womanhood. Ourika's ready acceptance of the marquise's words, in turn, corroborates this point of view. What Jemima is to Maria, the marquise appears to be to Ourika: a rational woman whose chief function in the text is to mitigate the protagonist's emotional excess. However, because the marquise is also the same figure who forecasts the role that racism will play in her life, it is telling that she later brushes it off and blames Ourika's suffering on her failure to cultivate and perform sensibility. By framing Ourika as an "unreasoning toy of instinct" who requires the help of white women to learn to control her feelings, the marquise—and through her, the text itself—naturalizes emotional excess in the black woman.[57] Moreover, the scene between them suggests that white women's power to define themselves as rational beings depends on maintaining existing racial hierarchies.

Ourika's inability to control her emotions nullifies any possibility of racial justice raised either by the figure of the black aristocratic heroine or by the French and Haitian revolutions, which occur on the text's periphery. At the start of the revolution in France, Ourika is optimistic about the potential of liberal principles to bring about racial equality: "I sensed that at the end of this great chaos I might find my true place. When personal destiny was turned upside down, all social caste overthrown, all prejudices had disappeared, a state of affairs might one day come to pass where I would feel myself less exiled."[58] But she grows disillusioned by "the ridiculousness of men who were trying to control the course of events . . . I soon stopped being the dupe of their false notion of fraternity. Realizing that people still found time, in all this adversity, to despise me, I gave up hope."[59] She is also initially hopeful about abolition, though this is undercut by a profoundly antiblack perspective on the Haitian Revolution:

> About this time talk started of emancipating the Negroes . . . I still cherished the illusion that at least somewhere else in the world there were others like myself. . . . But alas, I soon learned my lesson. The Santo Domingo massacres gave me cause for fresh and heartrending

sadness. Till then I had regretted belonging to a race of outcasts. Now I had the shame of belonging to a race of barbarous murderers.[60]

There are echoes here of Duras's own vexed political allegiances. Born into the aristocracy, her father, Guy de Coëtnempren, Count of Kersaint, was an early supporter of the French Revolution; maintaining plantations in Martinique put him in closer proximity to the economic interests of the bourgeoisie than to the nobility. He was thus labeled a "traitor to his class" and guillotined for publishing a pamphlet attacking inherited privilege.[61] Duras's mother, a white woman from Martinique, inherited her husband's plantations, which were eventually passed to Duras herself. She taught their daughters centrist values and was deeply disappointed when one of them, Félicité, married into a royalist family.[62] That Duras wrote a novel about a relatively (for its time) complex black heroine has sometimes led to the assumption that she supported abolition; however, as the above passages illustrate, *Ourika* is far from an abolitionist text. Moreover, although it reflects some liberal principles in its treatment of white women, the novella is uninterested in advancing racial equity.

The fact that Ourika's melancholy is finally assuaged by religion echoes white supremacist logics whereby enslaved people were forcibly "saved" by Christianity yet still not recognized as full human beings.[63] Ourika joins the convent because she feels grateful to God for sparing her the fate of other Africans: "He rescued me from savagery and ignorance. By a miracle of charity He stole me from the evils of slavery."[64] Throughout the text, she sees herself as unique among people of African descent. But by having her embrace religion only because she cannot adequately temper her emotions or exercise her capacity to reason, the text drives home its point that existing racial hierarchies are immutable. Religion can, in some sense, "save" her, but the embrace of Christianity will not elevate her in the judgment of white society. Thus, even as the figure of the black aristocratic heroine implicitly raises prescient questions about intersections between race, gender, and class, not a single character in the text—including the heroine herself—is finally able to view Ourika or her place in the world outside of logics associated with white womanhood.

As a response to the failure of the French Revolution and the loss of Haiti, Duras's novella negotiates the shattered promises of liberalism against a nostalgic desire to return to a social order that imagines the categories of race, class, and gender as immutable. Where Robinson's poetry exemplifies myopias that limit the capacity of the era's progressive thinkers to surmount the whiteness at liberalism's core, *Ourika* casts doubt on liberalism's capacity to bring about a just society in its failure to imagine a world in which its heroine might survive. Thus, *Ourika* highlights how applications of liberal principles in vindications of the rights of "women" remain dependent on existing hierarchies of race and class.

The liberal fantasy of collective, cross-racial unity in "womanhood" turns on the mutual acknowledgment of a shared condition of social death. Yet as Wilderson has taught us, "structures of ontological suffering stand in antagonistic... relation to one another (despite the fact that antagonists themselves may not be aware of the ontological position from which they speak)."[65] For Wilderson, the politico-ontological positions that he signifies as "Black/Slave, Red/'Savage' and White/Human" represent paradigms of power that precede the construction of particular identities, including those informed by gender.[66] The writers I have been discussing here attempt not to transform but to more fully inhabit the white/human position. To establish their own politico-ontological status, these women emphasized what they held in common with the fully authorized subject of rights—whiteness. In the process, they highlighted the political nonbeing of other(ed) women. As the next section shows, this was not limited to stories of black women, even as black women and men hold a singular relation to death in the racial imaginary of the modern world.

Flickering Whiteness in Felicia Hemans's Suicide Poems

Much of Felicia Hemans's writing about suicide strikes distinctly Wollstonecraftian notes in its emphasis on death as an escape from patriarchal tyranny—what Susan Wolfson describes as "the fatal binding of female freedom and female death."[67] Like Duras, Hemans engages the trope of suicide after much of the optimism of revolutionary rights discourses and abolition had dissipated. For Gary Kelly, this results in a shift from the individual to the world-historical: "The disappearance of individuals, nations, and empires into the abyss of time and history [operate as] a sublation of the individual life in the continuing life of a specific historical sociality, in particular the modern liberal nation-state and empire."[68] Kelly is right to note that many of Hemans's dead and dying women serve to imaginatively "bring about a future liberal state"; although liberalism's lofty promises are certainly bowed, for Hemans they are not broken.[69] But suicide is a special kind of death, necessarily individual, even as it can be made to speak to broader issues of society and sociality. Thus, Hemans's suicide poems remain uniquely focused on the question of individual subjectivity, of who "counts" and who does not in social structures that turn on casting women out. The world-historical dimension of these poems is to be found in the fact that they concern women from a range of cultures, eras, and ethnicities. Through repeated confrontations between whiteness and various iterations of what functionally amounts to an undifferentiated sense of "otherness" in nonwhiteness, the poems imagine a liberal (and decisively not liberated) global empire.

In this light, it pays to consider which women the poems themselves cast out. Consider, for example, the "Indian Woman's Death Song," which places the title figure at a distance from the narrator and reader, never closing that gap. The poem begins as a canoe is swept up by a powerful current. An unnamed speaker tells us that the canoe's speed is "fearful," even as the woman within it sits "proudly, dauntlessly, and all alone."[70] The description of the boat's speed in emotive terms—that is, as "fearful"—produces a feeling of distance, in part because it takes seven lines before a figure capable of feeling such an emotion is introduced. The first six lines, then, seem to suggest that this fear belongs to someone else—perhaps the reader or the poem's speaker but not the woman at the poem's center. Indeed, when the woman is finally introduced, she is described as feeling a "strange gladness," her hair waving "as if triumphantly."[71] The fear remains suspended elsewhere, as the woman's affect does not correspond to the feelings that the poem tells us are engendered by this scene. Compounding this estrangement, we are initially told that she is "alone," only to learn "that a babe lay sleeping at her breast" in the next line.[72]

This sense of distance is underscored by a headnote and two epigraphs. The headnote attributes Hemans's knowledge of Native American cultural practices to a travelogue, William Keating's *Narrative of an Expedition to the Source of the St. Peter's River . . . Under the Command of S. H. Long*, although there is not much cultural specificity in the woman's story. Rather, her tale more closely recalls sentiments expressed in the poem's epigraphs from Friedrich Schiller and James Fenimore Cooper. The excerpt from Cooper, "Let not my child be a girl, for very sad is the life of a woman," is echoed in the poem when the mother laments that her child was born for "woman's weary lot" and resolves to save them "from sorrow and decay" by killing them both.[73] Likewise, Schiller's exaltation of a woman who would rather die than live with a broken heart is echoed as the title figure reveals that her lover has left her and that she cannot live without him. As Ann Laura Stoler has shown, the regulatory discourses of romantic love and sexuality in nineteenth-century Europe were habitually "refracted through the discourses of empire and its exigencies."[74] Thus, Hemans's poem is arguably best understood as an attempt to negotiate the social situatedness of white women against a Native American woman's suicide.

Such a reading extends from Astrid Wind's trenchant analysis of representations of dead and dying Native Americans in terms of broader efforts to fortify the dominance of liberalism against other ways of life:

> Indians dying or dead became the major theme of literature dealing with natives at the turn of the eighteenth century when Europeans and Americans refused to understand them because the very understanding of the natives and their cultures would have eroded the myths that rationalized the progress of white civilization at the cost of native cultures.... In the context of the political and economical demands of the time ... the only Indian in [the] Anglo-American imagination, who would not halt the progress of white civilization, was a dead Indian.[75]

To be clear, the discourses Wind describes here are not interchangeable with those of black suicide that I emphasize in this book. Native American death, as Wind notes above, signifies the overcoming of an obstacle to white domination in the liberal imagination, whereas black suicide, as I have been arguing, more often operates to diffuse white anxieties about black freedom and social integration. What they share in common, however, are two important effects. Both fail to attend to the particularities of the cultures and peoples in whose voices they speak. Moreover, both obscure racist structures of thought and feeling by rendering sympathetically dying Native American figures (as noble and/or close to nature) and dying enslaved African-identified figures (as metaphysically liberated) while removing them from the discursive frame. When these deaths are depicted as self-inflicted, they often echo liberal rhetoric and can thus easily be (mis)taken for referenda on natural rights—as expressions of the individual will, rationality, and/or the capacity for inclusion. However, such readings often fail to adequately contend with the suicidal figures' a priori relations to civil society and thus ultimately reinforce social logics that variously turn on those figures' exclusions.

While a full discussion of the differences between these and other regimes of racialization in nineteenth-century British texts is beyond the scope of this project, I raise the issue here to highlight the underlying exclusivity of bourgeois white women's pursuit of "social life." Though its contexts and expressions vary, death is the sine qua non of the era's racial logics. Death by suicide, in turn, uniquely reinforces those logics by alternately sanctioning and foreclosing representation in liberal society depending on the framing of the suicidal figure in relation to the era's broader debates on individual rights, including the right to die. In this way, much like the texts by Robinson and Duras discussed above, "Indian Woman's Death Song" is not an expression of cross-racial affinity or solidarity authorized by a "democratic realm of death."[76] The similarities and differences between "Indian Woman's Death Song" and Hemans's treatment of suicide in her poetry about white women highlight the racial limits of such a democracy. Here, we see cultural differences leveled by the willingness of women broadly marked as nonwhite to embrace literal death, leaving only white womanhood alive."

Hemans's other suicide poems go out of their way to emphasize the whiteness of the women they center—even when those figures do not immediately lend themselves to being read as white. In the headnote to "Properzia Rossi," for example, Hemans writes that the poem was inspired by a painting in which the title figure's white breast is the brightest spot in the image.[77] Likewise, Hemans notes that "The Last Song of Sappho" is styled after a painting by Richard Westmacott the younger, son of the neoclassical sculptor of the same name. While the exact painting that Hemans looked at is not known, most nineteenth-century depictions of Sappho's leap follow the conventions of neoclassical sculpture and emphasize the supposed whiteness of Greek bodies.[78] This emphasis on whiteness is somewhat complicated in "The Bride of the Greek Isle" and "The Sicilian Captive." In these poems, Hemans highlights whiteness in her physical descriptions of the suicidal women but marks them as not white when they choose to die. The bride is described as having a "fair cheek's hue," yet at the moment of her death, she is likened to "an Indian bride" (in this case, Hemans presumably means South Asian, as the bride's self-immolation recalls the Hindu practice of sati).[79] The bride regrets her decision to die too late, and when she does, Hemans restores her whiteness:

> Proudly she stands, like an Indian bride
> On the pyre with the holy dead beside;
> But a shriek from her mother hath caught her ear,
> As the flames to her marriage-robe draw near,
> And starting, she spreads her pale arms in vain
> To the form they must never infold again.[80]

"The Sicilian Captive" likewise insists on the whiteness of its central figure, even as it, again, aligns her desire for death with nonwhiteness. The poem describes the title figure as having a "proud pale brow" and "marble cheek," despite the fact that Sicilians would not have been considered white.[81] It is only in her decision to die, motivated by a desire to return to her home country (echoing popular ideas about African beliefs in transmigration), that she is rendered nonwhite:[82]

> I may not thus depart–farewell! yet no, my country! no!
> Is not love stronger than the grave? I feel it must be so!
> My fleeting spirit shall o'ersweep the mountains and the main,
> And in thy tender starlight rove, and thro' thy woods again.
> Its passion deepens—it prevails!—I break my chain—I come
> To dwell a viewless thing, yet blest–in thy sweet air, my home![83]

In both "The Sicilian Captive" and "The Bride of the Greek Isles," life is associated with whiteness, while death—specifically the decision to choose death—is ascribed to those who are not white.

If self-destruction is a path to freedom for some, it is significant that Hemans takes great care to distance white womanhood from the act of suicide. In "Properzia Rossi" and "The Last Song of Sappho," Hemans emphasizes that she is re-creating other people's stories, rendering in poetic language what other artists had rendered visually. In "The Sicilian Captive" and "The Bride of the Greek Isles," the decision to kill oneself is framed as the purview of darker-skinned women, while white womanhood is extricated from the act of voluntary self-destruction and thus preserved. Thus, even as Hemans is critical of patriarchal structures writ large, her particular critique of white women's oppressions is sublimated through the bodies of nonwhite women. White women elicit sympathy because they are oppressed; however, they die as decidedly nonwhite. That they are in fact the same person emphasizes the extent to which the liberation of white women occurs at the expense of nonwhite women and, more broadly, the extent to which liberalism turns on racialized exclusions. Indeed, though rendered most obviously in Hemans's work, the mutable nature of whiteness, patriarchy, and the exclusions of both is implicit in all of the texts discussed thus far. These varied representations of suicide as, alternately, a signal of rationality and capacity for legibility (in *The Dying Negro*) and one of irrationality that justifies some people's continued subjugation (in the texts discussed in this chapter) hearken to important differences in how liberalism structures the marginalization of enslaved, displaced, and colonized peoples, and women of each group.

Revising Racial Sensibility in *The Story of Mattie J. Jackson*

This chapter has examined how liberal feminism turns on maintaining notions of racial difference, emphasizing how efforts to expand the bounds of liberalism to include white womanhood effectively also reinforced white supremacist ideologies. Building on the critique of sensibility made famous by Wollstonecraft, the white women writers discussed here indiscriminately projected an essentialized incompatibility with reason on nonwhite women. Even as some adopted postures of shared struggle, implicit in such postures is a structural relation of dominance. Within the established logics of the day, laying imaginary claim to the bodies of enslaved, displaced, and/or colonized women by writing their suicides lent white women writers a kind of proximal access to patriarchal authority. By way of conclusion, I want to emphasize that none of this was lost on black women.

With some exceptions, suicide and the strong emotions associated with it tend to figure in more muted ways in much of the era's writing by people of African descent.[84] As the next chapter explores in greater detail, one way in which black authors engaged the literary trope of suicide was to challenge European assumptions about why black people kill themselves: assumptions made popular by abolitionists. *The Story of Mattie J. Jackson* registers the subject of suicide at the level of form to challenge the transatlantic reach of the white supremacist protofeminist logics I have been discussing in this chapter. Jackson's text is noteworthy for how robustly it centers black women. The most important figure in Jackson's life is her mother, Ellen Turner, and much of the short narrative concentrates on their forced separations and hard-won reunions, as well as each woman's individual journey to freedom. The narrative is also notable because it was recorded by a black woman, Dr. L. S. Thompson, Jackson's stepmother. Thompson indicates her gender on the title page, identifying herself as "formerly Mrs. Schuyler," but she leaves the reader to discern that she is of African descent when she appears as a figure in Jackson's life toward the end of the *Story*. These elements combine to make Jackson's autobiography one that, in Joycelyn Moody's words, "'tests' readers' amenability to accepting the discursive authority of a nineteenth-century black woman."[85]

As in many other slave narratives, suicide registers as part of the narrator's lived reality but is not central to her story.[86] In Jackson's text, suicide is mentioned twice, both times on the fringes of the principle narrative. It is significant that both mentions of suicide are essentially apocryphal, having to do with people Jackson herself never met. The first instance concerns a failed suicide attempt. Early in the narrative, she relays a family legend about her grandfather, who had been emancipated after thirty years of enslavement only to be forced back into bondage. He tries to end his life "by perishing with cold and hunger" but is thwarted by his enslaver.[87] In Jackson's telling, this leads to a relatively positive turn: if he had not been found out, he would not have met the woman who would become her grandmother, with whom he "lived as happily as their circumstanced would permit."[88] Suicide is not framed here as a heroic pathway to freedom. Instead, the fact that he did *not* kill himself becomes quietly subversive in that it allows for several generations of familial relations. This implicit rebellion against what Patterson has termed *natal alienation*, a key factor in slaveholding cultures' ability to sustain institutions of enslavement, is made explicit in the close relationship between Jackson and Turner, as well as in the broader fact that Jackson attains what her grandparents could not and goes on to tell their family's story.[89]

The second suicide in Jackson's text is not thwarted, and her account of that suicide leads to a noteworthy break in the narrative. The poem below is one of only a few episodes to openly broach the subject of feeling, and it does so in reference to a figure well on the narrative's periphery. The poem, which is original to the *Story*, appears after Jackson mentions her second stepfather's first wife, who chose to die rather than live without her children:

> In agony close to her bosom she pressed,
> The life of her heart, the child of her breast—
> Oh love from its tenderness gathering might
> Had strengthened her soul for declining age.
> But she is free. Yes, she has gone from the land of the slave;
> The hand of oppression must rest in the grave.
> The blood hounds have missed the scent of her way,
> The hunter is rifled and foiled of his prey.[90]

The poem's indulgence of sentimental tropes stands in stark contrast to the rest of the narrative. In prose, this history is articulated plainly, and this echoes Jackson's straightforward recollections of the many separations her own family endured. Although Jackson discusses losing family and friends to death or forced separation, witnessing and surviving countless physical and psychological abuses, and watching her mother lose two husbands and several children, she rarely dwells on the strong emotions associated with these events. The poem thus shifts the text's tone dramatically, albeit momentarily.

The poem presents the unnamed woman as a grieving mother, a pathetic victim who lacks all agency in life but finally finds freedom in death. The woman's lack of agency and the poem's emphasis on her overwhelming emotions recall Robinson's Zelma and Duras's Ourika, both defined and ultimately undone by excessive feeling. Moreover, the poem's emphasis on the woman finding freedom in death links her to the uneasy relationship between whiteness, femininity, and death in Hemans's suicide poems, as well as to abolitionist texts like *The Dying Negro*, which valorize the self-destruction of black bodies even as they claim interest in improving black lives. Thus, when she repeats this woman's story in decidedly unsentimental prose, Jackson rescues her from the fates of real and fictional black women whose lives were—and in many ways, still are—reduced to sentimental tropes and sacrificed on the altar of white women's rights.

By setting her story about the agency and self-determination of multiple generations of black women against bourgeois liberal feminist tropes, Jackson (as well as Thompson, her amanuensis) indicates how far removed such representations actually are from the lived realities of black women and men. In the starkness of its contrast to the rest of Jackson's narrative, the verse interlude points to the limits of the white abolitionist imagination, as well as to problems in liberal feminist applications of its tropes to define and police the whiteness of "woman." *The Story of Mattie J. Jackson* recognizes that true liberation is not to be found by adhering to the logics of liberal modernity. As the next chapter will show, *The Interesting Narrative of the Life of Olaudah Equiano* presents an alternative.

chapter 3

Writ in Water

At the bottom of the Atlantic Ocean there's a
Railroad made of human bones.
Black ivory
Black ivory.
—Amiri Baraka, *Wise, Why's, Y's:*
The Griot's Song (Djeli Ya)

Here lies one whose name was writ in water.
—Grave of John Keats

Toward the end of *Clotel; or, the President's Daughter*, the first English-language novel by a writer of African descent (published in London in 1853), William Wells Brown's titular heroine, the illegitimate daughter of Thomas Jefferson and an enslaved woman named Currer, escapes capture by jumping into the Potomac River to her death. Brown uses Clotel's suicide to draw attention to the hypocrisy of a society that prides itself on liberal values but that enslaves African-identified people and refuses to acknowledge their humanity:

> Had Clotel escaped from oppression in any other land . . . no honour within the gift of the American people would have been too good to have been heaped upon the heroic woman. But she was a slave, and therefore out of the pale of their sympathy. They have tears to shed over Greece and Poland; they have an abundance of sympathy for "poor Ireland;" they can furnish a ship of war to convey the Hungarian

refugees from a Turkish prison to the "land of the free and home of the brave." They boast that America is the "cradle of liberty;" if it is, I fear they have rocked the child to death.[1]

The tragedy of Clotel's death is not just the fact of her suicide but the social conditions that necessitate it: had she been of almost any other ethnicity, Brown suggests, these conditions would be challenged by the liberal utopia that the United States claims to be. Addressing a culture obsessed with spectacles of voluntary death, Brown insists that the suicides of enslaved Africans are exceptional cases by reasserting, at the moment that Clotel's life ends, her blood ties to the president: "Thus died Clotel, the daughter of Thomas Jefferson, a president of the United States; a man distinguished as the author of the Declaration of American Independence, and one of the first statesmen of that country."[2] Clotel's suicide bears a unique relationship to the bounds of liberalism. While it's true that much of her suffering had been caused by the interlocking structures of white supremacy and patriarchy, her death exceeds the expressive capacity of liberal modernity.

Indeed, Clotel's suicide literally destabilizes Brown's novel, temporarily shifting its language from prose to poetry. In the poem that follows her suicide, Brown turns from the social conditions that drove Clotel's decision to die to what she might have felt in her final seconds of life. Where in the prose narrative Clotel's corpse washes up onto the shore and is unceremoniously buried, the poem lingers on her dying body:

> The dark and the cold, yet merciful wave,
> Receives to its bosom the form of the slave;
> She rises—earth's scenes on her dim vision gleam,
> Yet she struggleth not with the strong rushing stream:
> And low are the death-cries her woman's heart gives,
> As she floats adown the river,
> Faint and more faint grows the drowning voice,
> And her cries have ceased for ever!

A variety of frames associated with suicide converge in Clotel's final moments, and the point of their convergence is her death by water. Clotel's suicide evokes what by 1853 would have been familiar images of enslaved people's voluntary deaths (drawn from sources such as those I have been discussing) as well as more generalized associations between death, blackness, and the Atlantic Ocean. In Britain, this was galvanized by, among others, the 1781 Zong Massacre, in which enslavers alleging a shortage of drinking water threw 133 enslaved Africans overboard in order to claim an insurance payout. As Ian Baucom has discussed, responses to this case, both aesthetic and political, typify how "late-romantic-period Britons were learning to observe, make sense of, and screen themselves off from the greater violence of history."[3] Thus, for example, J. M. W. Turner's painting *Slavers Throwing Overboard the Dead and Dying—Typhoon Coming Up*, which was first exhibited in 1840, presents "a scene of death to which the spectator (in the role of liberal subject) is invited—to watch, sympathetically suffer, and then depart."[4] Somewhat similarly, Brown's poetic description of Clotel's suicide conjures a transcendental imaginary reminiscent of romanticism's aesthetic ethos, which upon closer inspection reveals itself to be rooted in liberalism. Baucom pointedly describes this as "British romanticism dallying in the courts of idealism and speaking the thoughts of liberalism."[5]

If, as we see in the second epigraph to this chapter, romanticism is fascinated with the posthumous haunting of authorial identity "writ in water," black writers offer a perspective on water as another kind of haunting. As Amiri Baraka indicates in the first epigraph to this chapter, the Middle Passage remains a living haunting for many writers of African descent. Here, names and legacies are not preserved for the ages but are violently stripped away.[6] This chapter considers how romanticism's fascination with water—which Samuel Baker has discussed as a moment "when a British literary elite saw the ocean as at once their nation's proper domain, the central geopolitical theater of their age, and the main natural force shaping their world"—is heralded by the literary (and literal) waters of the Middle Passage.[7] The chapter traces how Olaudah Equiano rewrites British representations of enslaved Africans seeking freedom in death by imagining, within the waters of the Atlantic Ocean, an alternative discursive space for subjectivities that do not depend on liberalism's exclusionary logics—in Baraka's terms, an underwater railroad that leads not to freedom within the bounds of liberalism but to life beyond those bounds.

By framing Equiano's own moments of suicidal thinking against the sentimentalism of *The Dying Negro*, *The Interesting Narrative of the Life of Olaudah Equiano* resists liberal notions of suicide as a pathway to freedom. Contrary to the condition of social death imposed on him by agents of the institution of slavery, Equiano's engagements with suicide lead to a powerful affirmation of black life on its own terms. Within the waters of the Atlantic Ocean, Equiano finds new frames for understanding what it means for him to choose, again and again, to stay alive.

In so doing, he troubles the proverbial waters of liberal individualism by asking what a project of freedom *not* oriented on "proving" one's capacity for legibility and integration might entail. Moving beyond discourses of state-sanctioned rights and freedoms, this chapter reads forms of being that exist outside of liberalism's purview, shifting the field of analysis from "the person" to "the human." It concludes by reading John Keats's name—that is, his poetics of/and posthumous fame—writ through Equiano's conception of water.

(Im)possible Life: Blackness and Romanticism

Having grown up navigating the literal and figurative waters of the Middle Passage, Equiano was part and parcel of the maritime economy of interdependent cultural and political formations that Paul Gilroy has famously called the Black Atlantic.[8] Equiano's subjectivity has been discussed using terms like diasporic, compound, and hybrid: as Paul Youngquist puts it, Equiano "shares with many sailors of the Black Atlantic the inability to be in any authentic way African, or American, or British, or whatever ... Citizen of the world, Equiano becomes a multitude."[9] In exploring that multiplicity, *The Interesting Narrative* foregrounds Equiano's blackness. I precisely do not mean his Africanness because, as Bryan Wagner reminds us, "Africa and its diaspora are much older than blackness. Blackness does not come from Africa. Rather, Africa and its diaspora become black at a particular stage of their history."[10] An antithesis to enlightenment ontological categories and epistemological frames, blackness is a constitutive (if, in many fields, still largely underacknowledged) element of the formation of "the west" and, by extension, liberal modernity.[11]

When he invokes *The Dying Negro* in chapter 5, Equiano positions *The Interesting Narrative* against then-popular discourses about the meaning and value of black life. Initially, Equiano asks death to "relieve me from the horrors I felt and dreaded, that I might be in that place 'Where slaves are free, and men oppress no more.'"[12] However, immediately following a nineteen-line excerpt from Day and Bicknell's poem, Equiano changes course: "The turbulence of my emotions ... gave way to calmer thoughts."[13] By distinguishing himself from his Anglo-European interlocutors, he challenges the assumed political efficacy of the strong emotions that underwrite Day and Bicknell's sentimental strategy. In this sense, although *The Dying Negro* and *The Interesting Narrative* ostensibly mean to achieve similar political ends, Equiano departs from the abolitionist modality of sensationalizing black death to spark outrage at the systematic exploitation and devaluation of black life. Instead, he challenges the ease with which readers consumed images of enslaved people's suicides.[14] Liberal strategies of "proving" African-identified people's capacity for social legibility and inclusion through self-destruction brutally foreclose any possibilities for black social existence apart from those sanctioned by the liberal state. If, as Achille Mbembe has taught us, "the ultimate expression of sovereignty resides . . . in the power and the capacity to dictate who may live and who must die," then framing the suicide of an enslaved person as a heroic affirmation of his social legibility only reproduces the sovereign power that drives the fantasy of liberation in the first place.[15]

Rejecting the epistemological and ideological assumptions and technologies that produce this discursive violence, Equiano's *The Interesting Narrative* moves toward a more positive articulation of black life. And while Equiano engages familiar abolitionist rhetoric to accomplish this, he distances himself from many white abolitionists' tendency toward caricature and reductivism. For example, Equiano opens *The Interesting Narrative* by claiming that he is "neither a saint, a hero, nor a tyrant."[16] This is a clear repudiation of the trope of the black martyr—which, as we have seen, effectively naturalizes the relation between blackness and death by dressing it up in descriptions of valor, courage, and sacrifice. By refusing popular British conceptions of what it means for an enslaved person to take his own life, Equiano makes the much more urgent statement that black life matters in its own right—that it can and must be disarticulated from Eurocentric ideologies that would define it in terms of lack, absence, or negation.

He achieves this by drawing on racialized discourses then associated with suicide to subvert Anglo-European ideas about why African-identified people kill themselves. Equiano first mentions suicide in chapter 2 when, having been taken from his family, he briefly escapes and hides out in a nearby thicket. There, he imagines that he might find a way home. His first thoughts of despair set in when he realizes that this will never happen: recalling an overheard conversation between his captors, he writes, "Most of them supposed I had fled towards home; but the distance was so great, and the way so intricate, that they thought I could never reach it, and that I should be lost in the woods. When I heard this I was seized with a violent panic, and abandoned myself to despair."[17] Crucially, when he realizes he is never going home again, he expresses despair but not, as he will do later, thoughts of suicide. As a narrative strategy, this deflects from the already widespread idea that Africans were driven to suicide by a shared belief in transmigration. Equiano distances himself from this belief in the first chapter: "I do not remember to have ever heard of it: some however believe in the transmigration of souls in a certain degree."[18] He underscores that distancing in the thicket by avoiding what to many European readers would have seemed like a natural connection between suicide and returning home.

The first time that he does articulate a desire to die, Equiano likewise undermines European conceptions about African peoples, this time concerning *how* they were presumed to kill themselves. Having gone days without food or water, Equiano writes, "I at length quitted the thicket, very faint and hungry, for I had not eaten or drank any thing all the day; and crept to my master's kitchen . . . and laid myself down in the ashes with an anxious wish for death to relieve me from all my pains."[19] Though he wants death to relieve his suffering from hunger, he does not act to kill himself; and indeed, underscores that point by commenting, in the next paragraph, on his new enslaver's suicidality following the death of his wife. This is contrary to the widespread notion among Europeans that Africans (especially the Igbo, Equiano's stated ethnicity of origin) favored starvation as a means of inflicting their own deaths. As Terri Snyder has shown, popular representations of the methods used to complete suicide reveal "notions of temperamental, ethnic, and racial characteristics that distinguished cultural outsiders . . . from Europeans."[20] According to Snyder, firearms were primarily associated with elite European men, hanging or drowning was attributed to white laboring-class men and white women of all social classes, and starvation or geophagy (eating dirt) became associated with enslaved Africans. In 1798, the English physician George Davidson described geophagy, which was then medically termed *Cachexia Africana*, as a particular "malady of West Indian slaves."[21] Davidson's description recalls George Cheyne's *The English Malady*, which set forth a theory of suicide as a particularly British penchant. Differentiating between Africans' and Europeans' methods of killing themselves thus enabled a way of distinguishing and maintaining perceived hierarchies between two supposedly suicide-prone cultures. Tellingly, Europeans did not acknowledge enslavement as a factor in why people of African descent killed themselves in such large numbers; rather, a common argument was that Africans were "ethnically predisposed to suicide."[22] Ironically, then, Anglo-Europeans came to rely on the same link between suicide and culture to demonstrate African peoples' "fitness" for enslavement, which earlier in the century had been considered part and parcel of English identity. Equiano's rejection of transmigration as motive and starvation as method undercuts both stereotypes.

Yet even as *The Interesting Narrative* begins to subvert European stereotypes about African minds, Equiano cannot escape the assaults on his own mind and body during his first voyage across the Atlantic. Twice repeating that he had "never experienced anything of the kind before," Equiano emphasizes the strangeness of these assaults:

> I was soon put down under the decks, and there I received such a salutation in my nostrils as I had never experienced in my life; so that, with the loathsomeness of the stench, and crying together, I became so sick and low that I was not able to eat, nor had I the least desire to taste anything. I now wished for the last friend, Death, to relieve me; but soon, to my grief, two of the white men offered me eatables; and, on my refusing to eat, one of them held me fast by the hands, and laid me across, I think, the windlass, and tied my feet, while the other flogged me severely. I had never experience anything of the kind before.[23]

In spite of the fact that he is, at this point in his life, still afraid of water ("I naturally feared that element the first time I saw it"[24]), he insists that he "would have jumped over the side" if not for an even bigger fear of being caught and whipped for the attempt.[25] Even if he had made the attempt, it likely would have been prevented by antisuicide nets commonly installed on slave ships (and in this way, enslaved people's capacity to choose whether to live or die was increasingly determined by enslavers and the environments they constructed). Shortly after this episode, when he witnesses the callous burial at sea of a white sailor—"they tossed him over the side as they would have done a brute"—his thoughts of suicide begin to evolve.[26]

In the following passage, Equiano reiterates, nearly verbatim, his first survey of the ship, describing again many of the same abject conditions he illustrated just four pages earlier (in the original 1789 printing; in most modern editions, these passages appear even closer together):

> The stench of the hold while we were on the coast was so intolerably loathsome, that it was dangerous to remain there for any time, and some of us had been permitted to stay on the deck for the fresh air; but now that the whole ship's cargo were confined together, it became almost pestilential. The closeness of the place, and the heat of the climate, added to the number in the ship, which was so crowded that each had scarcely room to turn himself, almost suffocated us. . . . The shrieks of the women, and the groans of the dying, rendered the whole a scene of horror almost inconceivable. Happily perhaps for myself I

was soon reduced so low here that it was thought necessary to keep me almost always on deck; and from my extreme youth, I was not put in fetters. In this situation, I expected every hour to share the fate of my companions, some of whom were almost daily brought upon deck at the point of death, which I began to hope would soon put an end to my miseries. Often did I think many of the inhabitants of the deep much more happy than myself; I envied them the freedom they enjoyed, and as often wished I could change my condition for theirs.[27]

Here, Equiano find himself wishing for death again, but rather than feeling powerless against the ship's various technologies of control, his suicidal longing leads him to reckon with the (im)possibility of black futurity. In this register, his reference to the "inhabitants of the deep" is a profoundly interesting turn of phrase, paying homage to African folktales of transatlantic flight while maintaining his self-professed disbelief in the transmigration of souls.[28]

Folktales of transatlantic flight abound among disparate peoples of the African diaspora. They tell of humans having access to magical powers that allow them to fly or, in some versions, walk over water back to Africa. One event informed by these beliefs, which has since also come to be strongly associated with suicide, occurred in 1803 on Georgia's St. Simon's Island, widely known today as Igbo Landing. This event was recalled by several formerly enslaved people interviewed for the Federal Writers' Project in the 1930s. One interviewee, "Uncle Jonah" Sunbury, remembers "a boatload" of enslaved people "tak[ing] wing and fly[ing] back home."[29] The event at Igbo Landing, wherein thirteen enslaved people drowned themselves, is widely read as a form of rebellion by collective suicide. However, as Floyd White, another Federal Writers' Project interviewee contends, if this was a rebellion, it failed: the people drowned.[30] Suicide, then, is not necessarily the right framework through which to interpret flying African legends, not least because it presumes a freely made choice. As Snyder argues, "to the extent that suicide was conscious and deliberate, it was selected from an egregiously narrow range of possibilities. . . . To say that slaves, ironically, chose [suicide] in order to die autonomously or to argue that slave self-destruction was an index of their humanity ignores both the chillingly fatal cost of slaves' self-destructive acts—they died—and the meanings of those deaths."[31] Flying African legends thus present discursive and epistemological possibilities that unsettle the differential logics through which Anglo-Europeans understood acts of voluntary death among enslaved peoples.[32]

Thus, even as Equiano, writing as a converted Christian, distances himself from African beliefs, his reference to the "inhabitants of the deep" nevertheless registers and pays them homage. Looking into the water during a moment of particular anguish, the phrase may well refer to the countless dead at the bottom of the ocean where, in this moment, he wishes to be. Yet this imagined communion with the dead is not sentimentalized as it inevitably would have been in contemporaneous abolitionist texts. Having already distanced himself from transmigration, we know it is not freedom in Africa that Equiano imagines when he stares into that water. Nor does Equiano frame freedom in death as a form of resistance, although as he makes clear elsewhere in *The Interesting Narrative*, he does not foreclose resistance as a motivating factor for others.[33] Equiano himself found other ways of resisting including, as Marcus Rediker has argued, by learning the workings of the ship and becoming indispensable to the crew.[34] Certainly, becoming a sailor offered a way for Equiano to stay alive. But in challenging racialized conceptions of why and how African people kill themselves so early in *The Interesting Narrative*, Equiano sets up the rest of the text to explore what it means for him to *live*. And so, when Equiano stares into the water, staring back at him is the very futurity that the politics and policies of enslavement—of denying a human being his claim to humanity, of turning his body into a commodity—mean to preclude.

Equiano's revision of popular ideas about enslaved people's suicides is, moreover, a radical recuperation of the flesh, as defined by Hortense Spillers, from liberalism's dichotomy between body and no body. When he stares into the water and doesn't jump, he demands that Anglo-European readers confront what it means that someone they have deprived of social life would keep choosing to live. By centering the flesh, Equiano anticipates Weheliye's critique of the primacy of the body in western notions of the legal and ontological construction of both personhood and the human. As discussed in this book's first chapter, Weheliye asks what a conception of the human might look like as an ontological totality: "a relational assemblage exterior to the jurisdiction of law given that the law . . . does not possess the authority to nullify the politics and poetics of the flesh found in the traditions of the oppressed."[35] Contrary to the body, on which so many of liberal modernity's social logics turn, the flesh offers Equiano a completely different basis for defining what it is to be human. The apparent impossibility, then, of Equiano's vision of life within the ocean's mortal depths registers how the violence of antiblackness produces, even as it means to negate, black social existence.

Within a western frame, "black life" has been rendered nearly as impossible a configuration as "inhabiting the deep." To reconcile black social existence with humanity demands the complete disordering of the social world as we know it. As Wilderson has argued, "One would have to lose one's Human coordinates and become Black. Which is to say, one would have to die."[36] Likewise, *The Interesting Narrative* highlights how asserting the value of black lives in a liberal frame conscripts those lives to the very dialectic that necessitates their status *as* black in the first place, thereby ensuring that "black lives" never attain "black life." For Wilderson, the epistemological borders between black and nonblack are impermeable within the terms of liberal modernity. To move beyond them requires the absolute destruction and reconstruction of society as we know it. *The Interesting Narrative* understands this intractability; however, in Equiano's hands, the singularity of the flesh signals possibilities beyond these bounds. This is why, in the waters of the Atlantic Ocean, a space of so much death, Equiano still manages to find life. But to articulate what he sees there in a framework not bound to liberal notions of humanity—defined as such contra (black) nonhumanity—Equiano must first distance himself from "the human" altogether. And thus, his reference to the "inhabitants of the deep" may also be quite literal.

Equiano's Black Ecology

Throughout the early chapters of *The Interesting Narrative*, Equiano is fascinated by the aquatic creatures that he encounters on the ship. These other life forms allow him to access an alternative ontological imaginary; thus, they offer a reprieve from the real and figurative encounters with death that structure so much of his existence on the ship. Building from the existing category confusion of the human with the nonhuman that drove the institution of slavery (i.e., turning human beings into nonhuman objects), Equiano's growing interest in aquatic life opens his text to the possibility of reading human being through an ethic and praxis of relation. Equiano thus transforms the enslaved African into what we might call an ecological subject—a subject that stands open to and is defined by the complexity of interrelations between the worlds of human and nonhuman beings.

Pseudoscientific racist discourses have authorized and disseminated the bestialization of blackness so much so that thinking about them together necessitates certain caveats. As Sharon Patricia Holland writes, "in the vocabularies of vulnerability applied to black agents, we can recognize a constant worry about the descent into animality."[37] However, Holland challenges this negative relation, showing that "there *are* narratives that place black being, black-ness in direct relation to the animal in modes of consideration, relation, and mutual observation that do not always already follow a prescription for violent trespass, possible descent or . . . negative mimetic relation."[38] I would suggest that Equiano's is one such narrative—a reclamation of a fuller scope of humanity than what is allowed by "enlightened" delimitations of blackness as antithetical to human being, achieved by attending to forms of nonhuman life. To be clear, Equiano does not actually equate blackness with animality. Rather, he engages the logics of categorization that undergird the era's pseudosciences of race to trouble the lines that within these logics demarcate who does and who does not "count" as human.

This begins with Equiano's recognition of the ocean as a life-sustaining force. Even as it is a mass grave for countless human beings, the ocean also provides sustenance to humans in the form of food and exists as a vast ecosystem unto itself. In this sense, Equiano's mode of thinking blackness ecologically also prefigures contemporary scientific findings that, as Christina Sharpe has discussed, indicate the continued atomic presence of enslaved people's bodies as part of the ocean's ecologies:

> The atoms of those people who were thrown overboard are out there in the ocean even today. They were eaten, organisms processed them, and those organisms were in turn eaten and processed, and the cycle continues. . . . The amount of time it takes for a substance to enter the ocean and leave the ocean is called residence time. Human blood is salty, and sodium . . . has a residence time of 260 million years. And what happens to the energy that it produced in the waters? It continues cycling like atoms in residence time. We, Black people, exist in the residence time of the wake.[39]

When Equiano encounters fish as a child on the first of many transatlantic voyages, he registers them as food: "One day they had taken a number of fishes; and when they had killed and satisfied themselves with as many as they thought fit, to our astonishment who were on the deck, rather than give any of them to us to eat as we expected, they tossed the remaining fish into the sea again, although we begged and prayed for some as well as we could, but in vain."[40] As the narrative progresses he begins to define his own life in terms of the lives of the fish he observes: the fish are also captured and discarded at the whims of European enslavers. Indeed, like many newly captured Africans, Equiano initially assumes that he has been captured and brought on board the ship to be eaten like the fish.[41]

Nor is this slippage between animal and human limited to Equiano's personal reflections. Ocean life also serves an important biopolitical function for the enslavers. In keeping enslaved people from eating the fish caught on the deck, white sailors mark their authority and delineate the captives as other than human and less than human (if not, at this point, altogether nonhuman). Monique Allewaert has developed a framework for reading the disciplining of enslaved bodies in terms of what she calls the parahuman, "an interstitial form of life that could be exploited for labor power in the way animals were . . . a perversion of the category of the human."[42] While eighteenth-century taxonomies of nature commonly categorized Africans simply as animals, Allewaert introduces the parahuman to recover the complex ways in which enslaved peoples negotiated their own humanity against European classificatory logics. Thus, she posits that the era of slavery introduced a new, if largely unacknowledged, understanding of the human that "loosens subjective identifications with either human or animal forms of being" and enables "an articulation of equality in diversity on a species level."[43] *The Interesting Narrative* hearkens toward such an understanding of a double suicide, which Equiano witnesses just after the episode in which the starving captives are denied fish to eat:

> Some of my countrymen, being pressed by hunger, took an opportunity, when they thought no one saw them, of trying to get a little privately; but they were discovered, and the attempt procured them some very severe floggings. One day . . . two of my wearied countrymen who were chained together (I was near them at the time), preferring death to such a life of misery, somehow made through the nettings and jumped into the sea: immediately another quite dejected fellow, who, on account of his illness, was suffered to be out of irons, also followed their example; and I believe many more would very soon have done the same if they had not been prevented by the ship's crew, who were instantly alarmed.[44]

The enslavers' deliberate category confusion between human being and object is underscored by the taxonomies used to justify racial enslavement. These logics are challenged when the starving captives move to steal the fish, unequivocally asserting their humanity. The flogging they receive is meant to discipline them from human being to object, but the three people who choose to die instead undermine that process. What is so precisely alarming about these suicides for the sailors is the enslaved men's refusal to be disciplined as objects. Two of the three men complete their refusals and drown; one is pulled back and "flogged ... unmercifully for thus attempting to prefer death to slavery."[45]

Following the double suicide and thwarted third attempt, Equiano starts to register the full strangeness of his circumstances, including his status as parahuman. This transition is marked by his evolving views on fish, from food that sustains human life to forms of life worthy of recognition as such in their own right: "I first saw flying fishes, which surprised me very much: they used frequently to fly across the ship, and many of them fell on the deck ... I was now more persuaded than ever that I was in another world, and that every thing about me was magic."[46] Ocean life increasingly inspires flights of fancy in Equiano, and through these, he imagines alternatives to enslavement and its underlying ideologies. At one point, he regards orcas as akin to gods: "I believed them to be the rulers of the sea ... the wind just then died away, and a calm ensued, and in consequence of it the ship stopped going. I supposed that the fish had performed this."[47] This marks a departure from his sense, just a few passages earlier, of himself as interchangeable with a captured and abused shark.[48] And it also suggests another reference point for Equiano: in addition to human beings who died on the Middle Passage and aquatic animals that alternately sustain (in multiple senses) and inspire him, Equiano's invocation of the "inhabitants of the deep" also calls forth the Afrodiasporic water spirit Mami Wata.

Though water deities are common in many African cultures, Mami Wata belongs, uniquely, to the African diaspora. There is some dispute regarding her exact origins, but most scholars agree that Mami Wata stories developed in West Africa in the fifteenth century, roughly conterminously with the beginnings of large-scale European exploitation of African peoples and resources. Mami Wata stories modify earlier tropes of water spirits as embodied in aquatic creatures by incorporating European water-related mythical imagery such as mermaids.[49] Even the spirit's name is said, by some, to be a pidgin English for "Mother of Water." In this sense, Mami Wata registers the variety of prediasporic African beliefs while also delineating a new cultural imaginary that exceeds their national bounds. However, as a number of critics stress, she is not, herself, "a pidgin phenomenon."[50] Though undeniably linked to and influenced by non-African cultures, Mami Wata stories and practices of worship did not develop for foreign consumption. Rather, she offers a window into how Africans understood their early encounter with Europeans.[51] Mami Wata registers perspectives that tend to get lost in Eurocentric accounts of African peoples and their histories. Insofar as she developed from African recalibrations of European cultural tropes—not the other way around—Mami Wata is an important symbol of African agency over European cultural imports. At the same time, she is a manifestation of the necessarily intercultural multiplicity that buttresses Afrodiasporic ontologies and epistemologies.

Exactly how Mami Wata registers relations between Africa and Europe varies considerably. In coastal Ghana, stories of Mami Wata's influence over inclement weather phenomena are registered as vengeance for the trade in enslaved Africans.[52] Elsewhere, Mami Wata embodies western obsessions with luxury, wealth, and power; in these stories, she represents values quite antithetical to those of precolonial Africans.[53] She has also been linked to versions of flying African folktales, as Michelle D. Commander explains below:

> During the slave trade, a group of Igbo Africans who, though shackled together on a slave ship, called on Mami Wata to "carry" them back home to Africa, a plea that she granted, endowing them with the needed strength to leap into the ocean. Their screams, the clinking of metal shackles against the body of the ship, and their impassioned entreaties to Mami Wata are thus fabled to endure in the Atlantic's sonic atmosphere, offering a radical, haunting reverberation.[54]

Equiano's thoughts of dying during his spiritual encounter with the "inhabitants of the deep" mark a moment of resistance, a stance against defining himself according to liberal principles. Though he does not name her, the spirit of Mami Wata propels him toward renewed agency and self-identification that proceeds from a position of encounter *with*, not *as*, the other. Calling on Mami Wata destabilizes his natal alienation. The spirits that Equiano encounters in the water return him, if not specifically to his Igbo roots, then to a broader Afrodiasporic heritage. Thus, they reestablish a component of the social life that the system of chattel slavery means to deny him—a life now neither wholly western nor wholly African but precisely diasporic. Part human and part fish, Mami Wata is likewise "a transcendent, transformative, transcultural, transnational, transgendered, trans-Atlantic being."[55] Acknowledging his own multiplicity enables Equiano to reconceptualize the human as relational and mediated through encounter not only with political subjects (as created by and understood within the liberal imaginary) but also with the panoply of intra- and interspecies nonsubjects (against which liberalism defines itself).

Bearing this relation to natural and supernatural aquatic life in mind, I return to the critical moment when Equiano looks into the water and sees freedom:

> I expected every hour to share the fate of my companions, some of whom were almost daily brought upon deck at the point of death, which I began to hope would soon put an end to my miseries. Often did I think many of the inhabitants of the deep much more happy than myself. I envied them the freedom they enjoyed, and as often wished I could change my condition for theirs.[56]

If this begins as a solipsistic moment, it evolves into a radically hopeful denial of the ontological impossibility of black life wrought by liberal modernity's association of blackness with (social) death. Whatever or whomever the "inhabitants" represent, Equiano's experience with "the deep" moves his narrative toward extra- or superhuman intimacy and agency. This encounter thus functions to bring into Equiano's purview the political efficacy of relation. Born(e) from the particular traumas of African enslavement, relation in this sense is diametrically opposed to the structures of exclusionary individualism, as Édouard Glissant explains:

> Straight from the belly of the slave ship into the violent belly of the ocean depths they went. But their ordeal did not die. . . .The unconscious memory of the abyss served as the alluvium for these metamorphoses. The populations that then formed, despite having forgotten the chasm, despite being unable to imagine the passion of those who foundered there, nonetheless wove this sail (a veil). They did not use it to return to the Former Land but rose up on this unexpected, dumbfounded land. They met the first inhabitants, who had also been deported by permanent havoc; or perhaps they only caught a whiff of the ravaged train of these people. . . .Thus, the absolute unknown, projected by the abyss . . . in the end became knowledge. Not just a specific knowledge . . . but knowledge of the Whole, greater from having been at the abyss and freeing knowledge of Relation within the Whole.[57]

Although Glissant recognizes the slave ship as a site of devastation, he also sees in it a generative quality, frequently referring to it as a womb.

As in Gilroy's framework of the Black Atlantic, Glissant frames the slave ship as a source of unanimity that through shared suffering joined multilingual and initially disconnected peoples. The abyss—the vast ocean of anguish endured and remembered by peoples of the African diaspora—enables not only the development of a unique set of identities but also points of entry into establishing connections with other subjugated peoples. This, in turn, enables more capacious forms of knowledge, "not just a specific knowledge, appetite, suffering, and delight of one particular people."[58] The abyss thus informs epistemologies beyond the western world's self-sanctioned, self-disseminated, and self-policed narratives of enlightened modernity.

What Glissant describes as "the Whole" or totality may just as well be discussed using the term *ecology*, based, as it is, in recognition of the interconnectedness of all human and nonhuman beings. Glissant's notion of relation shares deep affinities with the sense of interrelation between beings posited by ecological thinking. Equiano's emphasis on representing nonhuman beings as, by turns, metaphors and analogues for his own experience draws our attention to ecological spaces marked and sustained by mutually coexisting forms of life. It is toward such an ecology that Equiano himself drives in likening his experience on the ship with those that inhabit the deep. Thus, Equiano's conception of his own identities as African, English, diasporic, multiple—as well as his broader interrogation of the western project of "the human"—emerges from a pattern of interactions (an ecological relation) between the alien lives of nonhuman animals and superhuman spirits and the alienation of enslavement. Equiano's narrative positions itself against the individualism of "Man" and the false promises of liberal humanism, moving toward something akin to Glissant's notion of relation.

Yet contrary to Glissant's reclamation of the slave ship as a generative space, for Equiano, the ship remains a space of death. While one can argue that his experiences as a sailor eventually lead him to social integration and legibility, the life that he finds there—not to mention at the conclusion of the narrative when he marries a white woman and establishes himself as a member of English society—is only "life" according to liberal modernity's terms. The slave-ship-as-womb analogy may thus, at best, be read as a metaphor for what Jared Sexton describes as stalled birth, an endlessly "unbearable blackness" that creates the condition of possibility for the human, even as it is decidedly not human itself: "Racial blackness as the sine qua non of enslavement is devolved into a form of prenatal animation—'stuff floating' . . . in amniotic fluid somewhere between the embryonic and the fetal, between swelling and sucking, [akin to what Alain Badiou and Slavoj Žižek discuss as] 'a terrifying excess which, although it negates what we understand as 'humanity,' is inherent to being-human.'"[59] Thus, it is precisely not on the ship but in the ocean, through the human dead, nonhuman animals, and superhuman water spirits, that Equiano envisages black futurity and survival.

Black Optimism and Equiano's Poetic Turn

At its most radical, *The Interesting Narrative* invites readers to embrace the deep. I see this move as anticipating Moten's emphasis on "*life and optimism*" over and against Afropessimism's emphasis on death (even as Moten agrees with Sexton's appraisal of the two projects as, in terms of their larger political, ethical, and intellectual commitments, "not but nothing other than one another").[60] Where both projects understand blackness as ontologically exterior to civil society, Moten recalibrates the focus: rather than accepting blackness as the by-product of liberalism's imposition of social death on those against whom its subjects define themselves as living, Moten emphasizes that "black life is lived . . . in the burial ground of the subject by those who, insofar as they are not subjects, are also not . . . 'death-bound.'"[61] Which is to say, black life is not the condition of possibility for someone else's humanity. Rather, if we shift our epistemological grounding to recognize liberal modernity itself as the domain and dominion of death, social and otherwise, then "(the thinking and study of) blackness . . . bears the potential to end this funereal reign with an animative breath . . . [to] produce the absolute overturning, the absolute turning of this motherfucker out."[62] Thus, though he ultimately accedes (at least superficially) to the bounds of liberalism, Equiano's turn to the deep is cause for celebration "not because celebration is supposed to make us feel good or make us better, though there would be nothing wrong with that. It is, rather, because the cause for celebration turns out to be the condition of possibility of black thought. . . . Celebration is the essence of black thought, the animation of black operations, which are, in the first instance, our undercommon, underground, submarine sociality."[63] By the end of *The Interesting Narrative*, we might say that Equiano surfaces to become a respected member of English society (and this, perhaps, is its own kind of suicide, even as it facilitates his survival). But even where he accepts certain structures of whiteness to authorize his legibility in England and the British Atlantic world, he does so without completely abandoning his interrogation of those structures.

Although it occasionally includes excerpts from popular poetry, *The Interesting Narrative* itself is composed in prose with one significant exception: a long poem in the middle of chapter 10 entitled "Miscellaneous Verses; or, Reflections on the State of My Mind during My First Convictions of the Necessity of Believing the Truth, and of Experiencing the Inestimable Benefits of Christianity." Here, Equiano's negotiation of his conversion to Christianity irrupts from prose into lyrical verse and, much like the poetry of his close contemporary Phillis Wheatley, Equiano's is rife with double meanings. The poem embedded late in *The Interesting Narrative* revisits the autobiography's earlier engagement with the subject of suicide. Though it announces itself as a poem about religious awakening, Equiano's references to suicide continue to challenge the bounds of "Man," even as he appears to integrate and capitulate to western social norms.

Echoing reasons he had already given for why he chose to stay alive—namely, the antisuicide devices installed on slave ships and his disbelief in transmigration—Equiano recalls his life in bondage as one of perpetual melancholy with no agency:

> Prevented, that I could not die,
> Nor could to one sure refuge fly;
> An orphan state I had to mourn,-
> Forsook by all, and left forlorn.[64]

Importantly, he distances the mental state he describes here from the suicidal melancholy depicted by abolitionist poetry, declaring that spectators "by appearance could not know / The troubles that I waded through."[65] Further, Equiano ascribes his decision not to kill himself to the Christian deity: "I wish'd for death, but check'd the word, / And often pray'd unto the Lord."[66] If this refers to the moments of suicidality he had discussed in Part 1, then this is a revisionist moment and one of self-contradiction; but I read it as part of another rhetorical strategy. The following stanza suggests an explanation for why he chooses life that does not contradict what Equiano had established in Part 1:

> Unhappy, more than some on earth,
> I thought the place that gave me birth—
> Strange thoughts oppress'd—while I replied
> 'Why not in Ethiopia died?'[67]

Here, Equiano credits Africa, not Christianity or the west, with keeping him from killing himself. The dashes in the second and third lines above break up the grammar of the stanza, highlighting that it is "the place that gave me birth" that finally curbs his "strange thoughts" of suicide. The stanza thus gives an Afrocentric reason for his choosing to stay alive. The strained grammar of this stanza, particularly in the final question lacking a clear subject, suggests that African life and thought cannot be fully expressed by the rules of the English language. As such, it begs the question of whether the life Equiano leads and the identities he inhabits as he writes these words can be mapped onto the organizing structures of liberal modernity. If, in the context of the society that sanctions his publication, to be English is to be fully human, then of course it tracks that he would have his mostly white readers believe that a formerly enslaved African can become an English subject. Still, he continues to push against the bounds of this framework of the human as he had done earlier—by turning to the nonhuman animal.

Echoing his earlier communion with aquatic beings, Equiano now considers the freedom of aerial ones:

> Oft times I mus'd, and nigh despair,
> While birds melodious fill'd the air;
> 'Thrice happy songsters, ever free,'
> How blest were they, compared to me![68]

Where, in his encounter with the inhabitants of the deep, Equiano saw blackness in the water, here he locates it in the air, as "sable clouds began to rise." This is interrupted as "The English nation [calls him] to leave."[69] In framing England as a nation at a distance—not, for example, as "my" nation—Equiano underscores that his imagination remains independent of the dominating ideologies of the west. Thus, Equiano's engagement with the idea of suicide demands to be read not in terms of the liberal imaginary *to* which he addresses his autobiography but instead through the human dead, the nonhuman animals, and the superhuman spirits *with* and *through* whom he seems to be writing.

The transcendental capacity that Equiano finds in his communion with these figures helps him to revise well-meaning but ultimately ill-conceived sentiments that would reduce his life to a legal abstraction—a "slave" always already devoid of civic or social life—rather than a human being whose enslavement is naturalized by the society that takes it upon itself to write the terms of his liberation. In this sense,

Equiano's "inhabitants of the deep" function somewhat similarly to romantic notions about the capacity of the poetic imagination to transcend the material boundedness of being human. Equiano embraces the sea to open his reader's gaze beyond the limits that liberal modernity places on his humanity. I wonder whether and how twenty-first-century engagements with romanticism might follow that gaze further into the deep: to account for and allow black epistemologies to reorient the stories we tell about romanticism and to bring forward new possibilities for reading romanticism in expanded political and historical contexts. By way of conclusion, I would like to reframe one foundational example of romantic thought through the contra- or parahuman heuristics I have been discussing here.

Keats's Posthumous Life

Much has been made of John Keats's self-authored epitaph: "Here lies one whose name was writ in water." Recollections of the poet who claimed to be "in love with easeful death" have fed the association between artistic genius and what I have been calling romantic suicide, even as Keats's penchant for thinking about his own death is not, as some have argued, easily reducible to suicidality.[70] In his final letter, written to Charles Brown on November 30, 1820, Keats complains that the intensity of his illness has caused him to lead an already "posthumous existence."[71] Along similar lines, Joseph Severn later recalls that Keats would weep when he awoke and found himself still living.[72] Thus, Keats's ready embrace of death at the end of his short life, combined with his well-documented anxiety about his literary legacy ("I have left no immortal work behind me—nothing to make my friends proud of my memory"), animates a familiar narrative of Keats as the quintessential tortured artist who only came to be appreciated after his death.[73]

Keats's reputation as a frail, misunderstood genius who was finally undone by bad reviews persists as an organizing myth of British romanticism, and thus, to be "writ in water" has come to signal an ethereal literary legacy. This is coincidentally compounded by Percy Shelley's death by drowning and his own epitaph, "Nothing of him that doth fade, but doth suffer a sea-change, into something rich and strange," from Shakespeare's *The Tempest*. The metonymic relation between the trope of water—as a symbol of fluidity, atemporality, mutability—and the early death of a particular sort of poet blurs the line between the poetry and the men who wrote it. But what about those people whose lives and deaths are not recalled in books or marked by gravestones?

Reframed through Equiano's discussion of the inhabitants of the deep, to be writ in water opens a different critical register within which to read canonical romanticism. If the black ecological gaze enables alternatives to western conceptualizations of the human, it does so not only for people of African descent but also, necessarily, for Europeans. Such recalibrations are necessary for all of us who live in the afterlife of Atlantic slavery. Keats's rejection of the material world and his desire to transcend the boundedness of his humanity shares something in common with Equiano's (re)vision of the human. Indeed, though Keats invokes it as the archaic form of "written," the word "writ" also recalls the language of law and the primacy that liberal modernity places on the body. In this framework, Keats's appeal to immanence might be taken as an attempt to reconceptualize the human rather than to keep alive the restrictive and exclusionary ideal of tragic white masculinity.

In his most explicitly suicidal work, "Ode to a Nightingale," Keats rejects the human in the same manner as Equiano had done: by appealing to nonhuman animals. Keats's association of the nightingale with "the viewless wings of Poesy," coupled with his emphasis on her immortality, suggests that he is also calling up something extra- or superhuman. Equiano's turn to Mami Wata gives way to, in Keats, the Greek myth of Philomela in an asymptotically related effort to revise and open new understandings of the human. Sometimes named, but more often troped as a nightingale, robin, thrush, or some other singing bird, Philomela is enshrined in Anglo-European poetics as a symbol of that which is perpetually present but defies straightforward expression, thereby calling forth the necessity of poetry. Twentieth-century poet and critic Allen Grossman has argued that the western poetic tradition is founded on the complementary myths of Philomela and Orpheus. Orpheus becomes the emblematic poet of "humanity" after he loses everything that defines him as a man: his wife dies, mad women tear him apart (in many versions of the story, castrating him), and still he sings on. Implicitly, the Orphean paradigm turns on an understanding of humanity in terms of western male subjectivity. But as Grossman tells us, Philomela precedes this paradigm. Ovid's *Metamorphoses* introduces Philomela as a noble woman raped by the king Tereus, her sister's husband. To silence her, Tereus cuts out her tongue, but Philomela finds a way to tell her story by weaving it into a tapestry. Ultimately, Philomela is transformed into a nightingale and sings in perpetuity. Grossman points to a key moment in Virgil's *Georgics* when Orpheus encounters Philomela already in her nightingale form:

> Month in, month out, seven whole months, men say beneath a lofty cliff by lonely Strymon's shore [Orpheus] wept, and deep in icy caverns, unfolding this his tale, charming tigers, and making the oaks attend his strain; even as the nightingale, mourning beneath the poplar's shade, bewails the loss of her brood, that a churlish ploughman hath espied and torn unfledged from the nest: but she weeps all night long and, perched on a spray, renews her piteous strain, filling the region with sad laments.[74]

This episode suggests that Philomela is older than Orpheus. Her songs presuppose and announce his, but he is unable to recognize hers. In her transformation to a nightingale, she is freed from human being, and thus she sings from beyond it. This is the freedom that Keats seeks when he imagines that he might "drink, and leave the world unseen / And with [the nightingale] fade away into the forest dim."[75]

Unlike many contemporaneous engagements with the nightingale—wherein she is either held up as an abstract ideal (as in Charlotte Smith's *Elegiac Sonnets*) or made to speak in a language that isn't hers (as in Samuel Taylor Coleridge's "The Nightingale: A Conversation Poem")—Keats speaks not *about* or *as* but *to* the nightingale. The poem begins in a heavily enjambed first person that seems to teeter, by the third and fourth lines, on the edge of the third person: "My heart aches, and a drowsy numbness pains / my sense, as though of hemlock I had drunk, / Or emptied some dull opiate to the drains / One minute past, and Lethe wards had sunk."[76] It is not until the fifth line that the speaker addresses the nightingale directly, and even here, the address functions only to establish an audience for him to continue his own narrative of self-searching: "Tis not through envy of thy happy lot / But being too happy in thine happiness, / That thou. . . . Singest of summer in full-throated ease."[77] In the first stanza, the enjambment undergirds dizzying shifts between points of view, from the introspective lyricism of the opening, to the narrative mode in the middle, and finally to the outward-facing address of the stanza's conclusion. The poem carries on in this fashion, changing quickly and unexpectedly, without the ordering mechanisms of end-line or stanza breaks to mark shifts in perspective, temporality, and address, even as it is otherwise heavily structured through rhyme. Thus, the only consistently identifiable perspective becomes the reader's own. But even this is called into question when, in appealing to the nightingale, the speaker also reaches out to the reader.

In this way, Keats locates the reader in the position of the extrahuman subject, even as he precludes any reader's full identification with the mythic bird by reminding us of her immortality: "Thou wast not born for death, immortal Bird! / No hungry generations tread thee down; / The voice I hear this passing night was heard / In ancient days by emperor and clown."[78] For Helen Vendler, this moment suggests "a democratic diffusion: the song is audible to all alike."[79] However, there is also something decidedly undemocratic in the fact that the reader cannot but identify with the speaker, the inescapably human subject whose humanity is marked by the reason for his invocation of the nightingale in the first place, his increasingly debilitated body:

> The weariness, the fever, and the fret
> Here, where men sit and hear each other groan;
> Where palsy shakes a few, sad, last grey hairs,
> Where youth grows pale, and spectre-thin, and dies;
> Where but to think is to be full of sorrow
> And leaden-eyed despairs;
> Where beauty cannot keep her lustrous eyes,
> Or new love pine at them beyond to-morrow.[80]

Against these physical limitations, the speaker imagines flying "on the viewless wings of poesy."[81] In giving himself wings, the speaker seeks to become the nightingale. However, by virtue of the form of his address, any communion with the nightingale is also an appeal to the reader. And thus, our position within the poem is perplexed again, as we are forced to consider how to move from that which seems to define some and preclude others from being seen as fully human—our variously aged, gendered, racialized bodies—to something quite beyond them. Keats's nightingale thus signals the possibility but also the difficulty of thinking beyond the western frame of the human; thus, the poem ends with the speaker's return to the humanity he knows, which is to say, his own, relegating any possibilities opened by the nightingale to "a vision, or a waking dream,"[82] a figment of the imagination.

In the black radical tradition of which Equiano is a key progenitor, the imagination is strongly and sometimes singularly associated with freedom. Among other things, the imagination holds within it the potentiality of revising or dismantling the social logics that define blackness as negation. As Moten writes, "The imagination [and] the black . . . partake of the 'lawless freedom'" that exists against, and as an effect of, the logics of liberal modernity.[83] Phillis Wheatley espouses a similar idea in terms that at first blush may appear to be paradigmatically romantic:

> Imagination! who can sing thy force?
> Or who describe the swiftness of thy course?
> Soaring through air to find the bright abode,
> Th' empyreal palace of the thund'ring God,
> We on thy pinions can surpass the wind,
> And leave the rolling universe behind:
> From star to star the mental optics rove,
> Measure the skies, and range the realms above.
> There in one view we grasp the mighty whole,
> Or with new worlds amaze th' unbounded soul.[84]

Wheatley ascribes to the imagination the power to remake the world, not merely to escape it. The imagination enables her to write herself on her own terms rather than those ascribed to her by a white supremacist society. But I don't mean to suggest that either Wheatley or Equiano should be read as protoromantics. Even as Keats's affect and language may be comparable, in certain ways, to Equiano's or Wheatley's, when Keats returns to his embodied reality at the end of "Ode to a Nightingale," he returns to a social world in which his humanity is recognized and affirmed as such. And here, blackness and romanticism diverge in ways that are ultimately and fundamentally irreconcilable: to have the luxury of romanticizing suicide, the suicidal subject must first be legible as fully human.[85]

British romantic writers never did evacuate liberal epistemologies of the human, even as many of romanticism's most deeply held ideals about a world beyond material and political boundaries developed in implicit opposition to the same human(ism)s challenged by the black radical tradition. My point is not that the projects are similar but that the places where they diverge can illuminate both. Why don't we read the waters of the Middle Passage in the phrase "writ in water"? What if Keats's wish to be remembered through an act of erasure recalled Equiano's "inhabitants of the deep," who had no say in the matter? In their thinking about suicide, both authors reject fantasies of epistemological closure and ontological self-containment. How deeply ironic, then, that the liberal subject should so ardently court death (and here, I'm speaking not of Keats himself but of the culture that sanctions his literary authority), even as it holds nonsubjects in constant relation to it. In the next chapter, we'll see why liberal modernity can't have it both ways.

chapter 4

In Sympathy

> Look at the backflips people will do to find humanity in
> [Frankenstein's] monster.
> But when they saw a boy like mine, they had no love to spare.
> —Victor LaValle, *Destroyer*

My focus in this book so far has been on how literary representations of suicide at the turn of the nineteenth century functioned to authorize racialized political ontologies. I have examined how the trope of suicide was used to signal and police notions of political "being" and social "life" drawn from liberal rights discourses and how this is reflected in the consolidation of an anxious and untenable relation between blackness and death in the liberal imaginary. Black men were imaginatively called upon by white writers to prove their fitness for freedom by dying, while black women, whether framed as lovers, mothers, enslaved persons, or aristocrats, likewise ended their fictional lives through self-destruction. I have also shown how black writers, both in the nineteenth century and those currently working in the critical idioms of Afropessimism and black optimism, resist these tropes and pursue modalities of living in and beyond those imaginaries that delimit blackness through/to death. This chapter takes a broader, more speculative look at the relationship between racialization and suicide in liberal modernity.

In Mary Shelley's *Frankenstein*, liberalism seems to lead to suicide one way or another. On the one hand, suicide can be understood as the apotheosis of liberal individualism, such as we saw in David Hume's *On Suicide* and as we'll see again in Victor Frankenstein. On the other hand, suicide is the only logical end that the novel can offer the creature because of its investment in what I will argue is a flawed ethic of interracial sympathy. After establishing the relevance of suicide to *Frankenstein* through Mary Shelley's biography, this chapter routes the novel's reflections on liberal subjectivity and its racialized exclusions through theories of sympathy from Hume, Adam Smith, and most centrally, Percy Shelley. The chapter then examines how *Frankenstein* yokes the discourses of suicide and sympathy together in articulating an integrationist fantasy in which "monsters" may be "humanized" or "civilized" through appeals to sympathy. This fantasy, as deployed in *Frankenstein*, illuminates how the politico-ontological relation between blackness and death is produced by the liberal subject's own death drive. The chapter closes with a reading of Victor LaValle's *Destroyer*, a contemporary sequel of sorts to *Frankenstein* that I read as a response to the limitations of the original text's liberal grounding in its treatment of the interconnected issues of sympathy for the creature, Frankenstein's ill-fated individualism, and both characters' desires for death.

Frankenstein and the Suicide Debates

That suicide was a topic of interest for Shelley in the years leading up to her writing *Frankenstein* is evident from her journals. Her first mention of suicide appears on August 25, 1814, when she and Percy "hear of Patricksons [*sic*] killing himself... another of those cold blooded murders that like Maria Schooning we may put down to the world."[1] Patrickson was a protégé of Godwin's who killed himself on August 10, 1814. As Paula R. Feldman and Diana Scott-Kilvert explain, "Maria Schooning" likely refers to Maria Eleonora Schöning, the protagonist of a "harrowing story of female misfortune," written and published by Samuel Taylor Coleridge in *The Friend* in 1810:

> Maria is first raped as she sits weeping over her father's grave, and then befriended by a poor woman, Harlin. Maria persuades Harlin to join with her in a false confession of infanticide, so that she and Harlin can be executed, thus avoiding the sin of suicide, and Harlin's children can then be cared for by charity and not die of starvation. Overcome by remorse, Maria confesses the truth before her execution, but the magistrates do not believe her; Harlin is executed and Maria expires on the scaffold.[2]

Shelley's recollection of this narrative in her entry on Patrickson's suicide suggests that she affirms the opinion of her mother who, as discussed in this book's second chapter, famously wrote about suicide as an act of political resistance. In referencing Maria Schöning, a heroine not unlike the suicidal women of Wollstonecraft's fiction, Shelley seems to validate Patrickson's decision to end his life.

The specific way in which Shelley references Maria Schöning also highlights her interest in the socioeconomic dimension of the suicide debates. When Maria convinces Harlin to be executed instead of killing herself, she does so to ensure that Harlin's children are cared for. In the early nineteenth century, when a coroner deemed a person who committed suicide a felo-de-se (literally "felon to himself"), that person's property was forfeited to the state. This policy of forfeiture was notoriously corrupt, as wealthy people regularly swayed coroners against issuing felo-de-se verdicts to preserve family titles and fortunes. Shelley was soon to become entangled in an example of this corruption when in December 1816, the body of Harriet Shelley, Percy's first wife, washed up on the banks of the Thames. As local historian Henry George Davis would recall in his 1859 *Memorials of Hamlet of Knights*bridge, the entire affair "bears the marks of outside influence."[3] When the coroner's inquest was held—itself a "hushed up procedure"—"a verdict [was] returned, which saved her the revolting burial then awarded to the suicide."[4] The official verdict noted only that Harriet was "found dead in the Serpentine River," making no mention of her pregnancy by another man.[5] Moreover, no account of the inquest was given to the local newspapers, although it was common to report at least that an inquest had taken place, regardless of its outcome.[6] Percy's note to Mary five days after the inquest confirms that Harriet's death was in fact the result of suicide: "It seems that this poor woman—the most innocent of her abhorred and unnatural family—was driven from her father's house, & descended the steps of prostitution until she lived with a groom of the name of Smith, who deserting her, she killed herself."[7] No one was fooled by the attempted cover-up: as late as 1859, Davis still derides the actions of the Westbrook and Shelley families by invoking Thomas Hood's "The Bridge of Sighs," a poem about the suicide of a prostitute, to suggest that the local community was unconvinced by their efforts to conceal the fact of Harriet's suicide.[8]

Harriet's death brought Mary back to the topic of suicide in yet another way. The body was taken to the Fox and Bull Inn, then a receiving house of the Royal Humane Society. Founded in 1774, the Society worked to help prevent drowning deaths by disseminating information about resuscitative methods. Although not unique in its interests—Tim Marshall has described Europe at the end of the eighteenth century as a "resurrectionist culture" obsessed with the limits of biological life—the Royal Humane Society is uniquely pertinent to Shelley's novel.[9] Much of the science employed by Victor Frankenstein is similar to that used by the Society. Among their methods of resuscitation, the Society engaged turn-of-the-century interests in the animating potential of electricity as elucidated in, for example, the work of Luigi Galvani, John Hunter, and Ben Franklin (whose famous kite experiment Frankenstein cites in the first chapter of his narrative as an early inspiration of his interest in science).[10] Moreover, the Society actively promoted practices and techniques to revive people who attempted suicide by drowning.[11] By the time Mary Shelley wrote *Frankenstein*, the Society was considered a leader in efforts to curb what was then widely known as England's suicide problem.[12] In 1805, the physician Samuel Jackson Pratt reported that "more than five hundred suicides have been providentially restored by the medical assistants of the Humane Society."[13] Mary Wollstonecraft was one among this number.

Wollstonecraft was famously displeased with the Society's interference in her asserting, in Humean fashion, her right to die—a fact that haunted Mary Shelley all her life. Carolyn Williams has shown that Wollstonecraft's second suicide attempt (her first was earlier that year via an overdose of laudanum) was tinged, both in her planning and response to its failure, with what she saw as the intrusive work of the Royal Humane Society:

> When she set out to commit suicide, she expressed fears lest attempts be made to restore her to life. In October 1795, she wrote to Gilbert Imlay, "I go to find comfort, and my only fear is, that my poor body will be insulted by an endeavor to recall my hated existence. But I shall plunge into the Thames where there is the least chance of my being snatched from the death I seek". . . She jumped into the Thames off Putney Bridge, and lost consciousness before she was pulled out of the water. Her next letter expresses a coolly defiant refusal to endorse conventional responses to her situation: "I have only to lament, that, when the bitterness of death was past, I was inhumanly brought back to life and misery. . . . If I am condemned to live longer, it is a living death."[14]

Inevitably also in Shelley's purview was the suicide of her half-sister, Wollstonecraft's other daughter, Fanny Imlay, who died of an intentional laudanum overdose on October 9, 1816. In her suicide note, which was published on October 12, 1816, in Welsh newspaper *The Cambrian*, Imlay writes:

> I have long determined that the best thing I could do was to put an end to the existence of a being whose birth was unfortunate, and whose life has only been a series of pain to those persons who have hurt their health in endeavoring to promote her welfare. Perhaps to hear of my death will give you pain, but you will soon have the blessing of forgetting that such a creature ever existed.[15]

Scholars have speculated widely about the note's missing signature, but few have noted how closely Fanny's description of herself as a being of "unfortunate" birth whose life brings "a series of pain" is echoed throughout *Frankenstein*.[16] Indeed, given Shelley's deep familiarity with the topic, it is surprising that the role of suicide in her most famous novel is not more widely discussed.[17]

The novel concludes with the creature declaring his intention to kill himself, although importantly, we never find out if he does:

> "But soon," he cried, with sad and solemn enthusiasm, "I shall die, and what I now feel be no longer felt. Soon these burning miseries will be extinct. I shall ascend my funeral pile triumphantly, and exult in the agony of the torturing flames. The light of that conflagration will fade away; my ashes will be swept into the sea by the winds. My spirit will sleep in peace; or if it thinks, it will not surely think thus. Farewell."[18]

Insofar as the novel corroborates the creature's nonbelonging, it necessitates his expulsion from the social field: he has to die physically to underscore the absoluteness of his social death. At the same time, Mary Shelley was well versed in how authors of her day mobilized suicide to open the bounds of liberalism.[19] Read from this perspective, it is equally plausible that the creature's decision to kill himself signals his capacity for inclusion. That she leaves the completion of his suicide an open question renders both options possible depending on, among other things, whether one chooses to believe that he kills himself. In this sense, the novel becomes a litmus test for the reader's own politics, giving further credence to Rachel Feder's assertion that "you're never more yourself than when you're reading *Frankenstein*."[20] Complicating matters, however, is the fact that the creature is not the novel's only suicidal character.

Victor Frankenstein also repeatedly declares his intention to end his life: "I often endeavored to put an end to the existence I loathed and it required unceasing attendance and vigilance to restrain me from committing some dreadful act of violence."[21] While we never see Frankenstein attempt to end his life directly, he is only too eager to catch up to the creature so they can kill each other. Their pursuit of one another becomes, by the end of the novel, his only reason for staying alive:

> I had formed in my own heart a resolution to pursue my destroyer to death; and this purpose quieted my agony, and provisionally reconciled me to life.... I confess that is it the devouring and only passion of my soul... I devote myself, either in my life or death, to his destruction.... How I have lived I hardly know; many times have I stretched my failing limbs upon the sandy plain, and prayed for death. But... I dared not die.[22]

As the sections that follow demonstrate, the creature's and Frankenstein's suicidal desires are not separate impulses but are fundamentally linked. Read together, these discrete desires point to an irresolvable duality at the heart of liberalism: even as the liberal subject defines himself as socially "alive" against the politico-ontological and literal deaths of those he deems nonsubjects, suicide is the logical apotheosis of the rights and entitlements that define his own subjectivity and sanction his politico-ontological "life." Put another way, *Frankenstein* stages how the libidinal economy that overdetermines blackness as thanatological abjection in liberal modernity's social unconscious contains the possibility of its own destruction. To get here, Mary Shelley interpolates Percy Shelley's writings on love from 1815–1816, which draw heavily from eighteenth-century philosophies of sympathy.

The Social Function of Sympathy

Most of the action of *Frankenstein* is motivated by a thwarted desire for sympathy and love. In the background of *Frankenstein* are at least two unpublished essays by Percy Shelley, "Speculations on Morals" (ca. 1815) and "On Love" (1815).[23] At this early stage of Percy's career, "love" is not yet the philosophical doctrine of eternal human goodness that it would later become.[24] In 1815–16, Percy uses "love" to rethink theories of sympathy posited by eighteenth-century moral philosophers, focusing particularly on Hume and, to a lesser extent, Adam Smith.[25] For Hume, sympathy constitutes a mode of moral attunement. The dilemma of such attunement is that "the sentiment of others can never affect us, but by becoming, in some measure, our own."[26] Hence, sympathy can only teach a person to act morally by framing the object of sympathy in terms of the sympathizing self. Likewise, for Smith, sympathy is necessarily a fiction, for "our senses will never inform us of what [the other] suffers. They never did, and never can, carry us beyond our own person, and it is by the imagination only that we can form any conception of what are his sensations."[27] Like Hume, Smith emphasizes that the impetus toward sympathy derives from a benevolent desire to know others, even as the endeavor is ultimately a path back to the self.

No matter how well-intended, sympathy cannot but be filtered through the self and its attendant prejudices. David Marshall observes how the good intentions that drive people to want to sympathize may be used against them, leading people to be "deceived by hypocrites [who] know how to imitate the exterior signs and symptoms of feelings.... In reading or beholding the characters of others, one risks not only being misled but also being placed in the position of distance, difference, and isolation that sympathy is supposed to deny."[28] Saidiya Hartman extends this critique by emphasizing how the power differentials, inherent in any relation of sympathy, are particularly magnified in the attempted identification of subjects with those people positioned as non-/anti-/antesubjects: "The fungibility of the commodity makes the captive body an abstract and empty vessel vulnerable to the projection of others' feelings, ideas, desires, and values."[29] For Hartman, even when it is geared toward establishing parity, sympathy—like sentimentalism and sensibility, as discussed in previous chapters—underlines the fungibility of blackness in the liberal imaginary: the unconscious belief that the black body, whether enslaved or free, is always open to white possession and occupation. I bring this up here not to suggest that Mary Shelley analogizes the creature's existence to blackness, although there is much that could be said about the fungibility of the creature's corporeal form: a literal assemblage of other people's bodies. Rather, I raise Hartman's critique of cross-racial sympathy alongside Marshall's critique of sympathy as an indicator of moral attunement to highlight the inherent limitations of political engagements of sympathy in appeals for social recognition or integration. Indeed, as Manu Samriti Chander has demonstrated, "the British Romantic ideology of sympathy is founded on certain ineradicable antipathies."[30] Thus, when Percy Shelley extends Humean and Smithean theories of sympathy to put forward his own theory of subject production, he does so in unmistakably racist terms.

Following Hume and Smith, Percy takes the capacity for sympathy as an indication of the sympathizer's benevolence. A great deal of his "Speculations on Morals" recapitulates Hume's emphasis on sympathy as mediated through the imagination. For Hume, the imagination is a broad faculty of mind that reproduces "faint, languid" copies of impressions that in the experience of sympathy makes possible "the sentiments of others [to seem] our own."[31] For Percy, too, "Imagination or mind employed in prophetically imaging forth its objects, is that faculty of human nature on which every gradation of its progress... depends." However, in Percy's hands, sympathy also informs a theory of subject production that depends on an inherently racist program of so-called civilization. In "Speculations on Morals," he discusses the process of becoming attuned to that capacity as the province of the "civilized":

> The inhabitant of a highly civilized community will more acutely sympathize with the sufferings and enjoyments of others, than the inhabitant of a society of a less degree of civilization. He who shall have cultivated his intellectual powers by familiarity with the highest specimens of poetry and philosophy, will usually sympathize more than one engaged in the less refined functions of manual labour.[32]

More specifically, Percy is interested in how sympathy shapes subjects through texts. For him, the process by which one is constituted a sympathetic and thus not only a moral but a "civilized" being is tied to the reading of certain kinds of texts. According to this logic, where some strains of poetry and philosophy are the products of a universalist human ingenuity, so too are virtue and morality:

> The only distinction between the selfish man and the virtuous man is, that the imagination of the former is confined within a narrow limit, whilst that of the latter embraces a comprehensive circumference.... Virtue is thus intirely [sic] a refinement of civilized life; a creation of the human mind or, rather, a combination which it has made, according to elementary rules contained within itself, of the feelings suggested by the relations established between man and man.[33]

Percy maintains throughout "Speculations" that all people may possess the capacity for goodness, but as he notes above, goodness is developed socially.

These ideas are renegotiated by Mary Shelley in the creature's various (non-)experiences with sympathy—not only his perpetually thwarted desire for it but also his apparently innate capacity to freely extend it. For example, the creature's early interest in humans is sincere and naïve. He foregrounds how his presence in someone's life might benefit them rather than (as we will see in Frankenstein's actions) how that relationship would serve him: "I longed to discover the motives and feelings of these lovely creatures ... I thought (foolish wretch!) that it might be in my power to restore happiness to these deserving people."[34] Observing the De Lacey family, the creature endeavors to exercise what we might call true or disinterested sympathy, feeling only as they feel: "When they were unhappy, I felt depressed; when they rejoiced, I sympathized with their joys."[35] Yet as we have seen, pure sympathy is impossible. For Hume, Smith, and Percy Shelley, sympathy is at most an aspirational ideal. The creature, however, believes that he sympathizes with others without regard for himself, and more importantly, he *wants* to connect with others in this way.

Ironically, it is the creature's interest in others that motivates him to share, as it were, in Safie's education, which ultimately dampens his capacity for fellow feeling and makes him suicidal: "I found that these people possessed a method of communicating their experience and feelings to one another by articulate sounds. I perceived that the words they spoke sometimes produced pleasure or pain, smiles or sadness, in the minds and countenances of the hearers."[36] In learning the "godlike science" of language, the creature is introduced to a liberal framework into which he cannot assimilate, and once that is clear to him, the only source of alleviation he can see is his own death:

> The words [of Volney's *Ruins*] induced me to turn towards myself. I learned that the possessions most esteemed by your fellow-creatures were high and unsullied descent united by riches. A man might be respected with only one of these acquisitions; but without either he was considered, except in rare instances, as a vagabond and a slave, doomed to waste his powers for the profit of the chosen few. And what was I? Of my creation and creator I was absolutely ignorant; but I knew that I possessed no money, no friends, no kind of property. I was, besides, endowed with a figure hideously deformed and loathsome; I was not even of the same nature as man. I was more agile than they, and could subsist upon coarser diet; I bore the extremes of heat and cold with less injury to my frame; my stature far exceeded their's. When I looked around, I saw and heard of none like me. Was I then a monster, a blot upon the earth, from which all men fled, and whom all men disowned?[37]

By all indications, the creature is, at least physically, superior to human beings—he is larger, faster, stronger, and more resilient. But he learns to hate himself because he is taught that subjectivity is constituted through recognition and that recognition is regulated by social institutions. The single most important lesson that the creature gleans from his education, then, is that he does not fit into the structures that govern social life, and because of this, he believes he has no choice but to die: "I learned that there was but one means to overcome the sensation of pain, and that was death."[38] In coming to grips with what it means to be a subject and the fact that he cannot become one, the creature becomes suicidal.

Shelley is clear about the fact that the creature's death drive is socially conditioned. Before his "education," he strove to live: "Life, although it may only be an accumulation of anguish, is dear to me, and I will defend it."[39] But as his mind is colonized by liberal modernity, he becomes aware that he can die, and this awareness grows into the conviction that he must. This is especially clear when he reads Goethe's *Werther*:

> As I read . . . I applied much personally to my own feelings and condition. I found myself similar, yet at the same time strangely unlike the beings concerning whom I read, and to whose conversation I was a listener. I sympathized with, and partly understood them, but I was uninformed in mind; I was dependent on none, and related to none. The path of my departure was free; and there was none to lament my annihilation. My person was hideous, and my stature gigantic: what did this mean? Who was I? What was I? Whence did I come? What was my destination? These questions continually recurred, but I was unable to solve them.[40]

The creature's experience of reading *Werther* suggests that in order for Goethe's text to be understood, the appropriate reader must be there to understand it.[41] In the creature's case, instead of cultivating the subject of liberal modernity, his education brings into sharp focus the fact that he is not one, and this impels him to seek a way out of a world that, he is taught, he was never meant to inhabit. The great irony, of course, is that to anyone who cannot see him, he might have passed, as implied in De Lacey's assumption that the creature is not only European but French like him, "my countryman."[42] By thus highlighting inclusion as ultimately dependent on factors that cannot be conditioned, Shelley's text exposes the lie at the heart of the integrationist fantasy. In this sense it is a trenchant critique of liberalism. At the same time, *Frankenstein* is unable to imagine an option other than death for those marked as "nonsubjects" by liberal modernity. In this way, the text reinscribes the very logics it so brilliantly critiques.

When he asks for a mate, the creature explains that he wants to "excite the sympathy of some existing thing."[43] In so doing, he registers a desire for recognition. Frankenstein's destruction of the mate, in turn, indicates his refusal to grant him that possibility, either from him or anyone else. Frankenstein's destruction of the second creature has been read as motivated by a Malthusian worry that the two creatures would spawn a new species, but it is arguably better read as an example of liberal modernity's exclusionary logics. As Maureen McLane notes, it is not clear that the creature and his mate *can* reproduce; indeed, it seems reasonable to assume that if this were a real fear for Frankenstein, he could engineer the female creature in such a way as to render reproduction impossible.[44] Even more than he fears the creatures getting along, then, Frankenstein worries that the mate will reject the original creature in favor of "the superior beauty of man."[45] What the creature desires is the community they might form through their shared exclusion. But Frankenstein imagines that the second creature—for no discernible reason other than the fact that she is, ostensibly, female—would see the first creature as he does and would attempt, instead, to join mankind (never mind the fact that mankind would surely reject her). The myopia here is almost unimaginable except that we see it all the time: people in power unable to register positionalities that do not follow neatly from their own experiences.

The real issue, then, is not population but liberalism. Frankenstein's inability to step outside of himself, his failure to understand either creature for what they are or could become, register his absolute lack of sympathy. And crucially, as the novel's early emphasis on Frankenstein's schooling suggests, this myopia is cultivated at least partly by his education. As the next section will show, Frankenstein's individualism leaves no space for sympathy. How, then, can liberal modernity be expected to shape others through sympathy when its own subjects are closed to it? Shelley pursues this problem through another of Percy's 1815 essays, "On Love," which extends the questions raised in "Speculations on Morals" by considering what happens when the project of shaping subjects goes awry.

Friendly Antipathies

Percy develops his theory of "love" as a corollary to sympathy. In "On Love," the figure of the writer, the supposedly moral force who can shape the world through sympathy, also requires it from others; but the writer's attempt to find it reveals how little ordinary people understand each other, and worse still, how little the writer himself is understood:

> I know not the internal constitution of other men, nor even thine, whom I now address. I see that in some external attributes they resemble me, but when, misled by that appearance, I have thought to appeal to something in common, and unburthen my inmost soul to them, I have found my language misunderstood, like one in a distant and savage land. The more opportunities they have afforded me for experience, the wider has appeared the interval between us, and to a greater distance have the points of sympathy been withdrawn. With a spirit ill fitted to sustain such proof, trembling and feeble through its tenderness, I have everywhere sought sympathy, and have found only repulse and disappointment.[46]

It is, of course, easy to hear Frankenstein's creature here. But it is not just the creature who wishes to have someone understand his "inmost soul." The entirety of *Frankenstein* is driven by lonely people's desires for sympathy and recognition.

In the novel's opening pages, Walton admits to his intended reader, his sister Margaret, the same anxiety that Percy betrays in "On Love" about having one's feelings misunderstood in the medium of writing: "I have no friend, Margaret... I shall commit my thoughts to paper, it is true; but that is a poor medium for the communication of feeling. I desire the company of a man who could sympathize with me; whose eyes would reply to mine."[47] What Walton describes, and what will emerge even more profoundly when he meets Frankenstein, is the desire for what Percy calls "a miniature of our entire self... a soul within our own soul that describes a circle around its proper Paradise, which pain and sorrow and evil dare not overleap."[48] For Percy, love is not reading the other (i.e., sympathy) but finding someone who can properly read one's own self:

> [Love] is that powerful attraction towards all we conceive, or fear, or hope beyond ourselves, when we find within our own thoughts the chasm of an insufficient void, and seek to awaken in all things that are, a community with what we experience within ourselves. If we reason, we would be understood; if we imagine, we would that the airy children of our brain were born anew within another's; if we feel, we would that another's nerves should vibrate to our own, that the beams of their eyes should kindle at once and mix and melt into our own; that lips

of motionless ice should not reply to lips quivering and burning with the heart's best blood. This is Love.[49]

Love—which Walton will call friendship—is tantamount not to understanding but to *being understood*. Not coincidentally, in describing his loneliness to his sister, Walton recalls his background as a poet. In his second letter to Margaret, he relates that before he was an explorer he was "a poet, and for one year lived in a Paradise of my own creation; I imagined that I also might obtain a niche in the temple where the names of Homer and Shakespeare are consecrated. You are well acquainted with my failure, and how heavily I bore the disappointment."[50] Dejected by his inability to write, Walton wishes for a friend, hoping to be "read" in life if not in verse. And thus, when he meets Frankenstein, he believes him to be the friend he had sought.

Like Walton, Frankenstein's first education is in literature. And in a certain sense, so is the creature's. Before his initiation into language in the De Lacey cottage, the creature describes how he "tried to imitate the pleasant songs of the birds, but was unable. Sometimes I wished to express my sensations in my own mode, but the uncouth and inarticulate sounds which broke from me frightened me into silence again."[51] Walton, Victor, and the creature are all, in some sense, erstwhile poets. Shelley highlights that her central characters are all authors and readers such that even as he narrates his story to Walton, who in turn writes it down for Margaret (and enables our reading of it), Frankenstein positions the creature as the author of the narrative's end: the creature leaves literal textual traces, "marks in writing on the barks of trees, or cut in stone" to guide Frankenstein.[52] In their desire to die by each other's hand—depicted explicitly in terms of reading—they enter into exactly the relationship that Percy desires to have with his readers in "On Love" and that Walton seeks in Frankenstein. But who is writing whom into (non-)being here and to what end? Is not the creature, the abject "other," the author of Frankenstein's death just as surely as Frankenstein, the liberal subject, is the author of the creature's?

If we understand the relationship between Frankenstein and his creature through the dynamics of textual exchange—imagined by Percy as part of the social work of western poetry and philosophy—then Shelley's portrait is one of reading and writing gone awry. As discussed in this book's introduction, one of the most potent tools that liberal modernity has used to maintain its axes of power has been literary education. Almost as if to instrumentalize Percy's conception of perfect sympathy, literary texts have been deployed to cultivate "civilized" subjects without regard for what such a developmental model privileges and what (or whom) it leaves out. Shelley illustrates this in her novel by framing each narrator—Frankenstein, the creature, and Walton—in variously unreciprocated relations of textual exchange, thereby putting pressure on the positive link between sympathy and "civilization" asserted by her husband. Texts are at their most dangerous, she suggests, when authors claim to cover the entirety of the social field.

The novel's opening pages also link its exploration of love/friendship to the topic of suicide. When Walton finds Frankenstein on the brink of death, he describes how he and his crew "restored him to animation."[53] This not only anticipates the creation scene but also directly echoes Wollstonecraft's restoration by the Royal Humane Society. Frankenstein reiterates this language, thanking Walton for "benevolently restor[ing] me to life."[54] Walton is charmed by Frankenstein's gratitude, which he sees as indicative of deeper qualities of "benevolence and sweetness."[55] However, what most clearly emerges about Frankenstein's character over the course of the novel is his capriciousness and self-involvement. At no point in the novel does Frankenstein demonstrate the goodness that Walton projects onto him. Even Frankenstein's apparent gratitude is a misreading on Walton's part—by this point in the novel, Frankenstein's only desire is to kill the creature and to die himself. He admits to Walton that the only reason he made himself visible to the crew was on the off chance that the ship was headed south so that he could continue his pursuit; he is dismayed to learn they are northbound. When he is well enough, Frankenstein explains that he cannot be the friend Walton seeks because of this mission:

> I enjoyed friends, dear not only through habit and association, but from their own merits; and wherever I am, the soothing voice of my Elizabeth, and the conversation of Clerval, will be ever whispered in my ear. They are dead; and but one feeling in such a solitude can persuade me to preserve my life. If I were engaged in any high undertaking or design, fraught with extensive utility to my fellow-creatures, then could I live to fulfill it. But such is not my destiny; I must pursue and destroy the being to whom I gave existence; then my lot on earth will be fulfilled, and I may die.[56]

Thus, if Frankenstein is grateful to Walton for anything, it is for prolonging his life so that he may die as he intended: along with, and by the hand of, the creature.

To put a finer point on Frankenstein's self-involvement, it is worth pausing to appreciate the irony of Frankenstein's naming Elizabeth and Clerval to justify his obsession with the creature. While their deaths ostensibly serve to propel Frankenstein's revenge plot—and while Elizabeth and Clerval may well have been good friends to him—he was never a good friend to them. Frankenstein's relationships are motivated by a mix of self-interest and denial of his need for other people. For example, he admits to ignoring his responsibilities to Clerval and his family while in the throes of his research:

> The same feelings which made me neglect the scenes around me caused me also to forget those friends who were so many miles absent, and whom I had not seen for so long a time. I knew my silence disquieted them ... but I could not tear my thoughts from my employment. ... I wished, as it were, to procrastinate all that related to my feelings of affection.[57]

By "procrastinating" his social affections, Frankenstein posits feelings—at least those feelings relating to friendship and love—as mechanisms that can be turned off or ignored. However, when frightened by his own success, Frankenstein regains himself through his friendship with Clerval:

> Study had before secluded me from the intercourse of my fellow-creatures, and rendered me unsocial; but Clerval called forth the better feelings of my heart; he again taught me to love the aspect of nature, and the cheerful faces of children. Excellent friend! How sincerely did you love me, and endeavor to elevate my mind ... A selfish pursuit had cramped and narrowed me, until your gentleness and affection warmed and opened my senses.[58]

Later, Frankenstein admits his miscalculation to Walton: "If the study to which you apply yourself has a tendency to weaken your affections ... then that study is certainly unlawful, that is to say, not befitting the human mind."[59] In this declaration, Shelley underscores the novel's interest in social dynamics of reciprocity and the possibilities of relation between the self-contained, autonomous liberal subject and those through and against whom he defines himself.

If Frankenstein's isolation in the name of scientific progress is, by his own admission, his downfall, then the liberal individualist fantasy is called into question. Pondering the effects of his isolation, he speculates that "if no man allowed any pursuit whatsoever to interfere with the tranquility of his domestic affections, Greece had not been enslaved; Caesar would have spared his country; America would have been discovered more gradually; and the empires of Mexico and Peru had not been destroyed."[60] Here, crucially, the narrative breaks: "But I forget that I am moralizing in the most interesting part of my tale; and your looks remind me to proceed."[61] Thus, even as he attempts to convey a narrative of progress, Frankenstein cannot help but become aware of his story *as* a story, thereby inviting reflection on these grander narratives. Would it have been so bad if Greece were not enslaved, or the empires of Mexico and Peru not destroyed? How might it have altered the course of history if Europeans had occupied the territories they call "the Americas" more gradually, or not at all? In this moment, Shelley dares her readers to dream of a less self-interested world, one that the novel itself ultimately cannot imagine.

Thus, Frankenstein's friendships remain self-centered—he has friends when he needs them, but when he is occupied, he ignores them. Even his betrothal to Elizabeth is self-interested: he decides to marry her not only (nor even primarily) for love but rather to hasten his plan to die. When the creature promises to be with Frankenstein on his wedding night, Frankenstein assumes that the threat is directed at him and thus reasons that marrying Elizabeth would lure the creature to him: "The remembrance of the threat returned.... But death was no evil to me... and I therefore, with a contented and even cheerful countenance, agreed with my father, that if my cousin would consent, the ceremony should take place in ten days, and thus put, as I imagined, the seal to my fate."[62] Thus, when he agrees to the marriage, he thinks it is a step toward suicide: "When I thought that I prepared only my own death, I hastened that of a far dearer victim."[63] His decision is guided by a death wish that he frames as altruistic (to save his loved ones from being murdered by the creature), even knowing it would leave them bereft. But when Elizabeth and the others are gone, that ostensibly selfless motivation turns inward, and Frankenstein's life begins to revolve around a death wish motivated by self-loathing and despair.

In certain ways, the creature's suicidal motivations echo Frankenstein's. By the time he kills Elizabeth, the creature has vowed to ruin Frankenstein's life by severing his ties to his family and friends. However, even at his most destructive, the creature attributes more to those relationships than Frankenstein ever does. While Frankenstein occasionally loves his relations, that he also cavalierly forgets them in pursuit of "progress" suggests that sympathy and love do not motivate his life as strongly as they do the creature's. For even as the creature is, like Frankenstein, ultimately driven to suicide, his suicidality is informed by his perpetually thwarted desire for relation. Still, until the very end, he never stops seeking it. Despite the unceasing rejection he experiences, the creature is the only character in the novel who attempts to sympathize with others *in addition to* trying to get others to sympathize with (or, in Percy's terms, to love) him. It is deeply significant, then, that when Frankenstein dies, the creature tells Walton, "I seek not a fellow-feeling in my misery."[64] When he lived, even as the creature "destroyed [Frankenstein's] hopes" he "still desired love and fellowship."[65] But in rejecting Walton's invitation to stay, Shelley suggests that the love the creature sought was, ironically, borne out in the relationship he had with his creator. Their mutual commitment to each other's destruction is the expression of what Percy laments his inability to find in "On Love": a "soul within our own soul."[66]

By depicting both actors' suicides as the end result of the social functions of love and sympathy, *Frankenstein* exposes the rot at the heart of liberal modernity. In part, the novel highlights what Hartman identifies as "the facile intimacy" that drives the idea that liberalism can be revised to include those whom it has historically excluded through something like fellow feeling.[67] We see this in the fact that the creature becomes suicidal as a result of liberal society's refusal to "read" him (i.e., to sympathize with him), which in turn forecloses its willingness to "write" him in its image (i.e., to grant him the rights and entitlements that would authorize his inclusion). But crucially, sympathy for the creature is not Shelley's endgame. By linking the fates of creature and creator, Shelley also shows how those in possession of liberalism's entitlements are led to suicide in another way. If the creature is Frankenstein's undoing, he is also the triumph of the highest aspirations of liberal modernity—"progress," domination of the natural world, and through these the imagined substantiation of the supremacy of the white male individual. Thus, in a way, *Frankenstein* upholds the logical extension of Hume's "On Suicide"—that the apotheosis of liberal individualism is expressed in its self-destruction.

Blackness and the End(s) of Liberalism

Though I have called on Hartman's critique of liberalism, I have intentionally avoided analogizing the creature to blackness. Certainly, there is ample evidence to support comparisons of the creature to enslaved and emancipated people of African descent, as Jared Hickman, Debbie Lee, H. L. Malchow, Marie Mulvey-Roberts, Alan Lloyd Smith, and others have shown.[68] Nor is this a recent intervention: as Elizabeth Young has taught us, Frankensteinian imagery was widely deployed to both antiblack and antislavery ends in the nineteenth century.[69] In the terms outlined by these scholars, I might have delimited my discussion of suicide to Afropessimist debates about the ontological relation between blackness and death. But the creature has also been persuasively read in terms of other racial and ethnic discourses.[70] Where readings of the creature as an analogue of people of African, Asian, or Jewish descent are immensely valuable for what they teach us about nineteenth-century European notions about race and ethnicity, their sheer variety also highlights the fact that the creature exceeds any single framework of racial or ethnic identity. Thus, when Victor LaValle reimagines *Frankenstein* in his 2017 comic book series, *Destroyer*, in which an African American woman brings her son back to life, it is deeply significant that he does not conflate the creature with the reanimated child. In this way, LaValle also invites a timely reexamination of the original text's interest in "race."

Destroyer revels in the romantic contexts that produced *Frankenstein*: its characters have names like Percy and Byron, and the protagonist (the also brilliantly named Dr. Josephine Baker) is a descendent of Victor Frankenstein and a textbook Byronic hero. But as we see in the epigraph to this chapter, LaValle draws an important distinction between antiblackness and the social exclusion experienced by the creature. Dr. Baker builds on Frankenstein's dream of conquering death by reanimating her twelve-year-old son, Akai, who was murdered by police while walking home from a Little League game. But unlike Frankenstein's creature, who is flesh and bone, the reanimated Akai is part machine, designed such that the machine parts will eventually take over. LaValle carefully lays out the implications of this difference: the creature was built in Frankenstein's image—which is to say, in the image of western dreams of progress and white perfectibility—and as such, the creature, as Dr. Baker puts it, "is only human."[71] Akai is intentionally engineered as a counterpoint, enabling LaValle to do what Shelley implies but can't quite bring herself to do: by the end of *Destroyer*, every human, including Frankenstein's creature, is dead. Akai is the only character left, and he has the ability to reproduce himself to create a new world.

LaValle's distinction between antiblackness and social exclusion highlights the former not as an event or series of events but, as Christina Sharpe puts it, "total climate" produced not only by the "containment, regulation, punishment, capture, and captivity" of African-identified people in modern history but also by the persistence of cultural representations of blackness as "the symbol, par excellence, for the less-than-human being condemned to death," such as we saw in the abolitionist and proto-feminist texts discussed in previous chapters.[72] In their orientation toward black life outside the bounds of liberal modernity—the world as we know it—LaValle's and Sharpe's works parallel one another: (re)born of gratuitous violence, Akai is whole and, crucially, not human. *Destroyer* is not interested in garnering sympathy for the oppressed, nor is it exactly a story about black resistance. It is, instead, an optimistic vision on the order of Sharpe's notion of black being "in the wake"—of "inhabiting a blackened consciousness that would rupture the structural silences produced and facilitated by, and that produce and facilitate, Black social and physical death."[73] Akai's decision to destroy humanity as we know it also echoes Wilderson's emphasis on "the unbridgeable gap between Black being and Human life," as well as his insistence on the need for "a new language of abstraction to explain this horror [because the] explanatory power of Humanist discourse is bankrupt in the face of the Black."[74] Ultimately, then, LaValle reaches back to Frantz Fanon's declaration that to "change the order of the world" will finally require "an agenda for total disorder."[75]

Shelley's critique of liberalism is profoundly nuanced in ways that, in my view, far exceed the limits of much abolitionist and protofeminist thinking of the late eighteenth century, but it nevertheless remains tethered to humanist logics. More to the point, Shelley's text is not interested in blackness as such. A product of western social and scientific epistemologies, Frankenstein operates in the service of improving "humanity" while also ensuring its homogeneity. Thus, his refusal to sympathize with the creature inscribes the latter's alterity, marking his outcast status as permanent. And while it may be tempting to read this as indicative of the ontological relation between blackness and social death illuminated by Afropessimist thought, what it more precisely reveals is the related fact of how whiteness operates: how it thrives on and maintains its power through exclusion. As a result, the creature, along with whatever or whomever he represents, is rendered without agency. For instance, even after he demonstrates his ability to reason (a path to "liberation" only insofar as liberation depends on entry into liberal society), the creature remains dependent on his creator's access to European knowledges, as we see in his request for the mate. In showing the product of western ingenuity, the creature, talking back to his creator, Shelley critiques the social logics that enable Frankenstein and the culture he represents to maintain power by first creating and then endlessly modifying the categories and conditions that mark some as human and turn others into monsters. However, in the creature's turn to suicide, she also forecloses the possibility of life outside these logics. At best, we might read the fact that we don't actually see the creature kill himself as leaving space for that possibility, which LaValle picks up and carries to its logical conclusion.

The ontological relation between blackness and death, which is a structuring modality of liberal modernity, is not the same as the relation I have outlined between the creature and suicide: the latter relation is a response to that structure. Leaning too hard on the comparison veers into antiblackness just as surely as it may believe itself to be oriented toward antiracism. Following Wilderson, analogizing Frankenstein's creature to black people "erroneously locates Blacks in the world—a place where they have not been since the dawning of Blackness. This attempt to position the Black in the world by way of analogy is not only a mystification . . . but simultaneously also a provision for civil society, promising an enabling modality for Human ethical dilemmas."[76] In other words, the radicalism of eighteenth- and nineteenth-century European emancipatory discourses is necessarily underwritten by irreconcilable structural antagonisms that cannot be overturned or corrected by liberal appeals to sympathy or integration. Moreover, as the next and final chapter will show, more conventional "romantic" ideas about suicide also turn on these racialized discourses of social death and ontological negation.

chapter 5

Marvelous Boys

> Ah, how poets sing and die!
> Make one song and Heaven takes it;
> Have one heart and Beauty breaks it;
> Chatterton, Shelley, Keats and I—
> Ah, how poets sing and die!
> —Anne Spencer, "Dunbar"

When the Harlem Renaissance poet Anne Spencer invokes the British romantics, she rehearses the idea that these poets' early deaths contributed to their literary longevity. Listing herself among their ranks, Spencer ostensibly signals her desire to achieve the same exalted status.[1] Yet her choice of poets is peculiar: all three died young, but the death and legacy of one differs markedly from the others. While Percy Shelley and John Keats are remembered for their poetry, Thomas Chatterton is known primarily for killing himself. As early as 1818, William Hazlitt summed up the allure of the *idea* of Chatterton in precisely these terms:

> I never heard any one speak of any one of his works as if it were an old well-known favourite, and had become a faith and a religion in his mind. It is his name, his youth, and what he might have lived to have done, that excite our wonder and admiration. He has the same sort of posthumous fame that an actor of the last age has—an abstracted reputation which is independent of anything we know of his works.[2]

While the idea of his suicide haunts the work of many romantic and postromantic artists, Chatterton's poetry is not widely read or esteemed now, nor was it at the time that Spencer wrote. Chatterton's notoriety is tied, rather, to the myth of romantic suicide as a marker of literary genius.

By definition, the genius is unlike the majority, and thus it follows that he is unlikely to be widely understood or appreciated in his own time. Andrew Bennett has suggested that in emphasizing their own and one another's so-called genius, romantic poets effectively constructed the standards of taste by which subsequent generations would judge them. In so doing, they helped to shape the romantic canon as we have inherited it. The implied singularity of genius, Bennett argues, requires "deferred reception" because the original work of art "is both new and before its time" and as such, the poet who produces this work can only be understood in the future, usually posthumously.[3] Bennett is absolutely correct in his assessment of how certain white male poets' obsessions with their literary afterlives helped to create the romantic canon. However, the question of Chatterton's relevance to this canon remains: why is a preromantic poet, whose poetry is usually beside the point, so enduringly associated with romanticism? In one respect, the answer is fairly obvious: Chatterton was a convenient canvas onto which romantic poets projected fantasies about their own posthumous fame. But the idea of Chatterton also served—and continues to serve—an ideological function.

The myth of romantic suicide reproduces fantasies of the posterity and invulnerability, even in death, of bourgeois white masculinity. Thus, as this chapter argues, the figure of the singular genius has really been a representative man: an ideological symbol through which liberalism's social, epistemic, and ontological frameworks are reaffirmed and threats to their cohesion evacuated. The preceding chapters have shown that late eighteenth- and early nineteenth-century British literary culture was replete with stories of suicide. These were not limited to, nor even centrally focused on, the voluntary deaths of brilliant white men. Yet as the following will show, popular and scholarly recollections of this era isolate the figure of the suicidal genius from the wider social contexts discussed in this book and give him special status, thereby maintaining the exclusionary logics that the era's other representations of suicide precisely sought to challenge. This chapter revisits the evolution of the romantic suicide myth and considers how recent artistic interventions explode its underlying racial codes. Thus, understood in the frame developed here and throughout this book, Spencer's catalogue—"Chatterton, Shelley, Keats, and I"—is not an exaltation of a literary tradition to which she aspires to belong; it is an indictment of the logics that keep her out of it.

The Mythic Structure of Romantic Suicide

Throughout this book, I have referred to romantic suicide as a myth. This is no incidental turn of phrase. Myths produce and reinforce social structures and beliefs, yet their role in doing so is usually concealed from the general consciousness.[4] In this sense, the coveted status that Chatterton and figures like him hold in the western collective consciousness is nothing short of mythic. Chatterton has been described by scholars as "the most enduring image of Romanticism" and "a symbol of a fearless spirit that triumphed over death."[5] Across the western world, artists and critics have paid homage to the ideal of Chatterton as a tragic ingénue who lost a fatal struggle for acceptance by a society incapable of comprehending his genius. In the British romantic canon, Chatterton's suicide is recalled in Keats's *Endymion* and Shelley's *Adonais*, while Samuel Taylor Coleridge spent much of his adult life revising his "Monody on the Death of Thomas Chatterton." This chapter takes its title from William Wordsworth's description of Chatterton as "the marvellous boy [sic] / The sleepless Soul that perished in his pride"—two short lines in the twenty-stanza "Resolution and Independence" that have yielded arguably the most recognizable language associated with the dead poet.[6] He is also the subject of Alfred de Vigny's *Chatterton*, a drama heralded alongside Victor Hugo's *Hernani* as a crowning achievement of French romantic theater.[7] Throughout the twentieth century and into the twenty-first, Chatterton's suicide has inspired poetry, novels, drama and music in ways that have led scholars to view his literary afterlife as a blueprint of sorts for the posthumous reputations of later popular figures who died by suicide, including Ian Curtis, Robin Williams, and Kurt Cobain, to whom I turn later in this chapter; the posthumous legacy of Alexander McQueen, with whom this book opened, falls in line with these other icons.[8] Without exception, these works characterize Chatterton as the quintessentially romantic artist whose suicide was the ultimate extension of his "genius." In so doing, these narratives ensure the continued veneration of that elite cadre of white male "geniuses," the British romantics, with whom the idea of Chatterton's suicide remains intractably associated.

However, even a peripheral glance at the circumstances surrounding Chatterton's death should cast some doubt on the assumption that suicide was his intention. That this is not more widely acknowledged reflects the extent to which canonical British romanticism hinges on the myth of his suicide. As Michelle Faubert explains, Chatterton died from an overdose of arsenic, which was widely used for medicinal purposes at the time. Just four months earlier, Chatterton left a fake suicide note for his employer as part of a scheme to manipulate his way out of debt. But no suicide note was found at the scene of his death. It is thus entirely plausible that Chatterton died by accident. And yet, as Faubert asserts, generation after generation adheres to the received wisdom that he killed himself deliberately because "if Chatterton was not a suicide, then he ceases to be a mascot for romanticism."[9] This is to say, the idea of his suicide sustains a host of cultural fantasies that ground a privileged artistic and intellectual tradition.

The quintessential representation of Chatterton as the romantic suicide par excellence is Henry Wallis's 1856 oil painting, in which the novelist George Meredith poses as the dead poet (Figure 5.1). According to Andrew Radford and Mark Sandy, this painting "achieved iconic status for the poet and set the seal on the image which, in some sense, had been struggling to manifest itself since the poet's suicide in 1770."[10] Indeed, earlier representations of Chatterton's death differ markedly from this paradigmatic image. According to William L. Pressly, Wallis took some inspiration from a 1794 illustration by Henry Singleton, engraved for circulation by Edward Orme. Without disputing that Singleton's work exerted some influence on Wallis, it is worth noting that the Singleton image arguably shares more in common with another representation of Chatterton, produced in 1801 by Raphael Lamar West and engraved by Francesco Bartolozzi.[11] Taken together, these three images suggest a shift in how Chatterton's death was imagined and represented between the end of the eighteenth century and the mid-nineteenth century.

In the Wallis painting, though his eyes are closed, Chatterton faces the viewer. However, in the earlier illustrations by Singleton and West, Chatterton's eyes are open, and he looks away from the viewer, rendering unclear whether he is already dead or in the process of dying. Wallis depicts Chatterton as clearly dead; however, the orientation of his body toward the viewer, compounded by the painting's vivid colors, renders his suicide with a vibrancy that seems incongruous with its subject matter. It is not Chatterton eliciting this liveliness; the painting makes it clear that he is gone. Insofar as viewers are oriented toward the corpse, then, it is death itself that gives the painting its ironic vitality. By comparison, in Singleton's illustration it is unclear whether Chatterton is even the focus. He lays prostrate on the right side of the page, while on the left, a woman and child are entering his garret. The presence of these other characters suggests a drama to the scene beyond just that of the poet's death. Similarly, while Chatterton is the only figure in West's illustration, it is the light shining through the window and falling on Chatterton, rather than Chatterton himself, that emerges most prominently out of the otherwise heavily shaded image. The heavy-handed symbolism of

Figure 5.1. *The Death of Chatterton* by Henry Wallis, ca. 1856. *Source*: Yale Center for British Art, Paul Mellon Collection.

that light, drawing the eye to Chatterton's heart, functions much like the woman and child in Singleton's illustration, compelling the viewer to focus on something—anything—other than the fact of Chatterton's death. Moreover, because Chatterton faces away from the viewer in both illustrations, the viewer's focus is diffused rather than directed specifically toward the poet. In Wallis's painting, however, it is only the tragic fact of the poet's suicide that faces the viewer, both literally and metaphorically; every other detail is secondary to the titular subject whose lifeless body sprawls across the canvas. Thus, to paraphrase art historian Ron Brown, the Singleton and West images read more as *memento vivere* than Wallis's *memento mori*.[12]

Indeed, according to Brown, the first known image of Chatterton's suicide, John Flaxman's 1775 ink drawing *Thomas Chatterton Taking the Bowl of Poison from the Spirit of Despair*, completely circumvents his actual death. Flaxman's allegorical image of "a youth in a nightdress offered the cup by a crouching swarthy spirit and then being taken up by a goddess in a chariot" depicts Chatterton as "bypassing death to become immortal."[13] Thus, between the work by Flaxman in 1775 and Wallis's 1856 painting, there is a clear progression in emphasis from the drama of Chatterton's final moments to the reality of his death. Flaxman, Singleton, and West variously consider, without centering, what would become the aesthetic allure of the young poet's suicide. This thoroughly romantic position is presented in earnest by Wallis and echoed in the writings of his Victorian contemporaries.

One of Wallis's most ardent admirers, Dante Gabriel Rossetti, inscribes Chatterton's position in the romantic canon in his 1881 sonnet sequence, *Five English Poets*. The sequence exalts Chatterton, Blake, Coleridge, Keats, and Percy Shelley as representative of the moment in literary history we now inherit as British romanticism. Rossetti's sonnet on Chatterton is the first in the sequence and emphasizes his youth and the idea of his genius. Chatterton also appears in another poem by Rossetti, "Tiber, Niles, and Thames," which analogizes his suicide to the silencing of historically significant rulers.[14] Likewise, as Joseph Bristow and Rebecca N. Marshall discuss in their excellent book on the subject, Oscar Wilde hailed Chatterton as "the father of the Romantic movement in literature, the precursor of Blake, Coleridge and Keats, the greatest poet of his time"—a claim that, as Bristow and Marshall explain, had far more to do with the early politics of literary periodization than with the substance of Chatterton's relevance to those poets who were being labeled "romantic" in the late nineteenth century.[15]

All this is to say that while the canonical romantic poets' interest in Chatterton is indisputable, it was arguably these later artists, poets, and critics who developed the myth of Chatterton as paradigmatic of romantic suicide and, by extension, of romanticism itself. Romantic suicide was most thoroughly romanticized in the late nineteenth century. As Radford and Sandy explain, "Romantic myths of the artist as a solitary genius . . . were bequeathed to the Victorians as much as they were reinforced, even initiated, by Victorian editors and biographers." Victorians inscribed the "mythology and hagiography of Romantic authors" by consolidating facets of the bourgeois white male–focused art and culture they wanted future generations to remember through, among other things, the idea of Chatterton's suicide.[16] As a result, even today Chatterton remains, for some, "a glorious martyrdom to Europe's artists."[17]

The trouble with this well-worn narrative is that martyrs die for their beliefs. What exactly were Chatterton's beliefs? Do we know? Does it matter? Nick Groom has posited that Chatterton's exalted status in the history of English literature makes it difficult for scholars to properly analyze the poet's work on its own terms: "For the critic, Chatterton is too mercurial, too confusing: perpetually challenging the genres of writing, mixing national histories, national fictions, and national myths in a great post-Enlightenment creation of the past . . . Chatterton's iconicity has eclipsed his very work as a writer."[18] I would like to suggest something different. If Chatterton's iconicity has made it difficult for critics to read him, it is because we have our terms wrong. Chatterton is not a martyr; he is a sacrifice.

In his work on the social function of myths, René Girard theorizes that myths are founded on acts of sacrificial violence meant to strengthen a social order that feels itself disintegrating. The sacrificial object serves to "reinforce the social fabric."[19] In the construction and circulation of the myth of romantic suicide since the nineteenth century, Chatterton has operated as precisely such an object:

> [A] substitute for all the members of the community, offered up by the members themselves. The sacrifice serves to protect the entire community from *its own* violence. . . . The elements of dissension scattered throughout the community are drawn to the person of the sacrificial victim and eliminated, at least temporarily, by its sacrifice.[20]

The mythology that now attends Chatterton and, by extension, romantic suicide more broadly, emerged to consolidate the authority of the bourgeois white male subject at a moment when that authority was being questioned by competing liberal projects, including abolition and protofeminism. Moreover, as the next section demonstrates, Chattertonian figures of tortured, singular genius continue to circulate as mechanisms through which liberalism's rights and entitlements are policed and reinforced as the exclusive province of "Man."

At the turn of the nineteenth century, the hegemony of "Man" was threatened by writers who drew on liberal principles to render suicide a challenge to the authority of white male individualism. Stories about self-destruction produced in the era within and against which romanticism developed sought to challenge (even as they more often functionally maintained) the authority of "Man." That Chatterton was made (and continues to be) synonymous with romanticism, the most privileged western cultural category to emerge from that era, is arguably best explained by Girard's notion that the sacrifice "dies so that the entire community, threatened by the same fate, can be reborn in a new or renewed cultural order."[21] Thus, I would like to suggest that romantic suicide epitomizes a defensive ideology wherein the deification of white male solipsism reproduces an isolationist and exclusionary status quo.[22] And while it emerged from the nineteenth century, the myth of romantic suicide continues to circulate to strikingly similar ends today.

Conclusion: Black Lives and Dead White Guys

In my lifetime, no suicide has been so thoroughly romanticized as that of Kurt Cobain. That is, in the popular treatment of Cobain's life, and especially of his death, we see a clear recirculation of romantic literary tropes. One day after his body was found on April 8, 1994, the *New York Times* described him as the "hesitant poet of 'grunge rock,'" and the *Guardian* labeled him an "icon of alienation."[23] *Newsweek* recirculated this language as recently as 2018, with a headline memorializing him as "the poet of alienation" on the anniversary of his death.[24] In June of 1994, *Rolling Stone* took readers inside "Kurt Cobain's Downward Spiral: The Last Days of Nirvana's Leader," a subject revisited by Gus Van Sant in his 2005 film *Last Days*, a fictionalized portrayal of the events leading up to the death of a Cobain look-alike named, not incidentally, Blake.[25] Many news reports, particularly those from 1994, also articulated concerns about "copycat" suicides, echoing the eighteenth-century panic over Goethe's *Werther*, though studies have since demonstrated a decrease in suicides in the months following Cobain's death.[26] But the pièce de résistance is American artist Sandow Birk's 1994 painting, *The Death of Kurt Cobain*, which is modeled after Wallis's *The Death of Chatterton*. In Birk's depiction, Cobain's body is dressed and posed almost identically to Chatterton's, but his head is blown to bloody bits. A halo hovers above where his face would have been—a gruesome, pointed send-up of the mythology that mystifies the complexities of both writers' deaths, as well as their lives.[27] Since the day the world learned of Cobain's death, his work has been mediated and remediated through the narrative of romantic suicide. As a result, the art for which he was hailed the voice of his generation is now nearly impossible to disentangle from the much-publicized final line of his suicide note: "It's better to burn out than to fade away."[28]

It is worth noting, too, how well Cobain himself is now said to have understood the social script associated with romantic suicide. Charles Cross, Cobain's foremost biographer, quotes friends' and family members' recollections of Cobain expressing, from an early age, sentiments such as, "I'm going to become a superstar musician, kill myself, and go out in a flame of glory."[29] I would emphasize, as Cross does, that how much of this is truth and how much simply reflects the pervasiveness of romantic archetypes in his posthumous reputation is anyone's guess. It is true that Cobain's journals are rife with such sentiments, but these are often self-consciously tempered, as in the following: "To be positive at all times is to ignore all that is important, sacred or valuable.

To be negative at all times is to be threatened by rediculousness [sic] and instant discredibility [sic]."[30] The reality of suicide is complicated; romantic suicide is decidedly less so. Thus, I would argue that romantic suicide killed Kurt Cobain, but I don't mean Cobain the man. I have no right to speculate on why he chose to end his life, and it's not my intention to do that here. I'm talking about Cobain the legend: the posterchild for unruly brilliance and unbearable pain. It is the myth of romantic suicide, the very one I've been discussing in these pages, that keeps him locked inside this box even now, more than a quarter of a century after the traumatic moment of his passing.

If, as I have been arguing, the ideological function of romantic suicide has been to reinforce the dominance of the liberal subject, it is deeply ironic that Cobain should now be associated with this tradition. Cobain was no representative man. His appeal lay precisely in his subversion of hegemonic norms. He spoke out against rape culture, reflected publicly on his fluid sexuality, performed in drag and, long before it was fashionable in white progressive circles, he was writing about systemic racism and intersectionality.[31] In the liner notes to *Incesticide*, the collection of B-sides released shortly after *Nevermind* made Nirvana a household name, Cobain urged fans espousing homophobic, racist, or misogynistic views to "leave us the fuck alone. Don't come to our shows and don't buy our records."[32] Even so, the most commonly circulated facts about Cobain remain his drug use and suicide.[33]

However, at least one popular domain remembers him differently. Socially conscious hip-hop artists consistently see through the teen angst narratives that render Cobain's rage situational rather than what it was: a response to deeply rooted structural problems that keep our society unjust, unreasonable, and for many, fundamentally unlivable. Writing in 2014, Cross finds fifty-five hip-hop songs that sample Nirvana and dozens more that reference Cobain.[34] From established heavyweights like Jay-Z, Kendrick Lamar, Kool Keith, and Talib Kweli, to newer artists like the late Lil Peep, Trippie Redd, and Marcus Gloster, who performs under the moniker "Black Cobain," hip-hop's interest in Cobain runs deeper than, as some have claimed, the fact that his name conveniently rhymes with cocaine.[35] One particularly trenchant example is Denzel Curry's "Clout Cobain." The song is about fame and the entertainment industry's exploitation of young artists, and in this sense, it rehearses a familiar story. But the music video takes it somewhere else entirely.

Directed by Zev Deans, the video for "Clout Cobain" radiates deep respect for the late musician and was made in part to call attention to troubling ways in which his death is romanticized: "they glorify him for the wrong reasons," Curry told *Billboard* shortly after the video premiered in July of 2018.[36] But the video is also an indictment of the racial politics that undergird whose deaths get romanticized within the liberal imaginary and why. The video centers on Curry performing as part of a circus act. He wears a striped shirt reminiscent of the one worn by Cobain at the 1993 MTV Video Music Awards. His face is painted clown-white with an exaggerated smile and dark circle around his left eye, and thus the striped shirt also frames him as a mime or clown figure. Entering the stage on camelback, Curry is escorted by a man wearing a white shirt covered in frowning faces (a nod to Nirvana's smiley face logo, designed by Cobain in 1991). Shots of the audience, mostly young adults, recall the high school mosh pit in Nirvana's video for "Smells Like Teen Spirit." Audience members and fellow performers wear Cobain's iconic white oval sunglasses (which are in fashion again thanks in part to Curry's rebranding them "Clout Goggles").[37]

For most of its four minutes and nineteen seconds, the video explores themes now typically associated with Cobain: the ringleader steals money from Curry's pockets, industry workers promote drug use, and fans mindlessly absorb the latest trends. Though most of the video is in black and white, Deans employs selective color effects to make certain hues pop at key moments. The camera lingers on several fans wincing in pain as they get tattoos, which bleed bright red against the otherwise colorless scene. The raw feeling registered on their faces contrasts sharply with close-ups of other audience members, stone faced and apparently unimpressed with Curry's increasingly manic performance. These glimpses of people in pain join two other brief but significant shots from earlier in the video, which likewise punctuate what could otherwise be taken as another cautionary tale of drugs, fame, and empty consumerism.

At 0:36, we see Curry, a black man, in chains, being yanked onstage by the white ringleader. Then, at 2:17, the video cuts to an intertitle card that reads "Dance!!!" Curry begins to move in ways that recall conventions of minstrel performance. The racist iconography of the past then gives way to a more recent visual form. Beginning at 3:14, Curry is shown in the vertical frame of a cellphone video, waving a gun while livestreaming. Looking at this, it's hard not to connect the dots to the endless stream of cellphone recordings that show the fatal results of state-sanctioned violence disproportionately directed at African Americans. As his in-house audience roars with laugher and his digital audience floods his cellphone screen with "likes" (represented here by the Nirvana smileys), Curry stops, rolls his eyes, and drops the act. The camera pulls in on his face as he smears his makeup; the circle around his eye, which had appeared black, is revealed to be red, a bullseye. Curry renders his frustration increasingly palpable until, at 3:45, he raises the gun to his temple. The audience continues to cheer and laugh while the ringleader glares at the rogue performer. At 3:54, Curry pulls the trigger. With a spurt of dark red blood, his body falls out of the frame, and we watch the audience register what they've just witnessed. Following a protracted collective gasp, the camera pans slowly over Curry's body, up to his face, and then across to the blood pooling from his temple. Adding insult to fatality, there's popcorn in the blood.

Cobain functions here as a touchstone through which the video brings into focus the incongruities of a culture inured to the sight of bloodied and dying black bodies, which has yet to redress (or even really acknowledge) the lethal impacts of the war on drugs on communities of color, but insists on maintaining the romance of a white man's drug addiction and violent death by suicide. It achieves this by showing in brutal, graphic detail a version of what some Nirvana fans have been demanding for years. Since Cobain's death in 1994, the Seattle police department has received regular requests to release photos of his body. These come mostly from conspiracy theorists who believe the photos will prove that Cobain was murdered. In 2014, the twenty-year anniversary of his death, the Seattle police department reviewed the case, reaffirmed that it was a suicide, and released thirty-five photos taken at the scene. Two years later, photos of the shotgun Cobain used to kill himself were made public for the first time.[38] Both sets of photos were picked up by nearly every major news outlet and are now widely available online. Though not especially graphic—they don't show his face or head—they are nevertheless disturbing. Moreover, precisely because of what they do not show, they have done nothing to assuage conspiracy theorists.[39] So why release them at all? One detective associated with the case had the following to say when asked why they chose not to release the more graphic images: "What are people going to gain from seeing pictures of Kurt Cobain laying on the ground with his hair blown back, with blood coming out of his nose and trauma to his eyes from a penetrating shotgun wound? How's that going to benefit anybody?"[40] Indeed, it would benefit absolutely no one. What it would do, as Birk's painting of Cobain-as-Chatterton captures so incisively, is unravel the mythology that surrounds his suicide. It is significant, then, that Curry's video gives us precisely such a visual.

Of course, Curry's suicide in "Clout Cobain" is fictional, rendering this an admittedly imperfect comparison. Nevertheless, the lingering attention to his bloodied face and head in the context of a work that intentionally calls up Cobain speaks volumes about the racial logics of death in our modernity. A contemporary emblem of romantic suicide, Cobain is inscribed in cultural memory as more myth than man. Curry explodes that myth by calling attention to its inherently exclusionary presumptions. Dressed in one of Cobain's signature outfits, we might take Curry to stand in for Cobain, a "slave" to fame, even as the image of Curry in chains hearkens to the actual history of African enslavement and its afterlives. Thus, "Clout Cobain" links the mythmaking that renders Cobain immortal to the social logics that underwrite and turn on the daily (non)event of black death. In so doing, Curry demands that we consider why the death of a white man a quarter of a century ago continues to matter more than black lives do today. By the same token, some 250 years after Chatterton's death, his home city of Bristol, once a key hub of the trade in enslaved Africans, remains enraptured with its "poet genius" even as it is only recently beginning to reckon seriously with the far more death-driven contexts in which Chatterton and his contemporaries lived.[41] While conventional wisdom may complain that dead white "geniuses" have little to do with the afterlives of African enslavement, as this book has shown, that is simply not true.

By looking beyond romantic narratives of suicide, this book has endeavored to critique efforts to reckon with a wider set of meanings associated with suicide, as well as with the exclusionary ideologies that buttress liberal modernity's notions of who "counts" as a person, a subject, a citizen, and a human being. The urgency of thinking through these questions has never been more clearly spelled out. In late 2019, the US Congressional Black Caucus published a report on a striking rise in suicide among African American youth. Suicide is now the second leading cause of death among African Americans between the ages of ten and nineteen.[42] The report urges us to consider suicide a direct consequence of systemic racism. It is, of course, not wrong in its conclusions: suicide is, and has been since at least the eighteenth century, clearly connected to racial injustice. But while private pain cannot and should not be disarticulated from the social contexts in which it is experienced, as Wilderson reminds us, "The violence that saturates Black life isn't threatened with elimination just because it is exposed."[43] At their best, liberal legislators, poets, revolutionaries, and scholars imagine that the world as we know it can be transformed. But what worlds are possible beyond liberalism's bounds?

Notes

Introduction

1. On suicide notes in eighteenth-century print culture, see Eric Parisot, "Suicide Notes and Popular Sensibility in the Eighteenth-Century British Press," *Eighteenth-Century Studies* 47, no. 3 (2014): 277–91; and Michael Macdonald, "Suicide and the Rise of the Popular Press in England," *Representations* 22 (Spring 1988): 36–55. On changes in burial laws for suicides, see Barbara Gates, *Victorian Suicide: Mad Crimes and Sad Histories* (Princeton, NJ: Princeton University Press, 1987).
2. These findings were published in an 1883 essay in *Nature* called "Suicide of Scorpions." For more on this, see the second chapter of Jesse Bering's *Suicidal: Why We Kill Ourselves* (Chicago: University of Chicago Press, 2018).
3. David Constantine, introduction to *The Sorrows of Young Werther* by Johann Wolfgang von Goethe (New York: Oxford University Press, 2012), xxvii.
4. The following is a chronological list of books published on the subject in the last two decades: Georges Minois, *History of Suicide: Voluntary Death in Western Culture*, trans. Lydia G. Cochrane (Baltimore: Johns Hopkins University Press, 2001); Jeffrey R. Watt, ed., *From Sin to Insanity: Suicide in Early Modern Culture* (Ithaca, NY: Cornell University Press, 2004); Ron Brown, *The Art of Suicide* (London: Reaktion, 2004); John Weaver and David Wright, *Histories of Suicide: International Perspectives on Self-Destruction in the Modern World* (Toronto: University of Toronto Press, 2009); R. A. Houston, *Punishing the Dead? Suicide, Lordship, and Community in Britain, 1500–1830* (New

York: Oxford University Press, 2010); Alexander Murray, *Suicide in the Middle Ages* (New York: Oxford University Press, 2009); Ian Marsh, *Suicide: Foucault, History and Truth* (Cambridge: Cambridge University Press, 2010); Richard Bell, *We Shall Be No More: Suicide and Self-government in the Newly United States* (Cambridge, MA: Harvard University Press, 2012); Kelly McGuire, *Dying to Be English: Suicide Narratives and National Identity* (London: Pickering and Chatto, 2012); Jennifer Michael Hecht, *Stay: A History of Suicide and the Philosophies Against It* (New Haven, CT: Yale University Press, 2014); Marzio Barbagli, *Farewell to the World: A History of Suicide*, trans. Lucinda Byatt (Cambridge, UK: Polity, 2015); Terri Snyder, *The Power to Die: Suicide and Slavery in British North America* (Chicago: University of Chicago Press, 2015); and Andrew Bennett, *Suicide Century: Literature and Suicide from James Joyce to David Foster Wallace* (Cambridge: Cambridge University Press, 2017). Earlier book-length studies include, in addition to Gates's *Victorian Suicide*: Olive Anderson, *Suicide in Victorian and Edwardian England* (London: Clarendon, 1987); A. Alvarez, *The Savage God: A Study of Suicide* (New York: W. W. Norton, 1990); Michael MacDonald and Terence R. Murphy, *Sleepless Souls: Suicide in Early Modern England* (New York: Oxford University Press, 1991); and Victor Bailey, *This Rash Act: Suicide Across the Life Cycle in the Victorian City* (Stanford, CA: Stanford University Press, 1998).

5. Scholars who have debunked this myth include James Whitehead, *Madness and the Romantic Poet* (New York: Oxford University Press, 2017) and Duncan Wu, *30 Great Myths About the Romantics* (Chichester, UK: John Wiley, 2015). I realize that my categorization of the romantic genius as almost exclusively male may draw objections because women writers also adopted the persona. However, as Andrew Bennett has shown, when women contemporaries of those poets we now associate with romanticism adopted this persona, it was with the express aim of separating themselves from the male canon and its "gendering of genius and neglect." More recently, Tricia Lootens has shown how twentieth-century feminist literary critics used the trope of romantic suicide to establish some women writers as canonical: "Sylvia Plath killed herself and was born again to a dominant role in the world of letters." In these readings, and as I'll demonstrate in this book, suicide circulates as a cipher of privileges that reinscribes modernity's investment in patriarchy and whiteness. See Andrew Bennett, *Romantic Poets and the Culture of Posterity* (Cambridge: Cambridge University Press, 1999), 68; and Tricia Lootens, *The Political Poetess: Victorian Femininity, Race, and the Legacy of Separate Spheres* (Princeton, NJ: Princeton University Press, 2017), 58.

6. For images of McQueen's coats, see Andrew Bolton, *Alexander McQueen: Savage Beauty* (New Haven, CT: Yale University Press, 2011), 31–50.
7. Bolton, *Alexander McQueen*, 92, 112, 184.
8. Compare the accompanying web pages for the exhibition: while the show itself remains conceptually framed through the lens of romanticism, as per Bolton's vision, four of the V&A's ten subsections explicitly include the label "romantic," whereas in the earlier iteration at the Met, all the subsections are labeled "romantic." See Victoria and Albert Museum, "Alexander McQueen: Savage Beauty—About the Exhibition," accessed September 28, 2018, http://www.vam.ac.uk/content/exhibitions/exhibition-alexander-mcqueen-savage-beauty/about-the-exhibition; and Metropolitan Museum of Art, "Alexander McQueen: Savage Beauty," *The Metropolitan Museum of Art*, accessed February 28, 2015, http://blog.metmuseum.org/alexandermcqueen/about.
9. Frank B. Wilderson III, *Red, White, and Black: Cinema and the Structure of U.S. Antagonisms* (Durham, NC: Duke University Press, 2010), 21.
10. Wilderson, *Red, White, and Black*, 11.
11. Attending to recommendations set forth by P. Gabrielle Foreman et. al., I generally avoid calling people of African descent who were enslaved *slaves* so as to disarticulate the condition from the person. However, I use "suicidal slave," always in quotation marks, to underscore that this figure precisely normalizes such elisions. For more on this, see P. Gabrielle Foreman, et al., "Writing about Slavery/Teaching About Slavery: This Might Help," community-sourced document, accessed May 14, 2020, https://docs.google.com/document/d/1A4TEdDgYslX-hlKezLodMIM71My3KTNozxRvoIQTOQs.
12. In addition to Snyder's *The Power to Die*, see Brycchan Carey, *British Abolitionism and the Rhetoric of Sensibility: Writing, Sentiment, and Slavery, 1760–1807* (New York: Palgrave Macmillan, 2005); Michelle Faubert, "The Wollstonecraftian Plot: Female Suicide as Slave Protest," in *Romantic Bodyscapes: Embodied Selves, Embodied Spaces and Legible Bodies in the Romantic Age*, ed. Gerold Sedlmayr (Trier, Germany: Wissenschaftlicher Verlag Trier, 2015), 123–44; Moira Ferguson, *Subject to Others: British Women Writers and Colonial Slavery, 1670–1834* (London: Routledge, 1992); Lynn Festa, *Sentimental Figures of Empire in Eighteenth-Century Britain and France* (Baltimore: Johns Hopkins University Press, 2006); Margaret Higonnet, "Dialogues with the Dead: Enlightened Selves, Suicide, and Human Rights," *1616: Anuario de Literatura Comparada* 2 (2012): 189–208. Many others are referenced throughout this book.
13. For more on this, see the fourth chapter of McGuire's *Dying to Be English*.

14. Minois, *History of Suicide*, 267.
15. It is now generally accepted that there was no significant uptick in suicides following the publication of Goethe's novella. However, "the Werther effect" remains in circulation as a theory in the social sciences, informing the strict guidelines that reporters in many countries follow when writing about or discussing suicide. David Phillips originated the term in "The Influence of Suggestion on Suicide: Substantive and Theoretical Implications of the Werther Effect," *American Sociological Review* 39, no. 3 (1974): 340–54. Since then, aspects of the theory—from its historicity to its accuracy in predicting suicide rates—have been called into question. See Jan Thorson and Per-Arne Öberg, "Was There a Suicide Epidemic After Goethe's Werther?," *Archives of Suicide Research* 7, no. 1 (2003): 69–72; James Hittner, "How Robust is the Werther Effect? A Re-examination of the Suggestion-Imitation Model of Suicide," *Mortality* (August 2005): 193–200; and Michelle Faubert, "Werther Goes Viral: Suicidal Contagion, Vaccination, and Infections Sympathy," *Literature and Medicine* 34, no. 2 (Fall 2016): 389–417.
16. Quoted in Bruce Duncan, *Goethe's* Werther *and the Critics* (Rochester, NY: Camden House, 2005), 1; and Minois, *History of Suicide*, 181, respectively. Ironically, despite his own penchant for morbid themes and self-destructive behavior, Lord Byron lobbed a similar charge right back at Goethe: "It is moreover asserted that 'the predominant character of the whole body of English poetry is a *disgust* and contempt for life'—but I rather suspect that, by one single work of *prose, you* [Goethe] yourself have excited a greater contempt for life than all the English volumes of poesy that ever were written. Madame de Staël says that '*Werther* has occasioned more suicides than the most beautiful woman,' and I really believe that he has put more individuals out of this world than Napoleon himself." This quote appears in the ultimately rejected dedication to Byron's 1820 play *Marino Faliero*. See *The Works of Byron: Letters and Journals*, ed. Rowland E. Prothero, vol. 5 (New York: Charles Scribner's Sons, 1904), 102.
17. McGuire, *Dying to Be English*, 116.
18. See, particularly, McGuire, *Dying to Be English*; Bell, *We Shall Be No More*; and Snyder, *The Power to Die*. Although it is only recently that monographs have read the history of suicide through sociopolitical frameworks, Margaret Higonnet pioneered this approach in her 1985 article "Suicide: Representations of the Feminine," *Poetics Today* 6, no. 1–2 (1985): 103–18. This article opened conversations about the relationship between gender, rights discourses, sensibility, and the male-centered culture of romantic suicide. It is thus all the more surprising that there has been no book-length study on suicide and romanticism between then and now.

19. MacDonald and Murphy, *Sleepless Souls*, 2.
20. Watt, *From Sin to Insanity*, 8. In terms of influence on subsequent thinking about suicide, the only conceivable rival to Hume's text is Emile Durkheim's *On Suicide* (1897). Durkheim used statistical records to advance the theory that suicide rates are contingent upon the interplay of social forces. If we can control those forces, he argued, we can lower incidence of suicide at least to some degree. Durkheim's work remains influential in academic studies of suicide trends, as well as in the development of public policies on suicide education and prevention.
21. David Hume, *On Suicide* (New York: Penguin, 2005), 4–5.
22. Hume, *On Suicide*, 7. It is worth noting that in Catholicism, Protestantism, Anglicanism, Calvinism, and Lutheranism, suicide is strictly condemned. Other Christian denominations view it somewhat more leniently. For instance, Methodism (which, perhaps not coincidentally, developed in England toward the end of the eighteenth century) stresses compassion toward those who kill themselves, though it still considers the act itself to be sinful. For more on suicide and Christianity, see Minois, *History of Suicide*, 68–76.
23. Hume, *On Suicide*, 8–9.
24. Hume, 8–9.
25. Hume, 8–9.
26. Hume, 10.
27. Sylvia Wynter, "Unsettling the Coloniality of Being/Power/Truth/Freedom: Towards the Human, After Man, Its Overrepresentation—An Argument," *CR: The New Centennial Review* 3, no. 3 (Fall 2003): 260.
28. Quoted in John Immerwahr, "Hume's Revised Racism," *Journal of the History of Ideas* 53, no. 3 (1992): 481–82.
29. Immerwahr, "Hume's Revised Racism," 483.
30. Immerwahr, 483.
31. Immerwahr, 486. Aaron Garrett and Silvia Sebastiani also discuss these changes and their implications in "David Hume on Race," in *The Oxford Handbook of Philosophy and Race*, ed. Naomi Zack (New York: Oxford University Press, 2017), 31–43.
32. Henry Louis Gates Jr., *Figures in Black: Words, Signs and the 'Racial Self'* (New York: Oxford University Press, 1997), 18.
33. Wilderson, *Afropessimism* (New York: W. W. Norton, 2020), 224.
34. Wilderson, *Afropessimism*, 48.
35. Wilderson, 20–21.
36. Iyko Day, "Being or Nothingness: Indigeneity, Antiblackness, and Settler Colonial Critique," *Journal of the Critical Ethnic Studies Association* 1, no. 2 (Fall 2015): 102–21.
37. Mark Rifkin, *Fictions of Land and Flesh*, (Durham, NC: Duke University Press, 2019), 3, 5. Rifkin's first chapter offers a thorough overview

of commonalities and divergences between western academic and activist discourses of blackness and indigeneity. See also Glen Sean Coulthard, *Red Skin, White Masks: Rejecting the Colonial Politics of Recognition* (Minneapolis: University of Minnesota Press, 2014); Tiffany Lethabo King, *The Black Shoals: Offshore Formations of Black and Native Studies* (Durham, NC: Duke University Press, 2019); and Tiya Miles and Sharon P. Holland, eds., *Crossing Waters, Crossing Worlds* (Durham, NC: Duke University Press, 2006).

38. Fred Moten, "Chromatic Saturation," in *The Universal Machine* (Durham, NC: Duke University Press, 2018), 195–96.
39. Jared Sexton, "Ante-Anti-Blackness," *Lateral: Journal of the Cultural Studies Association* 1(2012), http://csalateral.org/section/theory/ante-anti-blackness-afterthoughts-sexton/.
40. Christina Sharpe, *In the Wake: On Blackness and Being* (Durham, NC: Duke University Press, 2016), 22.
41. Fred Moten, "Knowledge of Freedom," in *Stolen Life* (Durham, NC: Duke University Press, 2018), 33.
42. Saidiya V. Hartman and Frank B. Wilderson III, "The Position of the Unthought," *Qui Parle* 13, no. 187 :(2003) 2.
43. Audre Lorde, "The Master's Tools Will Never Dismantle the Master's House," in *Sister Outsider* (New York: Ten Speed, 2007), 110–14.
44. Wilderson, *Red, White, and Black*, 11.
45. Quoted in Siddhartha Mitter, "'What Does it Mean to Be Black and Look at This?' A Scholar Reflects on the Dana Schutz Controversy," *Hyperallergic*, March 24, 2017, https://hyperallergic.com/368012/what-does-it-mean-to-be-black-and-look-at-this-a-scholar-reflects-on-the-dana-schutz-controversy/. Sharpe is referring here to the analytic she develops for reading black existence as always occurring in relation to modernity's structural antiblackness, which she names through metaphorical engagements with elements of the Middle Passage—the slave ship, the hold, the weather: "The question for theory is how to live in the wake of slavery, in slavery's afterlives, the afterlife of property, how, in short, to inhabit and rupture this episteme with their, with out, knowable lives." Sharpe, *In the Wake*, 50.
46. Recognizing that the "liberal" in "liberal arts" predates the eighteenth-century liberalism this book focuses on, I make this assertion with an eye on Patrick Deneen's claim that in practice, this later sense of "liberal" has emerged as more prominent in universities today: "Under the guise of differences in race, an exploding number of genders, and a variety of sexual orientations, the only substantive worldview advanced is that of advanced liberalism: the ascent of the autonomous individual backed by the power and support of the state and its growing control over institutions, including schools and

universities." While Deneen advocates for a return to the ancient sense of the "liberal arts" as "the rescue of liberal education from liberalism," I see far more possibility in Stefano Harney and Fred Moten's call "to be in but not of" the university—to embrace what they variously call fugitive study, maroon study, black study, the undercommons, modalities that champion collectivity over university cultures that churn out state-sanctioned "autonomous individuals" committed to "enlightened" narratives of objectivity, civilization, and progress. See Patrick Deneen, *Why Liberalism Failed* (New Haven, CT: Yale University Press, 2018), 124, 130; also see Stefano Harney and Fred Moten, *The Undercommons: Fugitive Planning and Black Study* (Brooklyn, NY: Minor Compositions, 2013), 26.

47. Marlon Ross, "The Race of/in Romanticism: Notes Toward a Critical Race Theory," in *Race, Romanticism, and the Atlantic*, ed. Paul Youngquist (Burlington, VT: Ashgate, 2013), 34.

48. Generally speaking, critical race work in Anglo-European literary studies lags significantly behind American literary studies. However, scholars of premodern and early modern literature and culture have made significant headway in this area since at least the pathbreaking publication of Kim F. Hall's *Things of Darkness: Economies of Race and Gender in Early Modern England* (Ithaca, NY: Cornell University Press, 1995). More recently, the RaceB4Race conference series, created by Ayanna Thompson, has helped to substantially shift these fields by shining a light on antiracist scholarship in premodern and early modern studies and centering scholars of color. For more on this, see the following: https://www.ayannathompson.com/raceb4race.

49. Manu Samriti Chander, *Brown Romantics: Poetry and Nationalism in the Global Nineteenth Century* (Lewisburg, PA: Bucknell University Press, 2017), 101.

50. Chander, *Brown Romantics*, 154.

51. Bakary Diaby, "Black Women and/in the Shadow of Romanticism," *European Romantic Review* 30, no. 3 (2019): 253.

52. Eva Beatrice Dykes, *The Negro in English Romantic Thought: Or, A Study of Sympathy for the Oppressed* (Washington, DC: Associated, 1942), 153.

53. Robin DiAngelo, *White Fragility: Why It's So Hard for White People to Talk About Racism* (Boston: Beacon, 2018), 20.

54. Gauri Viswanathan, *Masks of Conquest: Literary Study and British Rule in India* (New York: Columbia University Press, 1989), 3.

55. Chander, *Brown Romantics*, 36–38.

56. Terry Eagleton, *Literary Theory: An Introduction*, 2nd ed. (Minneapolis: University of Minnesota Press, 1996), 23.

57. Eagleton, *Literary Theory*.

58. Paul Youngquist, "The African Queen," in *Race, Romanticism, and the Atlantic*, ed. Paul Youngquist (Burlington, VT: Ashgate, 2013), 81.
59. See, for example, Chander's *Brown Romantics* and Jared Hickman's *Black Prometheus: Race and Radicalism in the Age of Atlantic Slavery* (New York: Oxford University Press, 2016). Joel Pace and I discuss the limits of the term in "Introduction: New Directions in Transatlantic Romanticisms," *Symbiosis: A Journal of Transatlantic Literary and Cultural Relations* 23, no. 1 (Spring 2019): 5–19, while the Bigger Six Collective (of which I am a founding member) offers a counterargument for its utility in the coda to the same volume, pages 139–40.
60. These definitions are variously drawn from: bell hooks, *Teaching to Transgress: Education as the Practice of Freedom* (New York: Routledge, 1994); Richard Dyer, *White: Essays on Race and Culture* (New York: Routledge, 1997); Nell Irvin Painter, *The History of White People* (New York: W. W. Norton, 2010); and DiAngelo, *White Fragility*.
61. Thus, for example, bell hooks uses variations of the term "imperialist white supremacist capitalist hetero-patriarchy" to make visible the continually interlocking systems of subjugation that buttress liberal modernity. See, among others, hooks, *The Will to Change: Men, Masculinity, and Love* (New York: Washington Square, 2004) and *Feminism is for Everybody: Passionate Politics* (London: Pluto, 2000).
62. Sara Ahmed, *Living a Feminist Life* (Durham, NC: Duke University Press, 2017), 152–53.
63. Youngquist, "The African Queen," 82. Even as I write about defamiliarizing whiteness, I am reminded of Kehinde Andrews's claim that whiteness is akin to psychosis: it cannot be reasoned with and efforts to defamiliarize it merely reproduce it. He's right. The very existence of this work underlines his point that because "there are surely limits to the role that universities—bastions of Whiteness—can play in dismantling White supremacy," scholarly contributions to those efforts will always be necessarily insufficient. See "The Psychosis of Whiteness: The Celluloid Hallucinations of *Amazing Grace* and *Belle*," *Journal of Black Studies* 47, no. 5 (2016): 439.
64. Bennett, *Romantic Poets and the Culture of Posterity*, 78.
65. See Bennett, especially chapter 6.
66. Victor Hugo, "Author's Preface to the First Edition of *Hernani*," in *Dramas*, Vol. 1 of *The Works of Victor Hugo* (New York: Little, Brown, 1909), 3.
67. I'm thinking here of Amanda Anderson's *Bleak Liberalism*, which contends that liberalism has always been aware of these limitations and sets out to demonstrate that awareness through a reading practice meant to reconcile liberalism's twin poles of individual self-reflection and social analysis. In so doing, she ascribes liberalism's racial exclusions to blind spots that can be corrected as opposed to systemic logics

at its core. This is especially clear in her reading of Ralph Ellison's *Invisible Man*, which sidesteps Ellison's engagement with black radical thought. The black radical tradition precisely holds that blackness is a structural position located outside of and in opposition (or apposition) to liberalism. For example, as bell hooks argues, "Understanding marginality"—or, in Ellison's case, invisibility—"as a position and place of resistance is crucial for oppressed, exploited, colonized people. If we only view the margin as a sign marking despair, a deep nihilism penetrates in a destructive way the very ground of our being. It is there in that space of collective despair that one's creativity, one's imagination is at risk, there that one's mind is fully colonized, there that the freedom one longs for is lost." Anderson's reading implicitly denies the validity, if not also the existence, of such fugitive modes of social and political life. See Anderson, *Bleak Liberalism* (Chicago: University of Chicago Press, 2016) and hooks, "Choosing the Margin as a Space of Radical Openness," in *Yearning: Race, Gender, and Cultural Politics* (Boston: South End, 1990), 207.

68. Dwight A. McBride, *Impossible Witnesses: Truth, Abolitionism, and Slave Testimony* (New York: New York University Press, 2001), 21.

69. Fred Moten, "Black Op," in *Stolen Life* (Durham, NC: Duke University Press, 2018), 155–56. Attending to Moten's distinction in this essay and elsewhere between "blackness" as an analytical framework and "Blackness" as conventionally capitalized to signal a cultural identifier, I have chosen not to capitalize "black" and "blackness." I capitalize "Afropessimism" but not "black optimism" in keeping with the most recent conventional usage among their chief proponents, Wilderson and Moten, respectively. In a broader sense, I have understood the choice not to capitalize "black" in some work coming out of black studies as attestation of the field's, as well as African and Afrodiasporic people's, fugitive relations to the western academy. By contrast, disciplinary formations around certain other terms that are conventionally capitalized, such as "romanticism" and "the enlightenment," are as authorized by the same academy as they are complicit in its project of disseminating the intellectual, social, and political capital of "the west." My choice not to capitalize these three terms, while partly a move to unsettle that project's authority, is more precisely meant to bring forward and render formally the epistemic tensions and irreconcilabilities running through this book. When quoting from authors who have made different choices in these matters, I maintain their language as it appears in print.

70. Alexander Weheliye, *Habeas Viscus: Racializing Assemblages, Biopolitics, and Black Feminist Theories of the Human* (Durham, NC: Duke University Press, 2014), 4.

71. In choosing whether or not to capitalize certain words, my intent was to bring some of these frictions to the surface and make them visible at the level of form. See n. 69.
72. To cite all the relevant scholarship on romanticism and the rights discourses that informed the French, American, and Haitian revolutions would be next to impossible. A handful of book-length studies that explicitly consider liberalism as the groundwork for romanticism include: Nancy L. Rosenblum, *Another Liberalism: Romanticism and the Reconstruction of Liberal Thought* (Cambridge, MA: Harvard University Press, 1987); R. S. White, *Natural Rights and the Birth of Romanticism in the 1790s* (New York: Palgrave Macmillan, 2005); and Zoe Beenstock, *The Politics of Romanticism: The Social Contract and Literature* (Edinburgh: Edinburgh University Press, 2016).
73. Saidiya Hartman, *Scenes of Subjection* (New York: Oxford University Press, 1997), 122.
74. Charles W. Mills, *Black Rights/White Wrongs: The Critique of Racial Liberalism* (New York: Oxford University Press, 2017), 29. See also Charles W. Mills, *The Racial Contract* (Ithaca, NY: Cornell University Press, 1999) and Domenico Losurdo, *Liberalism: A Counter-History*, trans. Gregory Elliott (London: Verso, 2014). Part of Losurdo's overarching argument is that liberalism and racial enslavement emerged as the "twin birth" of modernity.
75. In terms of romantic studies, beyond those already mentioned, I would be remiss not to include Nikki Hessell's *Romantic Literature and the Colonised World: Notes from Indigenous Translations* (New York: Palgrave Macmillan, 2018). And, while not principally concerned with romanticism, Tricia Lootens's *The Political Poetess* also takes an explicitly antiracist stance in reading nineteenth-century British texts. There is, by now, little doubt that major changes are occurring in historically Eurocentric subfields of English studies. I hope that this book, whatever its flaws, contributes positively to these transformations.

Notes to Chapter 1

1. Thomas Day and John Bicknell, *The Dying Negro*, Gale Eighteenth Century Collections Online (CW3310391049) (London: John Stockdale, 1793), 1.
2. This explanation appears in the advertisement to the first edition. According to the English periodical *The Bibliographer*, "This story was told to Day by his friend John Bicknell, and the result was a poem entitled *The Dying Negro*." See "The Author of Sanford and Merton," *Bibliographer* 5 (January 1884): 31.

3. Paul Halliday, *Habeas Corpus: From England to Empire* (Cambridge, MA: Harvard University Press, 2010), 179.
4. Wilderson, *Red, White, and Black*, 44.
5. The chief precursor here is Aphra Behn's *Oroonoko*, although in that text, Oroonoko's attempted suicide is usurped and completed by his captors. More importantly, the text as a whole is decidedly not advocating for the abolition of slavery. If anything, Oroonoko's nobility frames his attempted suicide as exceptional, giving audiences license to feel for him without raising the idea that all enslaved Africans should be free. For more on the "noble African" trope, see Wylie Sypher, "The African Prince in London," *Journal of the History of Ideas* 2, no. 2 (1941): 237–47, as well as Laura Doyle's discussion of Equiano's engagement with that trope in *Freedom's Empire: Race and the Rise of the Novel in Atlantic Modernity, 1640–1940* (Durham, NC: Duke University Press, 2008). For an incisive reading of how the scene of Oroonoko's death signals Behn's and the novel's convoluted politics, see Megan Griffin, "Dismembering the Sovereign in Aphra Behn's *Oroonoko*," *ELH* 86, no. 1 (Spring 2019): 107–33.
6. Weheliye, *Habeas Viscus*, 3.
7. See William S. Laufer, *Corporate Bodies and Guilty Minds: The Failure of Corporate Criminal Liability* (Chicago: University of Chicago Press, 2008); and Gary Francione, *Animals as Persons: Essays on the Abolition of Animal Exploitation* (New York: Columbia University Press, 2008).
8. Carey, *British Abolitionism and the Rhetoric of Sensibility*, 76.
9. There is no exact transcription of the proceedings, and several contemporary accounts of the case survive, including one by Granville Sharp. Following scholarly precedent, my references to the case rely on the Lofft report: *Somerset v. Stewart*, 1 *Lofft* (King's Bench, 1772), 510.
10. For more on this history, see T. K. Hunter, "Geographies of Liberty: A Brief Look at Two Cases" in *Prophets of Protest: Reconsidering The History of American Abolitionism*, ed. Timothy Patrick McCarthy and John Stauffer (New York: New Press, 2006), 41–58.
11. On the historical and continuing impact of Mansfield's decision, see Justin Buckley Dyer, "After the Revolution: Somerset and the Antislavery Tradition in Anglo-American Constitutional Development," *Journal of Politics* 71, no. 4 (October 2009): 1422–34; Jenny S. Martinez, "Antislavery Courts and the Dawn of International Human Rights Law," *Yale Law Journal* 118, no. 3 (2008): 550–641; and Paul Waldau, "Will the Heavens Fall? De-Radicalizing the Precedent Breaking Decision," *Animal Law* 7 (2001): 75–117.
12. See Don Fehrenbacher, *Slavery, Law, & Politics: The Dred Scott Case in Historical Perspective* (New York: Oxford University Press, 1981):

28; and William R. Cotter, "The Somerset Case and the Abolition of Slavery in England," *History* 79, no. 255 (February 1994): 32.
13. Spirited reconsiderations of habeas corpus extend well into the present day. Consider, for instance, petitions for "world habeas corpus" that became prominent in the 1950s and 1960s, or, more recently, the controversy over violations of habeas corpus in Guantanamo Bay. For more on these particular examples, see Luis Kutner, *The Human Right to Individual Freedom: A Symposium on World Habeas Corpus* (Miami: University of Miami Press, 1970); and Anthony Gregory, *The Power of Habeas Corpus in America* (New York: Cambridge University Press, 2013).
14. On this long history, see also Edward Jenks, "The Story of Habeas Corpus," *Law Quarterly Review* 18 (1902): 64–77; William F. Duker, *A Constitutional History of Habeas Corpus* (Westport, CT: Greenwood, 1980); and Justin J. Wert, *Habeas Corpus in America: The Politics of Individual Right* (Lawrence: University Press of Kansas, 2011).
15. The later acts were largely clarifications of the 1679 Act. The Acts of 1803 and 1804 clarify the capacity of the judges of the King's Courts of Records and the Court of King's Bench to grant writs of habeas corpus; the Act of 1816 expedites the timeframe within which appeals of habeas corpus are to be heard; and the Act of 1862 limits issuances of writs of habeas corpus to England only, excluding the colonies from its reach. Full texts can be accessed at legislation.gov.uk.
16. Gregory, *Power of Habeas Corpus in America*, 32.
17. Gregory, 31.
18. Gregory, 35.
19. Quoted in Tony Wright, *Citizens and Subjects: An Essay on British Politics* (New York: Routledge, 2003), 16.
20. Kevin Gutzman, foreword to *The Power of Habeas Corpus in America*, by Anthony Gregory (Cambridge: Cambridge University Press, 2013), ix.
21. John Locke, *Second Treatise of Government* (Indianapolis: Hackett, 1980), 19.
22. Locke, *Second Treatise of Government*, 19.
23. Locke, 23.
24. This, of course, remains largely true today. As Margaret Jane Radin explains, "The premise underlying the personhood perspective is that to achieve proper self-development—to be a person—an individual needs some control over resources in the external environment." In a foundational text of critical race theory, Cheryl Harris traces how whiteness operates as a form of property in American legal history. See Radin, "Property and Personhood," *Stanford Law Review* 34, no. 5 (May 1982): 957–58; and Harris, "Whiteness as Property," *Harvard Law Review* 106, no. 8 (1993): 1707–91.

25. Isaac Kramnick, *Republicanism and Bourgeois Radicalism* (Ithaca, NY: Cornell University Press, 1990), 36.
26. Kramnick, *Republicanism*, 187.
27. Kramnick, 193.
28. Thomas Hallie Delamayne, *The Rise and Practice of Imprisonment in Personal Actions, Examined*, Gale Eighteenth Century Collections Online (CB3327352670) (London: J. Wilkie, 1772), 13.
29. Delamayne, *The Rise and Practice*, 81.
30. Delamayne, 20.
31. Samuel Estwick, *Considerations on the Negroe Cause Commonly So Called, Addressed to the Right Honourable Lord Mansfield, Lord Chief Justice of the Court of King's Bench*, Gale Eighteenth Century Collections Online (CW3323898286) (London: J. Dodsley, 1773), 89.
32. Estwick, *Considerations on the Negroe Cause*, 91.
33. Locke served as Secretary to the Council of Trade Plantations, was an investor in the Royal Africa and Bahama Adventure companies, and helped to draft the Fundamental Constitutions of Carolina. Beyond these obvious conflicts of interest, his stated opposition to slavery in general is contradicted by a defense of slavery in the *Second Treatise*, namely the justification of slavery as a form of punishment in chapter 4. Some critics claim that Locke's theory of slavery was intended to apply only to English absolutism and not to African enslavement. While I anticipate that some readers will have similar objections to the reading I offer here, I agree with Jennifer Rae Greeson's argument that Locke's economic involvement with transatlantic slavery should be viewed as seriously compromising his position as a champion of liberty and that his claims about property cannot and should not be divorced from his involvement with African enslavement. See Greeson, "The Prehistory of Possessive Individualism," *PMLA* 127, no. 4 (2012): 918–24. For more on Locke's relationship to slavery, see James Farr, "Locke, Natural Law, and New World Slavery," *Political Theory* 36, no. 4 (2008): 495–522; Jack Greene, "'Slavery or Independence': Some Reflections on the Relationship among Liberty, Black Bondage, and Equality in Revolutionary South Carolina," *South Carolina Historical Magazine* 80, no. 3 (July 1979): 193–214; and Jennifer Welchman, "Locke on Slavery and Inalienable Rights," *Canadian Journal of Philosophy* 25, no. 1 (March 1995): 67–81. On the relationship between suicide and slavery in Locke, see Gary D. Glenn, "Inalienable Rights and Locke's Argument for Limited Government: Political Implications of a Right to Suicide," *Journal of Politics* 46, no. 1 (February 1984): 80–105.
34. Greeson, "Prehistory," 918.
35. Fred Moten, "Erotics of Fugitivity," in *Stolen Life* (Durham, NC: Duke University Press, 2018), 253.

36. Locke, *Second Treatise*, 9.
37. Locke, 17.
38. In the absence of line numbers, I refer to the page numbers of the 1773 edition. I use the 1773 edition because of its historical proximity to the Somerset case, as well as its more sustained focus on the issue of suicide than subsequent editions. In subsequent editions, Day and Bicknell shift the poem's focus from the speaker's personal suffering (and therefore from his motivations to kill himself) to more general considerations of African enslavement.
39. Day and Bicknell, *Dying Negro*, 3.
40. Marcus Wood, *The Horrible Gift of Freedom: Atlantic Slavery and the Representation of Emancipation* (Athens: University of Georgia Press, 2010), 2–3. Italics in original.
41. Wood, *The Horrible Gift of Freedom*, 2.
42. Sharon Patricia Holland, *Raising the Dead: Readings of Death and (Black) Subjectivity* (Durham, NC: Duke University Press, 2000), 16.
43. Wood, *The Horrible Gift of Freedom*, 1.
44. Seymour Drescher, *Abolition: A History of Slavery and Antislavery* (New York: Cambridge University Press, 2009), 9–10.
45. Day and Bicknell, *Dying Negro*, 18.
46. Day and Bicknell, 18.
47. This was the case until Augustine declared suicide a sin in the fifth century. See Minois, *History of Suicide*, 23–31.
48. Celeste-Marie Bernier, *Characters of Blood: Black Heroism in the Transatlantic Imagination* (Charlottesville: University of Virginia Press, 2012), 21. Wood also discusses the trope of the black martyr in *Blind Memory: Visual Representations of Slavery in England and America, 1780–1865* (New York: Routledge, 2000).
49. Day and Bicknell, *Dying Negro*, 14.
50. While outside the scope of this chapter, it is worth pointing to the further possibility that the poem's condemnation of Christianity also echoes historical cases, including that of Somerset, who was baptized in what may have been a strategic move to help the case for establishing his personhood, as well as the unnamed man in the "item of news" the poem claims to be based on. For a rich account of the political applications of various theologies in transatlantic discourses of abolition, refer to Hickman, *Black Prometheus*.
51. Day and Bicknell, *Dying Negro*, 18–19.
52. Day and Bicknell, 19.
53. Day and Bicknell, 19.
54. On the wide reach of this trope, see Snyder, *The Power to Die* and Bell, *We Shall Be No More*.
55. Wilderson, *Red, White and Black*, 22.

56. See MacDonald, "Suicide and the Rise of the Popular Press in England."
57. Parisot, "Suicide Notes and Popular Sensibility," 279, 285.
58. Parisot, 285.
59. The ethical problems inherent in these strategies have been widely discussed. On the uses of such strategies in British abolitionist writing, see: Brycchan Carey and Peter J. Kitson, eds., *Slavery and the Cultures of Abolition* (Cambridge, UK: English Association, 2007); Paul Goring, *The Rhetoric of Sensibility of Eighteenth-Century Culture* (New York: Cambridge University Press, 2005); Christine Levecq, *Slavery and Sentiment: The Politics of Feeling in Black Atlantic Antislavery Writing, 1770–1850* (Hanover: University of New Hampshire Press, 2008); Ramesh Mallipeddi, *Spectacular Suffering: Witnessing Slavery in the Eighteenth-Century British Atlantic* (Charlottesville: University of Virginia Press, 2016); Srividhya Swaminathan and Adam R. Beach, eds., *Invoking Slavery in the Eighteenth-Century British Imagination* (Burlington, VT: Ashgate, 2013); Helen Thomas, *Romanticism and Slave Narratives* (New York: Cambridge University Press, 2000); and Marcus Wood, *Slavery, Empathy, and Pornography* (New York: Oxford University Press, 2002).
60. Hartman, *Scenes of Subjection*, 18–19.
61. Hartman, 20.
62. Festa, *Sentimental Figures of Empire*, 161.
63. This was not lost on the poem's contemporary readers. In 1775, Day and Bicknell revised the poem to make the speaker's suicide a function of a decidedly un-Christian ideology. Carey reads this version of the poem as "a rejection of his recent conversion to Christianity. In these later editions, the [speaker] offers himself as a sacrifice to unspecified, but clearly unchristian deities.... Perhaps mindful of the accusations of impiety the first edition received, Day [adds a pun on 'falling' into the third edition]. But, if the [speaker] is indeed falling towards damnation, it is a voluntary and calculated fall. No longer desiring the favours of a Christian God, the slave asks for 'no long eternity of happiness.' Instead, he wants freedom." See Carey, *British Abolitionism and the Rhetoric of Sensibility*, 83–84.
64. Snyder, *The Power to Die*, 9. Further discussions of suicide among enslaved Africans are to be found in: Alex Bontemps, *The Punished Self: Surviving Slavery in the Colonial South* (Ithaca, NY: Cornell University Press, 2001); Vincent Brown, *The Reaper's Garden: Death and Power in the World of Atlantic Slavery* (Cambridge, MA: Harvard University Press, 2008); Michael Gomez, *Exchanging Our Country Marks: The Transformation of African Identities in the Colonial and Antebellum South* (Chapel Hill: University of North Carolina Press,

1998); William D. Pierson, "White Cannibals, Black Martyrs: Fear, Depression, and Religious Faith as Causes of Suicide among New Slaves," *Journal of Negro History* 62, no. 2 (April 1977): 147–59; Marcus Rediker, *The Slave Ship: A Human History* (New York: Penguin, 2007); Eric Robert Taylor, *If We Must Die: Shipboard Insurrections in the Era of the Atlantic Slave Trade* (Baton Rouge: Louisiana State University Press, 2006); Stephanie E. Smallwood, *Saltwater Slavery: A Middle Passage from Africa to American Diaspora* (Cambridge, MA: Harvard University Press, 2007); and Daniel E. Walker, "Suicidal Tendencies: African Transmigration in the History and Folklore of the Americas," *Griot* 18, no. 2 (Spring 1999): 10–18.

65. Snyder, *Power to Die*, 45.
66. Quoted in Walker, "Suicidal Tendencies," 11.
67. Walker, 11.
68. Liberal modernity's inability to disarticulate its ideal of freedom from its deep-seated investment in the spectacle of black suffering is also enshrined in abolitionist iconography. For instance, in Josiah Wedgwood's abolitionist seal (easily the abolitionist era's most enduring and recognizable image), a kneeling bondsperson gazes up, presumably at his enslaver, with his hands clasped in a pose suggesting prayer or supplication. The stance is submissive, despairing, and dependent, suggesting that the enslaved African of the sentimental imagination must look outside of himself for his salvation. This representation of the enslaved in perpetually subordinate and submissive relation to enslavers is reproduced throughout abolitionist and emancipationist iconography. Such images undermine the agency of the person being represented and call attention instead to the dominant culture that keeps him kneeling at somebody else's feet. For more on this visual history, see Patricia A. Matthew, "Serving Tea for a Cause," *Lapham's Quarterly* 28 (February 2018), https://www.laphamsquarterly.org/roundtable/serving-tea-cause.
69. Were it not for the fact that it is written in the first person, it might also be possible to read *The Dying Negro* as an epitaph for the historical person it is based on. On a tertiary level, perhaps it can be read that way. However, the fact that it is written and narrated in the first person makes it, fundamentally, an act of ventriloquism—of "giving voice" to someone that it first has to imagine as voiceless.
70. In "Apostrophe, Animation, and Abortion," Johnson brings what she considers to be a fundamental relationship between apostrophe, animation, and death in western poetry to bear on contemporary debates about abortion in order to grapple with assumptions about the limits of human life implied through the uses of apostrophe in poetic and legal language. In "Anthropomorphism in Lyric and Law," Johnson

considers more broadly the possibility that "lyric and law might be seen as two very different ways of instantiating what a 'person' is." Both essays have been reprinted many times. "Anthropomorphism in Lyric and Law" first appeared in the *Yale Journal of Law and Humanities* 10, no. 2 (1998): 549–74 and was later reprinted in *Persons and Things* (Cambridge, MA: Harvard University Press, 2008); "Apostrophe, Animation, and Abortion" first appeared in *Diacritics* 16, no. 1 (1986): 29–47 and reprinted in *A World of Difference* (Baltimore: Johns Hopkins University Press, 1987) and also in several anthologies of literary and cultural criticism. My references to these essays refer to their first printings in the *Yale Journal of Law and Humanities* and *Diacritics*, respectively.

71. Johnson, "Anthropomorphism in Lyric and Law," 574.
72. Johnson, 556.
73. Moten, "Knowledge of Freedom," 33.
74. Vincent Brown, "Social Death and Political Life in the Study of Slavery," *American Historical Review* (2009): 1235. See also Jared Sexton, "The Social Life of Social Death: On Afro-Pessimism and Black Optimism," *InTensions* 5 (2011): 1–47.
75. Day and Bicknell, *Dying Negro*, 6.
76. Day and Bicknell, 6.
77. Day and Bicknell, 9.
78. Day and Bicknell, 4.
79. While somewhat beyond the scope of this discussion, suicide can also be viewed here as anticipating later associations between blackness and criminality. In their discussion of the speaker's final resting place, Day and Bicknell reframe liberalism's emphasis on property through the period's debate over what happens to the property of people who die by suicide. In England, this entailed forfeiture of any property to the state. This practice is part of a longer history that K. J. Kesselring argues is a defining feature of felony in English Common law: "Despite its ubiquity in legal discourse, the term 'felony' defies easy definition ... we can only define felony by its legal effects.... And forfeiture was the defining legal concept of felony." Thus, criminal laws were shaped, in part, around people's relationships to property, even as property also came to define, with increasing prominence, the very people these laws were meant to govern. Sir William Blackstone highlights this problem when he calls suicide a "peculiar species of felony." For Blackstone, suicide confounds easy categorization because it is a crime against both providence and law. He finally labels suicide "a felony committed to oneself" but admits that legal action against suicides is illogical because "human laws [cannot operate] on one who has withdrawn himself from their reach." The laws only affect

whatever and whomever the deceased leaves behind: reputations are tarnished by dishonorable burials, and families are destroyed by forfeiture. By the end of the eighteenth century, faith in the effectiveness of these laws had largely eroded. In 1771, the barrister William Eden, First Baron Auckland, called the practice of forfeiture "ineffectual and absurd," and moreover, "cruel" and "unjust... to heap sufferings on the head of innocence," which is to say, the surviving family. By 1826, the laws were overturned. Underscoring the increasing prominence of suicide within legal discourses of property, Blackstone's unease about and Eden's interest in reforming the laws that criminalized suicide highlights the extent to which the concept of suicide was associated not only with property and personhood but also criminality at the time Day and Bicknell wrote *The Dying Negro*. See Kesselring, "Felony Forfeiture in England, c. 1170–1870," *Journal of Legal History* 30, no. 3 (2009): 202–3; William Blackstone, *Commentaries on the Laws of England, Book the Fourth*, Gale Eighteenth Century Collections Online (CW3324351452)(Oxford: Clarendon, 1769), 189–90; and William Eden, *Principles of Penal Law*, Gale Eighteenth Century Collections Online (CW3324202367). (Dublin: John Milliken, 1772), 205.

80. Jared Sexton, "Ante-Anti-Blackness," http://csalateral.org/section/theory/ante-anti-blackness-afterthoughts-sexton/.
81. Sexton, "Ante-Anti-Blackness."
82. Weheliye, *Habeas Viscus*, 1–2.
83. Hortense Spillers, "Mama's Baby, Papa's Maybe: An American Grammar Book," *Diacritics* 17, no. 2 (Summer 1987): 65–81.
84. Holland, *Raising the Dead*, 58.
85. Weheliye, *Habeas Viscus*, 19.

Notes to Chapter 2

1. As previously indicated, at the time of writing, there exists no book-length study of suicide in British romanticism. There is, however, a substantial body of essay-length scholarship on suicide and gender in the period historically associated with romanticism. This work begins with Margaret Higonnet's "Suicide: Representations of the Feminine," which opened conversations about the relationship between women's rights discourses, sensibility, and the masculine culture of romantic suicide. Other relevant essays by Higgonet include: "Suicide as Self-Construction" in *Crossing the Borders: Madame de Staël*, ed. Avriel Goldberger, Madelyn Gutwirth, and Karyna Smurlo (New Brunswick, NJ: Rutgers University Press, 1991), 69–81; "Frames of

Female Suicide," *Studies in the Novel* 32, no. 2 (2000): 229–42; and "'This Winged Nature Fraught': Suicide and Agency in Women's Poetry," *Literature Compass* 12, no. 12 (December 2015): 683–89. In recent years, Michelle Faubert has been at the forefront of reenergizing the field's interest in suicide. In addition to essays already cited, her work on the subject includes: "Romantic Suicide, Contagion, and Rousseau's *Julie*," in *Romanticism, Rousseau, Switzerland: New Prospects*, ed. Diane Piccitto, Angela Esterhammer, and Patrick Vincent (New York: Palgrave Macmillan, 2015): 38–53; and "The Fictional Suicides of Mary Wollstonecraft," *Literature Compass* 12, no. 12 (2015): 652–59. On gender and suicide in eighteenth-century and Victorian England, see McGuire, *Dying to Be English* and chapter 2 of Lootens, *Political Poetess*, respectively. This list is not exhaustive, merely indicative of some influential voices in conversations on suicide and gender in romantic and romantic-adjacent texts and authors. It is worth noting that some nineteenth-century women also drew on romantic representations of white male suicidal genius as a way of claiming their place in the literary landscape of the day. The third chapter of Bennett's *Romantic Poets and the Culture of Posterity* gives an excellent overview of women's emulations of the conventionally masculine trope of suicidal genius.

2. William Blackstone, *The Commentaries of Sir William Blackstone*, Gale Eighteenth Century Collections Online (CW3325233304) (London, 1796), 77.

3. McGuire, *Dying to Be English*; Faubert, "The Wollstonecraftian Plot" and "Fictional Suicides." See also Anne Mellor, "'Am I Not A Woman and a Sister?': Slavery, Romanticism and Gender," in *Romanticism, Race, and Imperial Culture, 1780–1834*, ed. Alan Richardson and Sonia Hofkosh (Bloomington: Indiana University Press, 1996), 311–29.

4. Lootens, *Political Poetess*, 54. This is especially true in literary and historical scholarship informed by black feminism. For instance, Sasha Turner recently demonstrated how between the 1780s and 1834— the age of abolition and (British) emancipation but also the timeline conventionally associated with both romanticism and early liberal feminism—enslaved and free black women in Jamaica variously negotiated and leveraged their knowledge of the importance of enslaved women's bodies to the British Empire. More generally and foundationally, Hortense Spillers has theorized that the kinship structures imposed on enslaved people created forms of "ungendered" being that implicitly challenge hegemonic gender roles and other patriarchal structures of liberal modernity. See Turner, *Contested Bodies: Pregnancy, Childrearing, and Slavery in Jamaica* (Philadelphia: University of Pennsylvania Press, 2017); and Spillers, "Mama's Baby," 68.

5. Michelle Faubert, "A Family Affair: Ennobling Suicide in Mary Shelley's *Matilda*," *Essays in Romanticism* 20 (2013): 116.
6. See Cora Kaplan, "Mary Wollstonecraft's Reception and Legacies," in *The Cambridge Companion to Mary Wollstonecraft*, ed. Claudia Johnson (New York: Cambridge University Press, 2002), 246–70.
7. Janet Todd, "Reason and Sensibility in Mary Wollstonecraft's *The Wrongs of Woman*," *Frontiers* 5, no. 3 (1981): 17. My usage of "sensibility" here is similar to Kyla Schuller's discussion of "sentimentalism" in the US context. For Schuller, "Sentimentalism posits that the needs of the individuated subject can be reconciled to those of other individuated subjects through the guiding moral philosophy of sympathetic feeling . . . the sentimental state, [in turn] identifies the feelings of the civilized individual—and only the civilized individual—as the kernel of liberal democracy." Schuller delimits sensibility to medical discussions of the nervous system, while in her study sentimentalism encapsulates the capacity for sensibility and other behaviors and responses to mark social standing and individualism or the potential for it. Because Wollstonecraft names sensibility as the marker of self-discipline characteristic of the "civilized individual," I stay with that term above. However, as Markman Ellis reminds us, these terms, especially in the British context, "offer no obvious distinction . . . they amalgamate and mix freely a large number of varied discourses." See Schuller, *The Biopolitics of Feeling: Race, Sex, and Science in the Nineteenth Century* (Durham, NC: Duke University Press, 2018), 2; and Ellis, *The Politics of Sensibility: Race, Gender and Commerce in the Sentimental Novel* (New York: Cambridge University Press, 1996), 7–8.
8. Mary Wollstonecraft, *A Vindication of the Rights of Woman* (New York: Oxford World's Classics, 2008), 73.
9. Wollstonecraft, *Vindication*, 73.
10. Wollstonecraft, 99.
11. Wollstonecraft, *Maria*, in *Mary, A Fiction and The Wrongs of Women, or Maria*, ed. Michelle Faubert (Peterborough, ON: Broadview, 2012), 241, italics original.
12. Todd, "Reason and Sensibility," 19.
13. Wollstonecraft, *Vindication*, 166.
14. Wollstonecraft, *Maria*, 287.
15. Wollstonecraft, *Vindication*, 66.
16. Wollstonecraft, 228.
17. Todd, "Reason and Sensibility," 19.
18. Moira Ferguson, *Colonialism and Gender Relations: From Mary Wollstonecraft to Jamaica Kincaid* (New York: Columbia University Press, 1993), 15, 32.
19. Wollstonecraft, *Vindication*, 170.

20. Lootens, *Political Poetess*, 60.
21. Hazel V. Carby, *Cultures in Babylon: Black Britain and African America* (London: Verso, 1999), 68. Other foundational texts that speak to these issues include: Patricia Hill Collins, *Black Feminist Thought: Knowledge, Consciousness and the Politics of Empowerment* (New York: Routledge, 2000); Angela Davis, *Women, Race and Class* (New York: Vintage, 1983); bell hooks, *Ain't I A Woman: Black Women and Feminism* (Boston: South End, 1999); Akasha (Gloria T.) Hull, Patricia Bell Scott, and Barbara Smith, eds., *All the Women Are White, All the Blacks Are Men, but Some of Us Are Brave* (New York: Feminist Press at the City University of New York, 1982); Audre Lorde, "Age, Race, Class, and Sex: Women Redefining Difference," in *Sister Outsider* (New York: Ten Speed, 2007), 114–123; Audre Lorde, "An Open Letter to Mary Daly," in *This Bridge Called My Back, Fourth Edition: Writings by Radical Women of Color*, ed. Cherríe Moraga and Gloria Anzaldúa (Albany: State University of New York Press, 2015), 90–93; and Valerie Smith, *Not Just Race, Not Just Gender: Black Feminist Readings* (New York: Routledge, 1998).
22. Faubert, "Fictional Suicides," 655–56. In a strictly historicist framework, it is of course absurd to hold figures from the past responsible for ideas that had not yet been articulated. But even in such a framework, it must be said that conversations about gender parity do not begin solely with eighteenth-century white women. Moreover, not all forms of woman-centered activisms (feminism is too limited a term here) owe their existence to white liberal feminism. For more on this, see Vron Ware, *Beyond the Pale: White Women, Racism, and History* (London: Verso, 2015).
23. For example: Marisa J. Fuentes, *Dispossessed Lives: Enslaved Women, Violence, and the Archive* (Philadelphia: University of Pennsylvania Press, 2016); Saidiya Hartman, *Lose Your Mother: A Journey Along the Atlantic Slave Route* (New York: Farrar, Straus and Giroux, 2008); Lisa Lowe, *The Intimacies of Four Continents* (Durham, NC: Duke University Press, 2015); Jennifer Morgan, *Laboring Women: Reproduction and Gender in New World Slavery* (Philadelphia: University of Pennsylvania Press, 2004); Katherine McKittrick, *Demonic Grounds: Black Women and the Cartographies of Struggle* (Minneapolis: University of Minnesota Press, 2006); and Imani Perry, *Vexy Thing: On Gender and Liberation* (Durham, NC: Duke University Press, 2018).
24. Sara Ahmed, *Living a Feminist Life* (Durham, NC: Duke University Press, 2017), 157.
25. Mary Darby Robinson, *A Letter to the Women of England on the Injustice of Mental Subordination* (London: Longman, 1799), https://romantic-circles.org/editions/robinson/index.html, 94.

26. Robinson, "Letter," 9, italics in original.
27. Robinson, 18–19.
28. Robinson, 69.
29. Robinson, 12.
30. Robinson, 13.
31. Robinson, 13.
32. Mary Robinson, "The Storm," *Morning Post and Fashionable World* (February 3, 1796), http://spenserians.cath.vt.edu/TextRecord.php?textsid=38639, emphasis in original.
33. Shelley A. J. Jones, "Revision as Conversation in Mary Robinson's 'The Storm' and 'The Negro Girl,'" *CEA Critic* 71, no. 3 (Spring and Summer 2009): 37.
34. Higonnet, "'This Winged Nature Fraught,'" 684.
35. Mary Robinson, "The Negro Girl," in *Mary Robinson: Selected Poems*, ed. Judith Pascoe (Peterborough, ON: Broadview, 1999), 234–239, ll. 73–78.
36. Robinson, "Storm."
37. Robinson, "Negro Girl," ll. 85–90.
38. Robinson, "Negro Girl," l. 73.
39. Robinson, "Storm," emphasis in original.
40. For more on the text's background and the cultural craze it inspired, see Robin Mitchell, "'*Ourika* mania': Interrogating Race, Class, Space, and Place in Early Nineteenth-Century France," *Africa and Black Diaspora: An International Journal* 10, no. 1 (2017): 85–95; and Pratima Prasad, *Colonialism, Race, and the French Romantic Imagination* (New York: Routledge, 2009).
41. Mitchell, "'*Ourika* mania,'" 88.
42. Mitchell, 89.
43. Claire de Duras, *Ourika*, trans. John Fowles (New York: Modern Language Association of America, 1994), 4.
44. Duras, *Ourika*, 9.
45. Duras, 12.
46. Duras, 12.
47. Such readings include David O'Connell, "*Ourika*: Black Face, White Mask," *French Review* 47, no. 6 (Spring 1974): 47–56; Christopher Miller, *Blank Darkness: Africanist Discourse in French* (Chicago: University of Chicago Press, 1985); Mary Jane Cowles, "The Subjectivity of the Colonial Subject from Olympe de Gouges to Mme. de Duras," *L'Esprit Createur* 47, no. 4 (2007): 29–43; and Fowles's introduction to his translation, cited above. In addition to Mitchell and Prasad, Adeline Koh offers a compelling counter-reading in "Marriage, 'Metissage,' and Women's Citizenship: Revisiting Race and Gender in Claire de Duras' 'Ourika'," *French Forum* 38, no. 3 (Fall 2013): 15–30.

48. Duras, *Ourika*, 17.
49. Koh, "Marriage, 'Metissage,' and Women's Citizenship," 21.
50. Prasad, *Colonialism, Race, and the French Romantic Imagination*, 102.
51. Wollstonecraft, *Maria*, chapter 1.
52. Wollstonecraft, *Vindication*, 99.
53. Duras, *Ourika*, 40.
54. Duras, 42.
55. Duras, 42.
56. Duras, 43.
57. Duras, 46.
58. Duras, 19.
59. Duras, 20.
60. Duras, 21.
61. Francoise Massardier-Kenney, "Duras, Racism, and Class," in *Translating Slavery: Gender and Race in French Women's Writing, 1783–1823*, ed. Doris Y. Kadish and Francoise Massardier-Kenney (Kent, OH: Kent State University Press, 1994), 186.
62. Massardier-Kenney, "Duras, Racism, and Class."
63. Wheatley famously excoriates these logics in "On Being Brought from Africa to America" and elsewhere. For more on this, see Elizabeth J. West, *African Spirituality in Black Women's Fiction: Threaded Visions of Memory, Community, Nature, and Being* (Lanham, MD: Lexington, 2011).
64. Duras, *Ourika*, 21.
65. Wilderson, *Red, White and Black*, 5.
66. Wilderson, 24.
67. Susan Wolfson, *Borderlines: The Shifting of Gender in British Romanticism* (Stanford, CA: Stanford University Press, 2006), 60. While not an exhaustive list, other texts that touch on the theme of death and/as gender liberation in Hemans's work include: Myra Cottingham, "Felicia Hemans's Dead and Dying Bodies," *Women's Writing* 8, no. 2 (2001): 275–94; Anthony John Harding, "Felicia Hemans and the Effacement of Woman," in *Romantic Women Writers: Voices and Countervoices*, ed. Paula R. Feldman and Theresa M. Kelley (Hanover, NH: University Press of New England, 1995), 138–49; and Michael T. Williamson, "Impure Affections: Felicia Hemans's Elegiac Poetry and Contaminated Grief," in *Felicia Hemans: Reimagining Poetry in the Nineteenth Century*, ed. Nanora Sweet and Julie Melnyk (London: Palgrave Macmillan, 2001), 19–35.
68. Gary Kelly, "Death and the Matron: Felicia Hemans, Romantic Death, and the Founding of the Modern Liberal State," in *Felicia Hemans: Reimagining Poetry in the Nineteenth Century*, ed. Sweet and Melnyk (London: Palgrave Macmillan, 2001), 201.

69. Gary Kelly, "Introduction," *Felicia Hemans: Selected Poems, Prose, and Letters* (Peterborough, ON: Broadview, 2002), 28.
70. Felicia Hemans, "Indian Woman's Death Song," in *Records of Woman, With Other Poems*, ed. Paula R. Feldman (Lexington: University of Kentucky Press, 1999), 57–59, ll. 3, 7.
71. Hemans, "Indian Woman's Death Song," ll. 10–11.
72. Hemans, ll. 7–8.
73. Hemans, ll. 36, 39.
74. Ann Laura Stoler, *Race and the Education of Desire: Foucault's History of Sexuality and the Colonial Order of Things* (Durham, NC: Duke University Press, 1995), 7.
75. Astrid Wind, "'Adieu to All': The Death of the American Indian at the Turn of the Eighteenth Century," *Symbiosis: A Journal of Anglo-American Literary Relations* 2, no. 1 (April 1998): 51–52.
76. This common premise of liberal feminist scholarship on suicide is most clearly articulated in Higonnet, "Dialogues with the Dead" and "'This Winged Nature Fraught.'" Nancy Moore Goslee makes a similar argument, acknowledging but underemphasizing the troubling logics by which "allegories of culture" are turned into "allegories of gender, in which the [white] woman's plight is primary and the other interpretations subordinate to . . . her exploitation" in "Hemans's 'Red Indians': Reading Stereotypes," in *Romanticism, Race, and Imperial Culture, 1780–1834*, ed. Alan Richardson and Sonia Hofkosh (Bloomington: Indiana University Press, 1996), 249.
77. Felicia Hemans, "Properzia Rossi," in *Records of Woman, With Other Poems*, ed. Paula R. Feldman (Lexington: University of Kentucky Press, 1999), 29.
78. Felicia Hemans, "The Last Song of Sappho," in *The Poetical Works of Felicia Dorothea Hemans* (Oxford: Oxford University Press, 318 ,(1914. Nell Irvin Painter traces how these conventions were standardized in accordance with Eurocentric principles in *The History of White People* (New York: W. W. Norton, 2010).
79. Felicia Hemans, "The Bride of the Greek Isle," in *Records of Woman, With Other Poems*, ed. Paula R. Feldman (Lexington: University of Kentucky Press, 1999), 17–25, ll. 13, 216. Sati was viewed as controversial by Britons and banned by the British government in India in 1829. For more on this, see Lata Mani, *Contentious Traditions: The Debate on Sati in Colonial India* (Berkeley: University of California Press, 1998).
80. Hemans, "Bride of the Greek Isle," ll. 216–221.
81. Felicia Hemans, "The Sicilian Captive," in *Records of Woman, With Other Poems*, ed. Paula R. Feldman (Lexington: University of Kentucky Press, 1999), 90–94, ll. 23, 26. On Sicilian identity and racialization, see chapter 5 of Roberto Dainotto, *Europe (In Theory)* (Durham, NC: Duke University Press, 2007).

82. Lootens also suggestively reads "The Bride of the Greek Isle" in terms of the history of transatlantic slavery: "When is a 'Greek slave' not necessarily a Greek slave? At a moment of acute controversy around transatlantic slavery, it would seem: a moment, that is, like 1825, when Hemans's poem first appeared.... Slave runners' denials notwithstanding, generation after generation of kidnapped Africans, including women, had killed and were killing themselves in the Middle Passage." See Lootens, *Political Poetess*, 29.
83. Hemans, "Sicilian Captive," ll. 71–76.
84. The most notable exception to this claim is William Wells Brown's *Clotel, or the President's Daughter*, the first published English-language novel by a writer of African descent. While this is an abolitionist text that centers a biracial woman as its protagonist, it is not chiefly interested in women's rights and is thus beyond the scope of this chapter's discussion. There are also many qualifications to be made here about the role of the written text in Afrodiasporic storytelling, associations between suicide and problematic European tropes (such as the "tragic mulatto"), the relative paucity of material from which to draw definitive conclusions and the reasons for that paucity. As Mary Helen Washington writes, "We have seldom seen black women characters struggling over such questions as suicide, or racial violence as a means to freedom ... and that is because the women who raised these issues have been silenced, omitted, patronized, made invisible," quoted in Lootens, *The Political Poetess*, 70. See also Washington's discussion of the politics of anger and its manifestation as self-destruction in nineteenth-century writing by black women in Mary Helen Washington, *Black-Eyed Susans and Midnight Birds: Stories By and About Black Women* (New York: Doubleday, 1989).
85. Joycelyn Moody, *Sentimental Confessions: Spiritual Narratives of Nineteenth-Century African American Women* (Athens: University of Georgia Press, 2001), 124. Jackson's short narrative has not received much scholarly attention. In addition to Moody's reading, DoVeanna S. Fulton's *Speaking Power: Black Feminist Orality in Women's Narratives of Slavery* (Albany: State University of New York Press, 2006) discusses Jackson's resistance to various women enslavers, emphasizing how Jackson challenges assumptions about white women's compassion and virtue.
86. For instance, James Albert Ukawsaw Gronniosaw discusses only briefly his attempted suicide. Ignatius Sancho passively references the suicide of his father in his letters. The spiritual autobiography of Old Elizabeth emphasizes how religion subdues suicidal tendencies. And though Mary Prince, quoted in this chapter's epigraph, briefly considers suicide, these thoughts are quickly set aside. Rather than return to

Prince, I conclude my discussion with Jackson because hers is a more sustained (albeit still quite muted) focus on suicide. These and many other examples are available through the University of North Carolina's Documenting the American South project: https://docsouth.unc.edu.
87. Mattie J. Jackson, *The Story of Mattie J. Jackson* (Lawrence. KS: Sentinel Office, 1866), 4, https://docsouth.unc.edu/neh/jacksonm/jackson.html.
88. Jackson, *Story*.
89. Per Patterson's *Slavery and Social Death*, social death is partially achieved through natal alienation—the systematic isolation of enslaved people from their kin. Without kin, the enslaved are limited to a single legally authorized social relation: the enslaver.
90. Jackson, *Story*, 17–18.

Notes to Chapter 3

1. William Wells Brown, *Clotel; or The President's Daughter*, ed. M. Giulia Fabi (New York: Penguin, 2003), 185.
2. Brown, *Clotel*, 185. Notably, this is left out of the final edition of the novel, *Clotelle: or, the Colored Heroine*, published in Boston in 1867.
3. Ian Baucom, *Specters of the Atlantic: Finance Capital, Slavery, and the Philosophy of History* (Durham, NC: Duke University Press, 2005), 294.
4. Baucom, *Specters of the Atlantic*, 295.
5. Baucom, 290.
6. See Amiri Baraka, *Wise Why's Y's: The Griot's Song (Djeli Ya)* (Chicago: Third World, 1995).
7. Samuel Baker, *Written on the Water: British Romanticism and the Maritime Empire of Culture* (Charlottesville: University of Virginia Press, 2010), 3.
8. See Paul Gilroy, *The Black Atlantic: Modernity and Double Consciousness* (Cambridge, MA: Harvard University Press, 1995).
9. Paul Youngquist, "The Afro Futurism of DJ Vassa," *European Romantic Review* 16, no. 2 (2005): 188.
10. Bryan Wagner, *Disturbing the Peace: Black Culture and the Police After Slavery* (Cambridge, MA: Harvard University Press, 2009), 12.
11. To be sure, blackness is antonymous to the liberal state, though, as Wagner emphasizes, modern notions of race are often used to support antiblack state policies. It is worth reiterating here what differentiates "blackness" as an analytical framework from the cultural signifier sometimes delineated by the capitalized "Blackness." As Fred Moten

explains, "The implication here is not just that blackness and black culture are not the same; what is further and more importantly implied is that blackness and black people are not the same, however much it is without doubt the case that black people have a privileged relation to blackness, that black cultures are (under)privileged fields for the transformational expression and enactment of blackness." See Moten, "Knowledge of Freedom," 18.

12. As Vincent Carretta notes in his edition of the text, Equiano misquotes and conflates lines from three editions of the poem. Altogether, Equiano includes nineteen lines. See Olaudah Equiano, *The Interesting Narrative and Other Writings*, ed. Vincent Carretta (New York: Penguin, 2003), 97–98 and n. 277.

13. Equiano, *Interesting Narrative*, 98.

14. Though the theme of suicide recurs throughout *The Interesting Narrative*, it appears with particular frequency in the first volume, which details Equiano's capture into slavery and his early adventures as a sailor: the portion of his life, in other words, before he came to define himself as an Englishman and Christian subject to the social codes of liberal individualism.

15. Achille Joseph Mbembe, "Necropolitics," trans. Libby Meintjes, *Public Culture* 15, no. 1 (Winter 2003): 11.

16. Equiano, *Interesting Narrative*, 197.

17. Equiano, 213.

18. Equiano, 205.

19. Equiano, 214.

20. Snyder, *Power to Die*, 73.

21. Quoted in Snyder, *Power to Die*, 77.

22. Snyder, 12.

23. Equiano, *Interesting Narrative*, 56.

24. Equiano, 56.

25. Equiano, 56.

26. Equiano, 56.

27. Equiano, 58.

28. I am indebted to Jonathan Howard for first drawing my attention to this phrase many years ago. His work on it appears in "'Gone with the Ibos': The Blueness of Blackness in Paule Marshall's *Praisesong for the Widow*," *Callaloo* 39, no. 4 (Fall 2016): 898–918.

29. Georgia Writers' Project, *Drum and Shadows: Survival Studies among the Georgia Coastal Negroes* (Athens: University of Georgia Press, 1986), 116. This text provides transcriptions that claim to be faithful to the dialects of the people interviewed. Given the contentious history of these practices, I have chosen not to reproduce those transcriptions here. For more on this, see Catherine A. Stewart, *Long Past Slavery:*

Representing Race in the Federal Writers' Project (Chapel Hill: University of North Carolina Press, 2016).
30. Georgia Writers' Project, *Drum and Shadows*, 185.
31. Snyder, *Power to Die*, 17–18.
32. Jason R. Young similarly argues that "the communities and cultures in which flying African stories reside reveal wide fields of ontological and epistemological possibilities . . . proposing not only the existence of a mythic culture hero capable of escaping from slavery and racial oppression, but also the primacy of new worlds and possibilities away from the constraints of slavery and racial oppression." See Jason R. Young, "All God's Children Had Wings: The Flying African in History, Literature, and Lore," *Journal of Africana Religions* 5, no. 1 (2017): 61–62.
33. Both individual and group suicides were commonly framed as tactics of rebellion. Ottobah Cugoano, Equiano's contemporary, recalls being part of such a plan in his autobiography: "And when we found ourselves at last taken away, death was more preferable than life; and a plan was concerted amongst us, that we might burn and blow up the ship, and to perish all together in the flames: but we were betrayed by one of our own countrywomen." See Ottobah Cugoano, *Narrative of the Enslavement of Ottobah Cugoano, Narrative of the Enslavement of Ottobah Cugoano, a Native of Africa* (London: Hatchard, 1825), https://docsouth.unc.edu/neh/cugoano/cugoano.html.
34. Marcus Rediker, *The Slave Ship: A Human History* (New York: Penguin, 2007), 121–22.
35. Weheliye, *Habeas Viscus*, 136–37.
36. Wilderson, *Red, White, and Black*, 23.
37. Sharon Patricia Holland, "Vocabularies of Vulnerability," *Journal for Cultural Research* 22, no. 2 (2018): 206.
38. Holland, "Vocabularies of Vulnerability," 206.
39. Sharpe, *In the Wake*, 40–41.
40. Equiano, *Interesting Narrative*, 81–82.
41. On the common fear of white cannibalism among newly enslaved Africans, see Piersen, "White Cannibals, Black Martyrs: Fear, Depression, and Religious Faith as Causes of Suicide among New Slaves." *Journal of Negro History* 62, no. 2 (April 1977): 147–59.
42. Monique Allewaert, *Ariel's Ecology: Plantations, Personhood, and Colonialism in the American Tropics* (Minneapolis: University of Minnesota Press, 2013), 86. Allewaert frames the emergence of the parahuman in terms of the mutilation frequently performed on the bodies of enslaved people, arguing that because the Anglo-European gaze registered African bodies as always potentially unwhole, all enslaved Africans came to be regarded as not wholly human. Tracing the parahuman

through Creole folk tales of African Americans with missing body parts who form complex relations with animals, Allewaert reads the parahuman body as one "built on the intimacies borne through incompletion." See Allewaert, *Ariel's Ecology*, 99.
43. Allewaert, 108, 111.
44. Equiano, *Interesting Narrative*, 59.
45. Equiano, 59.
46. Equiano, 59.
47. Equiano, 66.
48. Equiano, 65.
49. Henry John Drewal, "Performing the Other: Mami Wata Worship in Africa," *Drama Review* 32, no. 2 (1988): 161.
50. Henry John Drewal, Charles Gore, and Michelle Kisliuk, "Siren Serenades: Music for Mami Wata and Other Water Spirits in Africa," in *Music of the Sirens*, ed. Linda Austern and Inna Naroditskaya (Bloomington: Indiana University Press, 2006), 295. My discussion relies mainly on Drewal's work on Mami Wata. A contrasting narrative of her origin is given in Barbara Paxton, "Mammy Water: New World Origins?," in *Baessler-Archiv, Neue Folge* 31 (1983): 407–446, as well as by some contemporary practitioners of Mami Wata worship. For example, Mama Zogbé (Vivien Hunter-Hindrew) holds that the name is not pidgin English but derives from ancient Egypt. See Mama Zogbé (Vivien Hunter-Hindrew), *Mami Wata: Africa's Ancient God/dess, Unveiled* (Martinez, GA: Mami Wata Healers Society of North America, 2007). While I follow the protocols of western academia in deferring to the scholarship cited above, I am ever mindful of the fact that these methods and epistemologies may not be the best way into this body of knowledge.
51. According to Drewal, this holds even today: "The Mami Wata phenomenon illustrates what Roy Wagner calls the invention of culture, an ongoing process of creating one's reality, of constructing meaning out of experience. Such invention never occurs in a vacuum or by accident, but rather emerges out of what already exists. Like anthropologists, Mami Wata Devotees 'study' others—overseas visitors—and generalize them from impressions, experiences, and other evidence.... That process is at the same time one of self-determination for Mami Wata devotees." See Drewal, "Performing the Other," 160.
52. Michelle D. Commander, *Afro-Atlantic Flight: Speculative Returns and the Black Fantastic* (Durham, NC: Duke University Press, 2017), 235, n. 5.
53. Barbara Frank, "Permitted and Prohibited Wealth: Commodity-Possessing Spirits, Economic Morals, and the Goddess." *Ethnology* 34, no. 4 (Fall 1995): 331–346.
54. Commander, *Afro-Atlantic Flight*, 2–3.

55. Drewal, Gore, and Kisliuk "Siren Serenades," 295.
56. Equiano, *Interesting Narrative*, 59.
57. Edouard Glissant, *Poetics of Relation*, trans. Betsy Wing (Ann Arbor: University of Michigan Press, 1997), 7–8.
58. Glissant, 8.
59. Jared Sexton, "Unbearable Blackness," *Cultural Critique* 90 no. 1 (2015): 171.
60. Moten, "Chromatic Saturation," 197, italics original.
61. Moten, 194.
62. Moten, 206, 197.
63. Moten, 197.
64. Equiano, *Interesting Narrative*, 194. In the absence of line numbers, I refer to page numbers.
65. Equiano, 195.
66. Equiano, 195.
67. Equiano, 195.
68. Equiano, 195.
69. Equiano, 195.
70. John Keats, "Ode to a Nightingale," in *The Complete Poems*, ed. John Barnard (London: Penguin, 2003), 346–348, l. 52. While some biographers have described Keats as suicidal toward the end of his life—see particularly Eric Wilson, *How to Make a Soul: The Wisdom of John Keats* (Evanston, IL: Northwestern University Press, 2015) and Sue Brown, *Joseph Severn, A Life: The Rewards of Friendship* (New York: Oxford University Press, 2009)—I would distinguish between his strong desire for death to relieve him of intense pain and suffering and an active attempt to take his own life. However, I submit that Brown's discussion of Keats's failed effort to convince Severn to give him a large quantity of laudanum blurs that distinction. Keats explicitly discusses the act of killing himself once, and this is in the context of a sarcastic rebuke of Benjamin Bailey in a June 1818 letter: "Yes, on my soul, my dear Bailey, you are too simple for the world—and that Idea makes me sick of it . . . I should not by rights speak in this tone to you for it is an incendiary spirit that would do so. Yet I am not old enough or magnanimous enough to annihilate self—and it would perhaps be paying you an ill compliment." See Grant F. Scott, ed., *Selected Letters of John Keats* (Cambridge, MA: Harvard University Press, 2002), 128–29.
71. Keats, *Selected Letters*, 485.
72. Joseph Severn, "To John Taylor, 6 March 1821," in *Joseph Severn: Letters and Memoirs*, ed. Grant F. Scott (New York: Routledge, 2016), 137–40.
73. Keats, *Selected Letters*, 422.
74. Quoted in Allen Grossman, *The Long Schoolroom: Lessons in the Bitter Logic of the Poetic Principle* (Ann Arbor: University of Michigan Press, 1997), 21.

75. Keats, "Ode to a Nightingale," ll. 19–20.
76. Keats, ll. 1–4.
77. Keats, ll. 5–7, 10.
78. Keats, ll. 61–64.
79. Helen Vendler, *The Odes of John Keats* (Cambridge, MA: Harvard University Press, 1983), 94.
80. Keats, "Ode to a Nightingale," ll. 23–30.
81. Keats, l. 33.
82. Keats, l. 79.
83. Moten, "Knowledge of Freedom," 15.
84. Phillis Wheatley, "On Imagination," in *The Collected Works of Phillis Wheatley*, ed. John C. Shields (New York: Oxford University Press, 1989), 65–69. ll. 13–22.
85. While the primary objects of her inquiry are beyond the scope of this discussion, Cristin Ellis offers a marvelous reading of the convergences and tensions of posthumanist and antiracist thought that is worth noting here. For Ellis, both frameworks "urge us to conceive . . . an episteme no longer premised upon the manufacture of a 'lesser' class of devalued and exploitable beings but, rather, one that embraces all being as one densely conjoined world," but when considered "from another angle . . . it is not clear that liberation is a term that can meaningfully be applied to an ontology of entanglement. Liberation, as we know it, implied disentanglement—an unburdening that restores us to a natural state of freedom, honoring our inherent right, as autonomous selves, to self-sovereignty. But none of these things—freedom, autonomy, sovereignty, the singular 'self'—remain readily legible in a world in which being is primordially relational." See Cristin Ellis, *Antebellum Posthuman: Race and Materiality in the Mid-Nineteenth Century* (New York: Fordham University Press, 2018), 159.

Notes to Chapter 4

1. Mary Shelley, *The Journals of Mary Shelley, 1814–1844*, eds. Paula R. Feldman and Diana Scott-Kilvert (Oxford: Clarendon, 1987), 40.
2. Mary Shelley, *Journals of Mary Shelley*, 40, n. 134.
3. George Henry Davis, *Memorials of Hamlet of Knightsbridge* (London: J. Russel Smith, 1859), 112.
4. Davis, *Memorials*, 113.
5. Bryan Rivers, "'Revolting Burial': A Victorian Commentary on the Harriet Shelley Inquest," *Notes and Queries* 52, no. 4 (December 2005): 480.
6. Rivers, "Revolting Burial," 480.

7. Rivers, "Revolting Burial," 480.
8. Bryan Rivers, "'Tenderly' and 'With Care': Thomas Hood's 'The Bridge of Sighs' and the Suicide of Harriet Shelley," *Notes and Queries* 53, no. 3 (September 2006): 327–329.
9. Tim Marshall, *Murdering to Dissect: Graverobbing, Frankenstein, and the Anatomy of Literature* (Manchester, UK: Manchester University Press, 1996), 9.
10. See particularly: Diana Coke, *Saved from a Watery Grave: The Story of the Royal Humane Society's Receiving House in Hyde Park, London* (London: Royal Humane Society, 2000); and Carolyn D. Williams, "'The Luxury of Doing Good': Benevolence, Sensibility, and the Royal Humane Society," *Pleasure in the Eighteenth Century*, ed. Roy Porter and Marie Mulvey Roberts (Basingstoke, UK: Macmillan, 1996), 77–107.
11. See Carolyn D. Williams, "'Inhumanly Brought Back to Life and Misery': Mary Wollstonecraft, *Frankenstein*, and the Royal Humane Society," *Women's Writing* 8, no. 2 (2001): 213–234.
12. For more on this, see McGuire, *Dying to Be English*, particularly the chapter on Eliza Haywood, one of the earliest social critics to comment on the so-called English malady.
13. Samuel Jackson Pratt, *Harvest-Home* (London: Richard Phillips, 1805), 552.
14. Williams, "Inhumanly Brought Back," 222–223.
15. Quoted in Janet Todd, *Death and the Maidens: Fanny Wollstonecraft and the Shelley Circle* (Berkeley: Counterpoint, 2007), 3.
16. Suggested explanations are as follows: the maid did it in order to avoid the taint of suicide on the premises; Fanny tore it off either because of a sense that she lacked an identity or to spare the Godwins embarrassment; Godwin did it; or, perhaps most sensationally, Percy did it because of a secret affair with Fanny. In addition to Todd's *Death and the Maidens*, see B. R. Pollin, "Fanny Godwin's Suicide Re-examined," *Etudes anglaises* 18, no. 3 (1965): 258–68.
17. Though suicide is sometimes mentioned in the context of broader discussions of *Frankenstein* (e.g., as in Ana M. Acosta's study of Genesis in eighteenth-century novels), only Richard K. Sanderson has read suicide as central to the novel. Sanderson reads suicide through the novel's allusion to Eve's suggestion in *Paradise Lost* that she and Adam either practice abstinence or mutually destroy each other. Thus, Sanderson posits that suicide is essential to the novel's interest in procreation. See Acosta, *Reading Genesis in the Long Eighteenth Century: From Milton to Mary Shelley* (Burlington, VT: Ashgate, 2006); and Sanderson, "'Glutting the Maw of Death': Suicide and Procreation in *Frankenstein*," *South Central Review* 9, no. 2 (Summer 1992): 49–64.

18. Mary Shelley, *Frankenstein*, ed. J. Paul Hunter (New York: W. W. Norton, 1995), 156.
19. See Faubert, "A Family Affair"; and Deanna Koretsky, "The Interracial Marriage Plot: Suicide and the Politics of Blood in Romantic-Era Women's Fiction," *Studies in the Literary Imagination* 51, no. 1 (Spring 2018): 1–18.
20. Rachel Feder, *Harvester of Hearts: Motherhood Under the Sign of Frankenstein* (Evanston, IL: Northwestern University Press, 2018), 3.
21. Mary Shelley, *Frankenstein*, 126–27.
22. Mary Shelley, 138–40.
23. On the nature of the Shelleys' working relationship, particularly in the years leading up to *Frankenstein*, see Mary Poovey, *The Proper Lady and the Woman Writer* (Chicago: University of Chicago Press, 1984), as well as Charles Robinson's edition of the novel, entitled *The Original Frankenstein* (New York: Vintage Classics, 2009), in which Robinson italicizes areas that Percy likely contributed to. Shelley herself notes many of their intellectual exchanges in her journals.
24. That is, the notion of love that unfolds in close association with Godwin's interest in "Necessity," which Percy would develop in *Prometheus Unbound* and other later works.
25. Although the Shelleys appear to have read more Hume than Smith, Percy's works suggest his familiarity with Smith. Percy cites Hume through much of his prose, including in "A Fragment on Miracles" (ca. 1813–15), "A Refutation of Deism" (1814), "Speculations on Morals" (1815), "On the Devil, and Devils" (ca. 1819), and *A Defence of Poetry* (1821). Further, the reading lists that Mary kept in her journals suggest that both Shelleys read Hume extensively between 1814 and 1817. Smith, on the other hand, is not listed in Mary's journals, nor does Percy cite Smith in his prose from this period. However, in his introductory essay on the development of Percy's thought in *Shelley's Prose*, David Lee Clark notes echoes of Smith in Percy's writing as early as 1812. See David Lee Clark, "Introduction," in *Shelley's Prose*, ed. David Lee Clark (Bel Air, CA: New Amsterdam, 1988).
26. David Hume, *A Treatise of Human Nature*, ed. Ernest C. Mossner (New York: Penguin, 1985), 441.
27. Adam Smith, *Theory of Moral Sentiments*, ed. Knud Haakonssen (New York: Cambridge University Press, 2002), 11.
28. David Marshall, *The Surprising Effects of Sympathy: Marivaux, Diderot, Rousseau, and Mary Shelley* (Chicago: University of Chicago Press, 1988), 181–82.
29. Hartman, *Scenes of Subjection*, 21.
30. Chander, *Brown Romantics*, 69.

31. Hume, *Treatise*, 593. See also M. Jamie Ferreira, "Hume and Imagination: Sympathy and 'the Other,'" *International Philosophical Quarterly* 34, no. 133 (March 1994): 39–57.
32. Percy Shelley, "Speculations on Morals," in *The Prose Works of Percy Bysshe Shelley*, ed. Richard Herne Shepherd (London: Chatto and Windus, 1906), 199.
33. Percy Shelley, "Speculations on Morals," 199.
34. Mary Shelley, *Frankenstein*, 77.
35. Mary Shelley, 75.
36. Mary Shelley, 74–75.
37. Mary Shelley, 80–81.
38. Mary Shelley, 81.
39. Mary Shelley, 66.
40. Mary Shelley, 66.
41. As discussed in this book's introduction, anxieties about the capacity of texts to affect minds in undesired ways were at the forefront of the Anglo-European cultural consciousness following the 1774 publication of Goethe's *The Sorrows of Young Werther*. In its references to *Werther*, *Frankenstein* can also be read as calling up the limits of the *bildung* tradition, a genre in which Goethe is a key figure. But Goethe's famed bildungsroman is not *Werther* but *Wilhelm Meister's Apprenticeship*. So, one could read the panic over *Werther* as stemming from the fact that the bourgeois subject the European novel was meant to shape is presented in that novella as so fragile that Werther would choose to commit suicide rather than cultivate and manage himself.
42. Mary Shelley, *Frankenstein*, 90.
43. Mary Shelley, 99.
44. Maureen McLane, *Romanticism and the Human Sciences* (New York: Cambridge University Press, 2000), 103.
45. Mary Shelley, *Frankenstein*, 114.
46. Percy Shelley, "On Love," in *Shelley's Poetry and Prose*, ed. Neil Fraistat and Donald H. Reiman (New York: W. W. Norton, 2002), 503.
47. Mary Shelley, *Frankenstein*, 10.
48. Percy Shelley, "On Love," 504.
49. Percy Shelley, 503–4.
50. Mary Shelley, *Frankenstein*, 8.
51. Mary Shelley, 69.
52. Mary Shelley, 142.
53. Mary Shelley, 14.
54. Mary Shelley, 15.
55. Mary Shelley, 14.
56. Mary Shelley, 147–48.
57. Mary Shelley, 33.

58. Mary Shelley, 43–4.
59. Mary Shelley, 33.
60. Mary Shelley, 33.
61. Mary Shelley, 33.
62. Mary Shelley, 132.
63. Mary Shelley, 133.
64. Mary Shelley, 154.
65. Mary Shelley, 154.
66. Percy Shelley, "On Love," 504.
67. Hartman, *Scenes of Subjection*, 19.
68. See H. L. Malchow, *Gothic Images of Race in Nineteenth-Century Britain* (Stanford, CA: Stanford University Press, 1996); Debbie Lee, *Slavery and the Romantic Imagination* (Philadelphia: University of Pennsylvania Press, 2002); Alan Lloyd Smith, "'This Thing of Darkness': Racial Discourse in Mary Shelley's *Frankenstein*," *Gothic Studies* 6, no. 2 (2004): 208–222; and Marie Mulvey-Roberts, *Dangerous Bodies: Historicizing the Gothic Corporeal* (Manchester, UK: Manchester University Press 2016).
69. See Elizabeth Young, *Black Frankenstein: The Making of an American Metaphor* (New York: New York University Press, 2008).
70. See, for example, Anne K. Mellor, "*Frankenstein*, Racial Science and the Yellow Peril," *Nineteenth-Century Contexts* 23, no. 1 (2008): 1–28; Cathy S. Gelbin, "Was Frankenstein's Monster Jewish?," *Publications of the English Goethe Society* 82, no. 1 (2013): 16–25; and Stephen Bertman, "The Role of the Golem in the Making of *Frankenstein*," *Keats-Shelley Review* 29, no. 1 (2015): 42–50.
71. Victor LaValle, *Destroyer* (Los Angeles: Boom! Studios, 2017).
72. Sharpe, *In the Wake*, 21.
73. Sharpe, 22.
74. Wilderson, *Red, White, and Black*, 55, 57.
75. Frantz Fanon, *The Wretched of the Earth*, trans. Richard Philcox (New York: Grove, 2004), 2.
76. Wilderson, *Red, White, and Black*, 37.

Notes to Chapter 5

1. Anne Spencer, "Dunbar," in *The Book of American Negro Poetry, With an Essay on the Negro's Creative Genius*, ed. James Weldon Johnson (New York: Harcourt, Brace, 1922), 174. For more on Spencer, see J. Lee Greene, *Time's Unfading Garden: Anne Spencer's Life and Poetry* (Baton Rouge: Louisiana State University Press, 1977); Maureen Honey, ed., *Shadowed Dreams: Women's Poetry of the Harlem Renaissance*

(New Brunswick, NJ: Rutgers University Press, 2006); Cheryl A. Wall, *Women of the Harlem Renaissance* (Bloomington: Indiana University Press, 1995); and Jane Baber White, *Lessons Learned from a Poet's Garden* (Hoboken, NJ: Blackwell, 2011).

2. William Hazlitt, "On Burns and the Old English Ballads," in *Lectures on the English Poets*, ed. Alfred Rayney Waller and Earnest Rhys (London: Taylor and Hessey, 1818; Project Gutenberg, 2005), July 24, 2012, http://www.gutenberg.org/cache/epub/16209/pg16209.html.

3. Bennett, *Romantic Poets and the Culture of Posterity*, 3.

4. Jungian psychology views myth as an expression of a culture's fears, goals, and dreams, a window into its collective unconscious. In a similar vein, religion scholar Bruce Lincoln has discussed myths as "an ideology in narrative form." See *Jung on Mythology*, ed. Robert A. Segal (Princeton, NJ: Princeton University Press, 1998); and Bruce Lincoln, *Theorizing Myth: Narrative, Ideology, and Scholarship* (Chicago: University of Chicago Press, 1999), 207.

5. See Nick Groom, "Introduction," in *Thomas Chatterton and Romantic Culture*, ed. Nick Groom (New York: Palgrave Macmillan, 1999), 3; and Maria Losada Friend, "Romantic Suicide: The Chatterton Myth and Its Sequels," *Encontro de Estudos Românticos* (2006): 124.

6. William Wordsworth, "Resolution and Independence," in *The Major Works*, ed. Stephen Gill (New York: Oxford World's Classics, 2008), 260–65. ll. 43–49. A number of works concerning Chatterton include some variation of the "marvelous boy" epithet in their title, while Michael MacDonald and Terrence R. Murphy's groundbreaking book on the history of suicide, *Sleepless Souls*, takes its title from the line that follows. See, among others, Peter Corris, *The Marvellous Boy* (New York: Random House, 1986); Karen Foxlee, *Ophelia and the Marvelous Boy* (New York: Alfred A. Knopf, 2014); Linda Kelly, *The Marvellous Boy: The Life and Myth of Thomas Chatterton* (London: Weidenfeld and Nicholson, 1971); and Charles Edward Russell, *Thomas Chatterton, The Marvellous Boy: The Story of a Strange Life, 1752–1770* (New York: Moffatt, Yard, 1908).

7. See chapter 12 of Kelly, *Marvellous Boy*.

8. Some literary titles include Peter Ackroyd, *Chatterton* (New York: Grove Atlantic, 1987); Neil Bell, *Cover His Face: A Novel of the Life and Times of Thomas Chatterton, the Marvelous Boy of Bristol* (London: Collins, 1943); Francis William Grattan, *Thomas Chatterton, the Marvellous Boy in the Foes and Woes of a Poet—A Four Act Drama* (Whitefish, MT: Kessinger, 2010); Barry MacSweeney, *Elegy for January: Thomas Chatterton, 1752–1770* (London: Menard, 1970); Charles Reznikoff, *Chatterton, The Black Death* (London: Forgotten Books, 2012); and Vita Sackville-West, *Chatterton: A Drama in Three*

Acts (London: Through Leaves, 2002). Matthew Dewey, Serge Gainsbourg, and Matthias Pintscher are among those who have written music inspired by Chatterton. Scholars who explicitly link Chatterton to Cobain include Jennifer Otter Bickerdike, *Fandom, Image and Authenticity: Joy Devotion and the Second Lives of Kurt Cobain and Ian Curtis* (New York: Palgrave Macmillan, 2014); P. David Marshall, *Celebrity and Power: Fame in Contemporary Culture* (Minneapolis: University of Minnesota Press, 2014); and Maureen McLane, *My Poets* (New York: Farrar, Straus and Giroux, 2012).

9. Michelle Faubert, "Fashionable Suicide in the Romantic Era," Fashionable Diseases: Medicine, Literature, and Culture, ca. 1660–1832: A Leverhulme Trust Project at the Universities of Northumbria and Newcastle, MP3 audio, accessed February 15, 2015, http://www.fashionablediseases.info/downloads/suicide.MP3.
10. Andrew Radford and Mark Sandy, "Introduction: Romanticism and the Victorians," in *Romantic Echoes in the Victorian Period*, ed. Andrew Radford and Mark Sandy (Burlington, VT: Ashgate, 2008), 8.
11. William L. Pressly, *The Artist as Original Genius: Shakespeare's "Fine Frenzy" in Late-Eighteenth-Century British Art* (Newark: University of Delaware Press, 2007), 165–71. See also Joseph Bristow and Rebecca Marshall, *Oscar Wilde's Chatterton: Literary History, Romanticism, and the Art of Forgery* (New Haven, CT: Yale University Press, 2015), 85–88. The Singleton and West images are both held by the National Portrait Gallery, London, and available for viewing on their website, npg.org.uk.
12. Ron M. Brown, *The Art of Suicide* (London: Reaktion, 2001), 99. Inga Bryden also discusses the Wallis image as an example of *memento mori*. See Inga Bryden, "The Mythical Image: Chatterton, King Arthur, and Heraldry," in *Thomas Chatterton and Romantic Culture*, ed. Nick Groom (New York: St. Martin's Press, 1999), 64–78.
13. Brown, *Art of Suicide*, 138.
14. See *The Complete Poetical Works of Dante Gabriel Rossetti*, ed. William M. Rossetti (Boston: Little, Brown, 1899), 261, 266.
15. Quoted in Bristow and Marshall, *Oscar Wilde's Chatterton*, 110.
16. Radford and Sandy, "Introduction: Romanticism and the Victorians," 2–3. See also Julie Crane, "'Wandering between Two Worlds': The Victorian Afterlife of Thomas Chatterton," in *Romantic Echoes in the Victorian Period*, ed. Andrew Radford and Mark Sandy (Burlington, VT: Ashgate, 2008), 27–38.
17. Gates, *Victorian Suicide*, 23.
18. Groom, "Introduction," in *Thomas Chatterton and Romantic Culture*, 5.
19. René Girard, *Violence and the Sacred*, trans. Patrick Gregory (Baltimore: Johns Hopkins University Press, 1979), 8.

20. Girard, *Violence and the Sacred*, italics in original, 8.
21. Girard, 255.
22. My thinking here also draws on Roland Barthes's notion of myths as tools used by the ruling class to conserve its way of life: "The bourgeoisie hides the fact that it is the bourgeoisie and thereby produces myth; revolution announces itself openly as revolution and thereby abolishes myth," in *Mythologies*, trans. Annette Lavers (New York: Farrar, Straus and Giroux, 1972), 149.
23. See Timothy Egan, "Kurt Cobain, Hesitant Poet of 'Grunge,' Dead at 27," *New York Times*, April 9, 1994, https://www.nytimes.com/1994/04/09/obituaries/kurt-cobain-hesitant-poet-of-grunge-rock-dead-at-27.html; and Jonathan Freedland, "Kurt Cobain: An Icon of Alienation," *Guardian*, republished April 5, 2014, https://www.theguardian.com/music/from-the-archive-blog/2014/apr/05/kurt-cobain-an-icon-of-alienation.
24. *Newsweek*, "Kurt Cobain: Poet of Alienation—How *Newsweek* Grappled with the Musician's Suicide in 1994," *Newsweek*, April 5, 2018, https://www.newsweek.com/kurt-cobain-poet-alienation-how-newsweek-grappled-musicians-suicide-1994-873712.
25. See Neil Strauss, "Kurt Cobain's Downward Spiral: The Last Days of Nirvana's Leader," *Rolling Stone*, June 2, 1994, https://www.rollingstone.com/music/music-news/kurt-cobains-downward-spiral-the-last-days-of-nirvanas-leader-99797; and Gus Van Sant, dir., *Last Days* (New York: HBO Films, 2005).
26. Factors for this include the CDC's insistence on including information about suicide prevention resources in discussions of Cobain's death—now a standard practice in reporting on suicide—as well as his widow Courtney Love's public reading of his suicide note in the days after his death. Charles Cross suggests that Love's response "took away any glamour that might have been associated with the act and showed how much pain was left for others after his suicide." See David A. Jobes, et al., "The Kurt Cobain Suicide Crisis: Perspectives from Research, Public Health, and the News Media," *Suicide and Life-Threatening Behavior* 26, no. 3 (1996): 260–71; and Charles Cross, *Here We Are Now: The Lasting Impact of Kurt Cobain* (New York: HarperCollins, 2014), 149.
27. The painting can be seen on the artist's website, part of his History Paintings series, accessed April 13, 2020, https://sandowbirk.com. The painting is also discussed in David S. Rubin, *It's Only Rock and Roll: Rock and Roll Undercurrents in Contemporary Art* (New York: Prestel, 1996).
28. Quoted in Michael Azerrad, *Come As You Are: The Story of Nirvana* (New York: Doubleday, 2001), 349.

29. Charles Cross, *Heavier Than Heaven: A Biography of Kurt Cobain* (New York: Hachette, 2001), 34.
30. Kurt Cobain, *Journals* (New York: Riverhead, 2001), 18.
31. Cobain, *Journals*, 167–170.
32. Quoted in Cross, *Here We Are Now*, 57–58.
33. In a Google search for "Kurt Cobain" on May 28, 2019, the second hit after his Wikipedia page is another Wikipedia page dedicated solely to his suicide. The fourth is a website dedicated to his suicide note. Of the top four suggestions for additional searches, two are questions about how he died, one is about his health problems, and one asks where he is buried.
34. Cross, *Here We Are Now*, 40.
35. Brandon Soderburg, "The Rap on Kurt: Hood Pass 4 Life," *SPIN*, July 18, 2011, https://www.spin.com/2011/07/rap-kurt-hood-pass-4-life/.
36. John Norris, "Denzel Curry in his New Album 'Ta13oo,' Why Kurt Cobain is Glorified for the Wrong Reasons & His Connection to Trayvon Martin," *Billboard*, August 8, 2018, https://www.billboard.com/articles/columns/hip-hop/8469090/denzel-curry-ta13oo-album-clout-cobain-interview.
37. Jake Woolf, "The White Sunglasses You're Seeing Everywhere Now Have a New Name," *GQ*, July 25, 2017, https://www.gq.com/story/kurt-cobain-sunglasses-clout-coggles.
38. "Kurt Cobain Death Scene Photos," CBS News, accessed March 29, 2019, https://www.cbsnews.com/pictures/new-kurt-cobain-death-scene-photos/.
39. See, for example, Camila Domonoske, "Court Dismisses Latest Attempt to Acquire Kurt Cobain Death Scene Photos," *NPR*, May 16, 2018, https://www.npr.org/sections/thetwo-way/2018/05/16/611801099/court-dismisses-latest-attempt-to-acquire-kurt-cobains-death-scene-photos.
40. Casey McNerthney and Amy Clancy, "Seattle Police Re-Examine Cobain Suicide, Develop Scene Photos," *KIRO 7*, March 20, 2014, https://www.kiro7.com/news/only-kiro-7-seattle-police-re-investigate-kurt-cob/81808273.
41. In 2020, 250 years after Chatterton's death, a number of tributes to the poet have been organized by scholars and fans. By contrast, though Bristol's involvement in the triangular trade is well known to scholars, large-scale efforts to reckon with this part of the city's past are relatively recent, as journalist Aamna Mohdin discusses in her article about Olivette Otele, the nation's first black woman history professor, who began her post at Bristol University in 2020. See Steven Morris, "Bristol Celebrates its Poet Genius Who Died at Just 17," *Guardian*, March 30, 2020, https://www.theguardian.com/uk-news/2020/mar/30/

bristol-celebrates-poet-thomas-chatterton-who-died-at-17; "Chatterton250: A Call for Odes and Elegies," Keats-Shelley Association of America, February 18, 2020, https://k-saa.org/chatterton250-a-call-for-odes-and-elegies; and Aamna Mohdin, "UK's First Black Female History Professor to Research Bristol's Slavery Links," *Guardian*, October 30, 2019, https://www.theguardian.com/education/2019/oct/30/olivette-otele-uk-first-black-female-history-professor-to-research-bristol-slavery-links.

42. Congressional Black Caucus, *Ring the Alarm: The Crisis of Black Youth Suicide in America* (Washington, DC: CBC, 2019), https://watson-coleman.house.gov/uploadedfiles/full_taskforce_report.pdf. The report is the result of a task force launched by Congresswoman Bonnie Watson Coleman in April of 2019. The only other such resource to make explicit the link between suicide and racial injustice is *Widening the Lens: Exploring the Role of Social Justice in Suicide Prevention: A Racial Equity Toolkit*, also published in 2019 by the Massachusetts Coalition for Suicide Prevention, https://www.masspreventssuicide.org/wp-content/uploads/2019/09/WideningTheLensToolkit.pdf.

43. Wilderson, *Afropessimism*, 225.

Bibliography

Ackroyd, Peter. *Chatterton*. New York: Grove Atlantic, 1987.
Acosta, Ana M. *Reading Genesis in the Long Eighteenth Century: From Milton to Mary Shelley*. Burlington, VT: Ashgate, 2006.
Ahmed, Sara. *Living a Feminist Life*. Durham, NC: Duke University Press, 2017.
Allewaert, Monique. *Ariel's Ecology: Plantations, Personhood, and Colonialism in the American Tropics*. Minneapolis: University of Minnesota Press, 2013.
Alvarez, A. *The Savage God: A Study of Suicide*. New York: W. W. Norton, 1990.
Anderson, Amanda. *Bleak Liberalism*. Chicago: University of Chicago Press, 2016.
Anderson, Olive. *Suicide in Victorian and Edwardian England*. New York: Oxford University Press, 1987.
Andrews, Kehinde. "The Psychosis of Whiteness: The Celluloid Hallucinations of *Amazing Grace* and *Belle*." *Journal of Black Studies* 47, no. 5 (2016): 435–53.
"The Author of Sanford and Merton." *Bibliographer*, no. 5 (January 1884): 30–34.
Azerrad, Michael. *Come As You Are: The Story of Nirvana*. New York: Doubleday, 2001.
Bailey, Victor. *This Rash Act: Suicide Across the Life Cycle in the Victorian City*. Stanford, CA: Stanford University Press, 1998.
Baker, Samuel. *Written on the Water: British Romanticism and the Maritime Empire of Culture*. Charlottesville, VA: University of Virginia Press, 2010.
Balzac, Honoré de. *Le Peau de Chagrin*. In Vol. 10 of *La Comédie Humaine*, edited by Pierre Georges Castex, 5–294. Paris: Gallimard, 1979.

Baraka, Amiri. *Wise Why's Y's: The Griot's Song (Djeli Ya)*. Chicago: Third World, 1995.
Barbagli, Marzio. *Farewell to the World: A History of Suicide*. Translated by Lucinda Byatt. Cambridge, UK: Polity, 2015.
Barthes, Roland. *Mythologies*. Translated by Annette Lavers. New York: Farrar, Straus and Giroux, 1972.
Baucom, Ian. *Specters of the Atlantic: Finance Capital, Slavery, and the Philosophy of History*. Durham, NC: Duke University Press, 2005.
Beenstock, Zoe. *The Politics of Romanticism: The Social Contract and Literature*. Edinburgh: Edinburgh University Press, 2016.
Behn, Aphra. *Oroonoko*, edited by Janet Todd. London: Penguin, 2003.
Bell, Neil. *Cover His Face: A Novel of the Life and Times of Thomas Chatterton, the Marvellous Boy of Bristol*. London: Collins, 1943.
Bell, Richard. *We Shall Be No More: Suicide and Self-Government in the Newly United States*. Cambridge, MA: Harvard University Press, 2012.
Bennett, Andrew. *Romantic Poets and the Culture of Posterity*. New York: Cambridge University Press, 1999.
———. *Suicide Century: Literature and Suicide from James Joyce to David Foster Wallace*. New York: Cambridge University Press, 2017.
Bering, Jesse. *Suicidal: Why We Kill Ourselves*. Chicago: University of Chicago Press, 2018.
Bernier, Celeste-Marie. *Characters of Blood: Black Heroism in the Transatlantic Imagination*. Charlottesville: University of Virginia Press, 2012.
Bertman, Stephen. "The Role of the Golem in the Making of *Frankenstein*." *Keats-Shelley Review* 29, no. 1 (2015): 42–50.
Bickerdike, Jennifer Otter. *Fandom, Image and Authenticity: Joy Devotion and the Second Lives of Kurt Cobain and Ian Curtis*. New York: Palgrave Macmillan, 2014.
The Bigger Six Collective. "Coda: From Coteries to Collectives." *Symbiosis: A Journal of Transatlantic Literary and Cultural Relations* 23, no. 1 (Spring 2019): 139–40.
Birk, Sandow. *The Death of Kurt Cobain*. Oil painting, 1994. Accessed April 13, 2020. https://sandowbirk.com/history-paintings.
Blackstone, William, Sir. *Commentaries on the Laws of England, Book the Fourth*. Gale Eighteenth Century Collections Online (CW3324351452). Oxford: Clarendon, 1769.
———. *The Commentaries of Sir William Blackstone*. Gale Eighteenth Century Collections Online (CW3325233304). London, 1796.
Bohls, Elizabeth A. "Standards of Taste, Discourses of 'Race', and the Aesthetic Education of a Monster: Critique of Empire in *Frankenstein*." *Eighteenth-Century Life* 18, no. 3 (1994): 23–36.
Bolton, Andrew. *Alexander McQueen: Savage Beauty*. New Haven, CT: Yale University Press, 2011.

Bontemps, Alex. *The Punished Self: Surviving Slavery in the Colonial South.* Ithaca, NY: Cornell University Press, 2001.
Botting, Fred. *Making Monstrous: Frankenstein, Criticism, Theory.* Manchester, UK: Manchester University Press, 1991.
Bristow, Joseph, and Rebecca Marshall. *Oscar Wilde's Chatterton: Literary History, Romanticism, and the Art of Forgery.* New Haven, CT: Yale University Press, 2015.
Brown, Marshall. "*Frankenstein*: A Child's Tale." *NOVEL: A Forum on Fiction* 36, no. 2 (2003): 145–75.
Brown, Ron M. *The Art of Suicide.* London: Reaktion, 2001.
Brown, Sue. *Joseph Severn, A Life: The Rewards of Friendship.* New York: Oxford University Press, 2009.
Brown, Vincent. *The Reaper's Garden: Death and Power in the World of Atlantic Slavery.* Cambridge, MA: Harvard University Press, 2008.
———. "Social Death and Political Life in the Study of Slavery." *American Historical Review* (2009): 1231–49.
Brown, William Wells. *Clotel; or The President's Daughter: A Narrative of Slave Life in the United States*, edited by M. Giulia Fabi. New York: Penguin, 2003.
———. *Clotelle; or, the Colored Heroine.* Boston: Lee and Sheppard, 1867.
Bryden, Inga. "The Mythical Image: Chatterton, King Arthur, and Heraldry." In *Thomas Chatterton and Romantic Culture*, edited by Nick Groom, 64–78. New York: St. Martin's Press, 1999.
Burton, Robert. *The Anatomy of Melancholy.* Oxford: Clarendon, 1989.
Byron, Lord (George Gordon). *The Giaour.* In *Lord Byron: The Major Works*, edited by Jerome McGann, 207–47. New York: Oxford World's Classics, 2008.
———. Vol. 5, *The Works of Byron: Letters and Journals*, edited by Rowland E. Prothero. New York: Charles Scribner's Sons, 1904.
Carby, Hazel V. *Cultures in Babylon: Black Britain and African America.* London: Verso, 1999.
Carey, Brycchan. *British Abolitionism and the Rhetoric of Sensibility: Writing, Sentiment, and Slavery, 1760–1807.* New York: Palgrave Macmillan, 2005.
Carey, Brycchan, Markman Ellis, and Sara Salih, eds. *Discourses of Slavery and Abolition: Britain and its Colonies, 1760–1838.* New York: Palgrave Macmillan, 2004.
Carey, Brycchan, and Peter J. Kitson, eds. *Slavery and the Cultures of Abolition: Essays Marking the Bicentennial of the British Abolition Act of 1807.* Rochester, NY: D.S. Brewer, 2007.
CBS News. "Kurt Cobain Death Scene Photos." Accessed March 29, 2019. https://www.cbsnews.com/pictures/new-kurt-cobain-death-scene-photos/.

Chander, Manu Samriti. *Brown Romantics: Poetry and Nationalism in the Global Nineteenth Century*. Lewisburg, PA: Bucknell University Press, 2017.

Chander, Manu Samriti, and Patricia A. Matthew, eds. "Abolitionist Interruptions." Special issue, *European Romantic Review* 29, no. 4 (2018): 431–556.

Cheyne, George. *The English Malady*, edited by Roy Porter. New York: Routledge, 2013.

Clark, David Lee. "Introduction." In *Shelley's Prose*, edited by David Lee Clark, 3–36. Bel Air, CA: New Amsterdam, 1988.

Cobain, Kurt. *Journals*. New York: Riverhead, 2001.

Coke, Diana. *Saved from a Watery Grave: The Story of the Royal Humane Society's Receiving House in Hyde Park, London*. London: Royal Humane Society, 2000.

Coleman, Deirdre. *Romantic Colonization and British Anti-Slavery*. New York: Cambridge University Press, 2009.

Collins, Patricia Hill. *Black Feminist Thought: Knowledge, Consciousness and the Politics of Empowerment*. New York: Routledge, 2000.

Commander, Michelle D. *Afro-Atlantic Flight: Speculative Returns and the Black Fantastic*. Durham, NC: Duke University Press, 2017.

Congressional Black Caucus. *Ring the Alarm: The Crisis of Black Youth Suicide in America*. Washington, DC: CBC, 2019. https://watson-coleman.house.gov/uploadedfiles/full_taskforce_report.pdf.

Constantine, David. Introduction to *The Sorrows of Young Werther*, by Johann Wolfgang von Goethe, vii–xxviii. New York: Oxford University Press, 2012.

Cook, Daniel. *Thomas Chatterton and Neglected Genius, 1760–1830*. New York: Palgrave Macmillan, 2013.

Corris, Peter. *The Marvellous Boy*. New York: Random House, 1986.

Cotter, William R. "The Somerset Case and the Abolition of Slavery in England." *History* 79, no. 255 (February 1994): 31–56.

Cottingham, Myra. "Felicia Hemans's Dead and Dying Bodies." *Women's Writing* 8, no. 2 (2001): 275–94.

Coulthard, Glen Sean. *Red Skin, White Masks: Rejecting the Colonial Politics of Recognition*. Minneapolis: University of Minnesota Press, 2014.

Cowles, Mary Jane. "The Subjectivity of the Colonial Subject from Olympe de Gouges to Mme. de Duras." *L'Esprit Créateur* 47, no. 4 (2007): 29–43.

Crane, Julie. "'Wandering between Two Worlds': The Victorian Afterlife of Thomas Chatterton." In *Romantic Echoes in the Victorian Period*, edited by Andrew Radford and Mark Sandy, 27–38. Burlington, VT: Ashgate, 2008.

Cross, Charles. *Heavier than Heaven: A Biography of Kurt Cobain*. New York: Hachette, 2001.

———. *Here We Are Now: The Lasting Impact of Kurt Cobain*. New York: HarperCollins, 2014.

Cugoano, Ottobah. *Narrative of the Enslavement of Ottobah Cugoano, a Native of Africa*. London: Hatchard, 1825. https://docsouth.unc.edu/neh/cugoano/cugoano.html.
Dainato, Roberto. *Europe (In Theory)*. Durham, NC: Duke University Press, 2007.
Davis, Angela Y. *Women, Race, and Class*. New York: Vintage, 1983.
Davis, David Brion. *The Problem of Slavery in the Age of Revolution, 1770–1823*. Ithaca, NY: Cornell University Press, 1975.
Davis, George Henry. *Memorials of Hamlet of Knightsbridge*. London: J. Russel Smith, 1859.
Day, Iyko. "Being or Nothingness: Indigeneity, Antiblackness, and Settler Colonial Critique." *Journal of the Critical Ethnic Studies Association* 1, no. 2 (Fall 2015): 102–21.
Day, Thomas, and John Bicknell. *The Dying Negro*. Gale Eighteenth Century Collections Online (CW3310391049). London: John Stockdale, 1793.
Delamayne, Thomas Hallie. *The Rise and Practice of Imprisonment in Personal Actions, Examined*. Gale Eighteenth Century Collections Online (CB3327352670). London: J. Wilkie, 1772.
Deneen, Patrick. *Why Liberalism Failed*. New Haven, CT: Yale University Press, 2018.
Diaby, Bakary. "Black Women and/in the Shadow of Romanticism." *European Romantic Review* 30, no. 3 (2019): 249–54
———. "Feeling Black, Feeling Back: Fragility and Romanticism." *Symbiosis: A Journal of Transatlantic Literary and Cultural Relations* 23, no. 1 (Spring 2019): 117–38.
DiAngelo, Robin. *White Fragility: Why It's So Hard for White People to Talk About Racism*. Boston: Beacon, 2018.
Domonoske, Camila. "Court Dismisses Latest Attempt to Acquire Kurt Cobain Death Scene Photos." *NPR*, May 16, 2018. https://www.npr.org/sections/thetwo-way/2018/05/16/611801099/court-dismisses-latest-attempt-to-acquire-kurt-cobains-death-scene-photos.
Doyle, Laura. *Freedom's Empire: Race and the Rise of the Novel in Atlantic Modernity, 1640–1940*. Durham, NC: Duke University Press, 2008.
Drescher, Seymour. *Abolition: A History of Slavery and Antislavery*. New York: Cambridge University Press, 2009.
———. *Econocide: British Slavery in the Era of Abolition*. Chapel Hill: University of North Carolina Press, 2010.
Drewal, Henry John. "Performing the Other: Mami Wata Worship in Africa." *Drama Review* 32, no. 2 (1988): 160–85.
Drewal, John Henry, Charles Gore, and Michelle Kisliuk. "Siren Serenades: Music for Mami Wata and Other Water Spirits in Africa." In *Music of the*

Sirens, edited by Linda Austern and Inna Naroditskaya, 294–316. Bloomington: Indiana University Press, 2006.

Duker, William F. *A Constitutional History of Habeas Corpus*. Westport, CT: Greenwood, 1980.

Duncan, Bruce. *Goethe's Werther and the Critics*. Rochester, NY: Camden House, 2005.

Duras, Claire de. *Ourika*. Translated by John Fowles. New York: Modern Language Association of America, 1994.

Durkheim, Emile. *On Suicide*. Translated by Robin Buss. New York: Penguin, 2006.

Dyer, Justin Buckley. "After the Revolution: Somerset and the Antislavery Tradition in Anglo American Constitutional Development." *Journal of Politics* 71, no. 4 (October 2009): 1422–34.

Dyer, Richard. *White: Essays on Race and Culture*. New York: Routledge, 1997.

Dykes, Eva Beatrice. *The Negro in English Romantic Thought: Or, A Study of Sympathy for the Oppressed*. Washington, DC: Associated, 1942.

Eagleton, Terry. *Literary Theory: An Introduction*. Minneapolis: University of Minnesota Press, 1996.

Eden, William. *Principles of Penal Law*. Gale Eighteenth Century Collections Online (CW3324202367). Dublin: John Milliken, 1772.

Egan, Timothy. "Kurt Cobain, Hesitant Poet of 'Grunge,' Dead at 27." *New York Times*, April 9, 1994. https://www.nytimes.com/1994/04/09/obituaries/kurt-cobain-hesitant-poet-of-grunge-rock-dead-at-27.html.

Ellis, Cristin. *Antebellum Posthuman: Race and Materiality in the Mid-Nineteenth Century*. New York: Fordham University Press, 2018.

Ellis, Markman. *The Politics of Sensibility: Race, Gender and Commerce in the Sentimental Novel*. New York: Cambridge University Press, 1996.

Equiano, Olaudah. *The Interesting Narrative and Other Writings*, edited by Vincent Carretta. London: Penguin, 2003.

Estwick, Samuel. *Considerations on the Negroe Cause Commonly So Called, Addressed to the Right Honourable Lord Mansfield, Lord Chief Justice of the Court of King's Bench*. Gale Eighteenth Century Collections Online (CW3323898286). London, 1773.

Fanon, Frantz. *The Wretched of the Earth*. Translated by Richard Philcox. New York: Grove Press, 2004.

Farr, James. "Locke, Natural Law, and New World Slavery." *Political Theory* 36, no. 4 (2008): 495–522.

Faubert, Michelle. "A Family Affair: Ennobling Suicide in Mary Shelley's *Matilda*." *Essays in Romanticism* 20 (2013): 101–28.

———. "Fashionable Suicide in the Romantic Era." Fashionable Diseases: Medicine, Literature, and Culture, ca. 1660–1832: A Leverhulme Trust Project at the Universities of Northumbria and Newcastle. MP3 audio.

Accessed February 15, 2015. http://www.fashionablediseases.info/downloads/suicide.MP3.

———. "The Fictional Suicides of Mary Wollstonecraft." *Literature Compass* 12, no. 12 (2015): 652–59.

———. "Romantic Suicide, Contagion, and Rousseau's *Julie.*" In *Romanticism, Rousseau, Switzerland: New Prospects*, edited by Diane Piccitto, Angela Esterhammer, and Patrick Vincent, 38–53. New York: Palgrave Macmillan, 2015.

———. "Werther Goes Viral: Suicidal Contagion, Vaccination, and Infections Sympathy." *Literature and Medicine* 34, no. 2 (Fall 2016): 389–417.

———. "The Wollstonecraftian Plot: Female Suicide as Slave Protest." In *Romantic Bodyscapes: Embodied Selves, Embodied Spaces and Legible Bodies in the Romantic Age*, edited by Gerold Sedlmayr, 123–44. Trier, Germany: Wissenschaftlicher Verlag Trier, 2015.

Feder, Rachel. *Harvester of Hearts: Motherhood Under the Sign of Frankenstein.* Evanston, IL: Northwestern University Press, 2018.

Fehrenbacher, Don. *Slavery, Law, & Politics: The Dred Scott Case in Historical Perspective.* New York: Oxford University Press, 1981.

Ferguson, Moira. *Colonialism and Gender Relations: From Mary Wollstonecraft to Jamaica Kincaid.* New York: Columbia University Press, 1993.

———. *Subject to Others: British Women Writers and Colonial Slavery, 1670–1834.* London: Routledge, 1992.

Ferreira, M. Jamie. "Hume and Imagination: Sympathy and 'the Other.'" *International Philosophical Quarterly* 34, no. 133 (March 1994): 39–57.

Festa, Lynn. *Sentimental Figures of Empire in Eighteenth-Century Britain and France.* Baltimore: Johns Hopkins University Press, 2006.

Flaxman, John. "Thomas Chatterton Taking the Bowl of Poison from the Spirit of Despair." Drawing, 1775. The Trustees of the British Museum. https://www.britishmuseum.org/collection/object/P_1962-0714-32.

Flint, Kate. *The Transatlantic Indian: 1776–1930.* Princeton, NJ: Princeton University Press, 2008.

Foreman, P. Gabrielle. "Writing About Slavery/Teaching About Slavery: This Might Help." Unpublished manuscript. Accessed May 14, 2020. https://docs.google.com/document/d/1A4TEdDgYslX-hlKezLodMIM-71My3KTNozxRvoIQTOQs.

Foxlee, Karen. *Ophelia and the Marvelous Boy.* New York: Alfred A. Knopf, 2014.

Francione, Gary. *Animals as Persons: Essays on the Abolition of Animal Exploitation.* New York: Columbia University Press, 2008.

Frank, Barbara. "Permitted and Prohibited Wealth: Commodity-Possessing Spirits, Economic Morals, and the Goddess." *Ethnology* 34, no. 4 (Fall 1995): 331–46.

Frazer, Michael L. *The Enlightenment of Sympathy.* New York: Oxford University Press, 2010.

Freedland, Jonathan. "Kurt Cobain: An Icon of Alienation." *Guardian*, republished April 5, 2014. https://www.theguardian.com/music/from-the-archive-blog/2014/apr/05/kurt-cobain-an-icon-of-alienation.

Friedrich, Caspar David. *Wanderer Over the Sea of Fog*. Painting, oil on canvas, ca. 1817. Kunsthalle Hamburg, Germany. https://online-sammlung.hamburger-kunsthalle.de/de/objekt/HK-5161.

Friend, Maria Losada. "Romantic Suicide: The Chatterton Myth and Its Sequels." *Encontro de Estudos Românticos* 14 (2006): 123–30.

Fuentes, Marisa J. *Dispossessed Lives: Enslaved Women, Violence, and the Archive*. Philadelphia: University of Pennsylvania Press, 2016.

Fulford, Tim. *Romantic Indians: Native Americans, British Literature, and Transatlantic Culture, 1756–1830*. New York: Oxford University Press, 2006.

Fulford, Tim, and Kevin Hutchings, eds. *Native Americans and Anglo-American Culture, 1750– 1850: The Indian Atlantic*. New York: Cambridge University Press, 2009.

Fulford, Tim, and Peter J. Kitson, eds. *Romanticism and Colonialism: Writing and Empire, 1780–1830*. New York: Cambridge University Press, 1998.

Fulton, DoVeanna S. *Speaking Power: Black Feminist Orality in Women's Narratives of Slavery*. Albany: State University of New York Press, 2006.

Garrett, Aaron, and Silvia Sebastiani. "David Hume on Race." In *The Oxford Handbook of Philosophy and Race*, edited by Naomi Zack, 31–43. New York: Oxford University Press, 2017.

Gates, Barbara T. *Victorian Suicide: Mad Crimes and Sad Histories*. Princeton, NJ: Princeton University Press, 1988.

Gates, Henry Louis, Jr. *Figures in Black: Words, Signs and the 'Racial Self.'* New York: Oxford University Press, 1997.

Gelbin, Cathy S. "Was Frankenstein's Monster Jewish?" *Publications of the English Goethe Society* 82, no. 1 (2013): 16–25.

Georgia Writers' Project. *Drum and Shadows: Survival Studies Among the Georgia Coastal Negroes*. Athens: University of Georgia Press, 1986.

Gilroy, Paul. *The Black Atlantic: Modernity and Double Consciousness*. Cambridge, MA: Harvard University Press, 1995.

Girard, René. *Violence and the Sacred*. Translated by Patrick Gregory. Baltimore: Johns Hopkins University Press, 1979.

Glenn, Gary D. "Inalienable Rights and Locke's Argument for Limited Government: Political Implications of a Right to Suicide." *Journal of Politics* 46, no. 1 (February 1984): 80–105.

Glissant, Edouard. *Poetics of Relation*. Translated by Betsy Wing. Ann Arbor: University of Michigan Press, 1997.

Gomez, Michael. *Exchanging Our Country Marks: The Transformation of African Identities in the Colonial and Antebellum South*. Chapel Hill: University of North Carolina Press, 1998.

Goring, Paul. *The Rhetoric of Sensibility of Eighteenth-Century Culture.* New York: Cambridge University Press, 2005.
Goslee, Nancy Moore. "Hemans's 'Red Indians': Reading Stereotypes." In *Romanticism, Race, and Imperial Culture, 1780–1834*, edited by Alan Richardson and Sonia Hofkosh, 237–57. Bloomington: Indiana University Press, 1996.
Grattan, Francis William. *Thomas Chatterton, the Marvelous Boy in the Foes and Woes of a Poet: A Four Act Drama.* Whitefish, MT: Kessinger, 2010.
Greene, J. Lee. *Time's Unfading Garden: Anne Spencer's Life and Poetry.* Baton Rouge: Louisiana State University Press, 1977.
Greene, Jack. "'Slavery or Independence:' Some Reflections on the Relationship Among Liberty, Black Bondage, and Equality in Revolutionary South Carolina." *South Carolina Historical Magazine* 80, no. 3 (July 1979): 193–214.
Greeson, Jennifer Rae. "The Prehistory of Possessive Individualism." *PMLA* 127, no. 4 (2012): 918–24.
Gregory, Anthony. *The Power of Habeas Corpus in America: From the King's Prerogative to the War on Terror.* New York: Cambridge University Press, 2013.
Gregory, Dick. *The Shadow That Scares Me.* New York: Doubleday, 1968
Griffin, Megan. "Dismembering the Sovereign in Aphra Behn's *Oroonoko*." *ELH* 86, no. 1 (Spring 2019): 107–33.
Grinnell, George. "Equiano's Refusal: Slavery, Suicide Bombing and Negation." *European Romantic Review* 27, no. 3 (June 2016): 365–74.
Gronniosaw, James Albert Ukawsaw. *A Narrative of the Most Remarkable Particulars in the Life of James Albert Ukawsaw Gronniosaw, an African Prince, as Related by Himself.* Bath, UK: G. Wye, 1772. https://docsouth.unc.edu/neh/gronniosaw/gronnios.html.
Groom, Nick. "Introduction." In *Thomas Chatterton and Romantic Culture*, edited by Nick Groom, 3–14. New York: Palgrave Macmillan, 1999.
Grossman, Allen. *The Long Schoolroom: Lessons in the Bitter Logic of the Poetic Principle.* Ann Arbor: University of Michigan Press, 1997.
Gutzman, Kevin. "Foreword." In *The Power of Habeas Corpus in America*, by Anthony Gregory, ix–xi. New York: Cambridge University Press, 2013.
Hall, Kim F. *Things of Darkness: Economies of Race and Gender in Early Modern England.* Ithaca, NY: Cornell University Press, 1995.
Halliday, Paul D. *Habeas Corpus: From England to Empire.* Cambridge, MA: Harvard University Press, 2010.
Harding, Anthony John. "Felicia Hemans and the Effacement of Woman." In *Romantic Women Writers: Voices and Countervoices*, edited by Paula R. Feldman and Theresa M. Kelley, 138–49. Hanover, NH: University Press of New England, 1995.
Harney, Stefano, and Fred Moten. *The Undercommons: Fugitive Planning and Black Study.* Brooklyn, NY: Minor Compositions, 2013. http://

www.minorcompositions.info/wpcontent/uploads/2013/04/undercommons-web.pdf.

Harris, Cheryl. "Whiteness as Property." *Harvard Law Review* 106, no. 8 (1993): 1707–91.

Hartman, Saidiya V. *Lose Your Mother: A Journey Along the Atlantic Slave Route.* New York: Farrar, Straus and Giroux, 2008.

———. *Scenes of Subjection: Terror, Slavery, and Self-Making in Nineteenth-Century America.* New York: Oxford University Press, 1997.

Hartman, Saidiya V., and Frank B. Wilderson, III. "The Position of the Unthought." *Qui Parle* 13, no. 183 :(2003) 2–201.

Hazlitt, William. "On Burns and the Old English Ballads." In *Lectures on the English Poets*, edited by Alfred Rayney Waller and Earnest Rhys. London: Taylor and Hessey, 1818. Project Gutenberg, 2005. Accessed July 24, 2012. http://www.gutenberg.org/cache/epub/16209/pg16209.html.

Hecht, Jennifer Michael. *Stay: A History of Suicide and the Philosophies Against It.* New Haven, CT: Yale University Press, 2013.

Hemans, Felicia. "The Bride of the Greek Isle." In *Records of Woman, with Other Poems*, edited by Paula R. Feldman, 17–25. Lexington: University of Kentucky Press, 1999.

———. "Indian Woman's Death Song." In *Records of Woman, with Other Poems*, edited by Paula R. Feldman, 57–59. Lexington: University of Kentucky Press, 1999.

———. "The Last Song of Sappho." In *The Poetical Works of Felicia Dorothea Hemans*, 318. Oxford: Oxford University Press, 1914.

———. "Properzia Rossi." In *Records of Woman, with Other Poems*, edited by Paula R. Feldman, 29. Lexington: University of Kentucky Press, 1999.

———. "The Sicilian Captive." In *Records of Woman, with Other Poems*, edited by Paula R. Feldman, 90–94. Lexington: University of Kentucky Press, 1999.

Hessell, Nikki. *Romantic Literature and the Colonised World: Lessons From Indigenous Translations.* New York: Palgrave Macmillan, 2018.

Hickman, Jared. *Black Prometheus: Race and Radicalism in the Age of Atlantic Slavery.* New York: Oxford University Press, 2016.

Higonnet, Margaret. "Dialogues with the Dead: Enlightened Selves, Suicide, and Human Rights." *1616: Anuario de Literatura Comparada* 2 (2012): 189–208.

———. "Frames of Female Suicide." *Studies in the Novel* 32, no. 2 (2000): 229-42.

———. "Suicide: Representations of the Feminine." *Poetics Today* 6, no. 1/2 (1985): 103–18.

———. "Suicide as Self-Construction." In *Crossing the Borders: Madame de Staël*, edited by Avriel Goldberger, Madelyn Gutwirth, Karyna Smurlo, 69–81. New Brunswick, NJ: Rutgers University Press, 1991.

———. "'This Winged Nature Fraught': Suicide and Agency in Women's Poetry." *Literature Compass* 12, no. 12 (December 2015): 683–89.

Hittner, James. "How Robust Is the Werther Effect? A Re-Examination of the Suggestion Imitation Model of Suicide." *Mortality* 10 (August 2005): 193–200.

Holland, Sharon Patricia. *Raising the Dead: Readings of Death and (Black) Subjectivity*. Durham, NC: Duke University Press, 2000.

———. "Vocabularies of Vulnerability." *Journal for Cultural Research* 22, no. 2 (2018): 204–8.

Honey, Maureen, ed. *Shadowed Dreams: Women's Poetry of the Harlem Renaissance*. New Brunswick, NJ: Rutgers University Press, 2006.

hooks, bell. *Ain't I A Woman: Black Women and Feminism*. Boston: South End, 1999.

———. *Black Looks: Race and Representation*. New York: Routledge, 2015.

———. *Yearning: Race, Gender, and Cultural Politics*, 203–9. Boston: South End, 1990.

———. *Feminism is for Everybody: Passionate Politics*. London: Pluto, 2000.

———. *Teaching to Transgress: Education as the Practice of Freedom*. New York: Routledge, 1994.

———. *The Will to Change: Men, Masculinity, and Love*. New York: Washington Square, 2004.

Houston, R. A. *Punishing the Dead? Suicide, Lordship, and Community in Britain, 1500–1830*. New York: Oxford University Press, 2010.

Howard, Jonathan. "'Gone with the Ibos': The Blueness of Blackness in Paule Marshall's *Praisesong for the Widow*." *Callaloo* 39, no. 4 (Fall 2016): 898–918.

Hugo, Victor. "Author's Preface to the First Edition of *Hernani*." Vol. 1 of *The Works of Victor Hugo, Dramas*, 3–6. New York: Little, Brown, 1909.

Hull, Akasha (Gloria T.), Patricia Bell Scott, and Barbara Smith, eds. *All the Women Are White, All the Blacks Are Men, but Some of Us Are Brave*. New York: Feminist Press at the City University of New York, 1982.

Hume, David. *On Suicide*. New York: Penguin, 2005.

———. *Treatise of Human Nature*, edited by Ernest C. Mossner. New York: Penguin, 1985.

Hunter, T. K. "Geographies of Liberty: A Brief Look at Two Cases." In *Prophets of Protest: Reconsidering the History of American Abolitionism*, edited by Timothy Patrick McCarthy and John Stauffer, 41–58. New York: New Press, 2006.

Hutchings, Kevin. *Romantic Ecologies and Colonial Encounters in the British Atlantic World, 1770–1850*. Quebec: McGill-Queen's University Press, 2009.

Immerwahr, John. "Hume's Revised Racism." *Journal of the History of Ideas* 53, no. 3 (1992): 481–86.

Jackson, Mattie J. *The Story of Mattie J. Jackson*. Lawrence, KS: Sentinel Office, 1866. https://docsouth.unc.edu/neh/jacksonm/jackson.html.

Jenks, Edward. "The Story of Habeas Corpus." *Law Quarterly Review* 18 (1902): 64–77.
Jobes, David A., Alan L. Berman, Patrick W. O'Carroll, Susan Eastgard, and Steve Knickmeyer. "The Kurt Cobain Suicide Crisis: Perspectives from Research, Public Health, and the News Media." *Suicide and Life-Threatening Behavior* 26, no. 3 (1996): 260–71.
Johnson, Barbara. "Anthropomorphism in Lyric and Law." *Yale Journal of Law and Humanities* 10, no. 2 (1998): 549–74.
———. "Apostrophe, Animation, and Abortion." *Diacritics* 16, no. 1 (1986): 29–47.
———. *Persons and Things*. Cambridge, MA: Harvard University Press, 2008.
———. *A World of Difference*. Baltimore: Johns Hopkins University Press, 1987.
Jones, Shelley A. J. "Revision as Conversation in Mary Robinson's 'The Storm' and 'The Negro Girl.'" *The CEA Critic* 71, no. 3 (Spring and Summer 2009): 37–54.
Jung, Carl. *Jung on Mythology*, edited by Robert A. Segal. Princeton, NJ: Princeton University Press, 1998.
Kaplan, Cora. "Mary Wollstonecraft's Reception and Legacies." In *The Cambridge Companion to Mary Wollstonecraft*, edited by Claudia Johnson, 246–70. New York: Cambridge University Press, 2002.
Kaplan, Louise J. *The Family Romance of the Imposter-Poet Thomas Chatterton*. Berkeley and Los Angeles: University of California Press, 1989.
Keats, John. "Ode to a Nightingale." In *The Complete Poems*, edited by John Barnard, 346–48. London: Penguin, 2003.
———. *Selected Letters of John Keats*, edited by Grant F. Scott. Cambridge, MA: Harvard University Press, 2002.
Keats-Shelley Association of America. "Chatterton250: A Call for Odes and Elegies." February 18, 2020. https://k-saa.org/chatterton250-a-call-for-odes-and-elegies.
Kelly, Gary. "Death and the Matron: Felicia Hemans, Romantic Death, and the Founding of the Modern Liberal State." In *Felicia Hemans: Reimagining Poetry in the Nineteenth Century*, edited by Nanora Sweet and Julie Melnyk, 196–211. London: Palgrave Macmillan, 2001.
———. "Introduction." In *Felicia Hemans: Selected Poems, Prose, and Letters*, edited by Gary Kelly, 15–85. Peterborough, ON: Broadview, 2002.
Kelly, Linda. *The Marvellous Boy: The Life and Myth of Thomas Chatterton*. London: Weidenfeld and Nicholson, 1971.
Kesselring, K. J. "Felony Forfeiture in England, c. 1170-1870." *Journal of Legal History* 30, no. 3 (2009): 201–26.
King, Tiffany Lethabo. *The Black Shoals: Offshore Formations of Black and Native Studies*. Durham, NC: Duke University Press, 2019.
Kitson, Peter J. "'Bales of Living Anguish': Representations of Race and the Slave in Romantic Writing." *ELH* 67, no. 515 :(2000) 2–37.

———. *Romantic Literature, Race, and Colonial Encounter.* New York: Palgrave Macmillan, 2007.
Koh, Adeline. "Marriage, 'Metissage,' and Women's Citizenship: Revisiting Race and Gender in Claire de Duras' 'Ourika.'" *French Forum* 38, no. 3 (Fall 2013): 15–30.
Koretsky, Deanna. "The Interracial Marriage Plot: Suicide and the Politics of Blood in Romantic-Era Women's Fiction," *Studies in the Literary Imagination* 51, no. 1 (Spring 2018): 1–18.
Koretsky, Deanna, and Joel Pace. "Introduction: New Directions in Transatlantic Romanticisms." *Symbiosis: A Journal of Transatlantic Literary and Cultural Relations* 23, no. 1 (Spring 2019): 5–19.
Kramnick, Isaac. *Republicanism and Bourgeois Radicalism: Political Ideology in Late Eighteenth-Century England and America.* Ithaca, NY: Cornell University Press, 1990.
Kutner, Luis. *The Human Right to Individual Freedom: A Symposium on World Habeas Corpus.* Miami: University of Miami Press, 1970.
Laufer, William S. *Corporate Bodies and Guilty Minds: The Failure of Corporate Criminal Liability.* Chicago: The University of Chicago Press, 2008
LaValle, Victor, dir. *Destroyer.* Los Angeles: Boom! Studios, 2017.
Lee, Debbie. "Black Single Mothers in Romantic Literature and History." In *Race, Romanticism, and the Atlantic,* edited by Paul Youngquist, 165–82. Burlington, VT: Ashgate, 2013.
———. *Slavery and the Romantic Imagination.* Philadelphia: University of Pennsylvania Press, 2002.
Lootens, Tricia. *The Political Poetess: Victorian Femininity, Race, and the Legacy of Separate Spheres.* Princeton, NJ: Princeton University Press, 2017.
Levecq, Christine. *Slavery and Sentiment: The Politics of Feeling in Black Atlantic Antislavery Writing, 1770–1850.* Durham: University of New Hampshire Press, 2008.
Lincoln, Bruce. *Theorizing Myth: Narrative, Ideology, and Scholarship.* Chicago: University of Chicago Press, 1999.
Locke, John. *Second Treatise of Government.* Indianapolis: Hackett, 1980.
Lorde, Audre. "Age, Race, Class, and Sex: Women Redefining Difference." In *Sister Outsider,* 114–23. New York: Ten Speed, 2007.
———. "An Open Letter to Mary Daly." In *This Bridge Called My Back, Fourth Edition: Writings by Radical Women of Color,* edited by Cherríe Moraga and Gloria Anzaldúa, 90–93. Albany: State University of New York Press, 2015.
———. "The Master's Tools Will Never Dismantle the Master's House. In *Sister Outsider,* 110–14. New York: Ten Speed, 2007.
Losurdo, Domenico. *Liberalism: A Counter-History.* Translated by Gregory Elliott. London: Verso, 2014.

Lowe, Lisa. *The Intimacies of Four Continents*. Durham, NC: Duke University Press, 2015.
MacDonald, Michael. "Suicide and the Rise of the Popular Press in England." *Representations* 22 (Spring 1988): 36–55.
MacDonald, Michael, and Terence R. Murphy. *Sleepless Souls: Suicide in Early Modern England*. New York: Oxford University Press, 1991.
Macpherson, C. B. *The Political Theory of Possessive Individualism: Hobbes to Locke*. New York: Oxford University Press, 2011.
MacSweeney, Barry. *Elegy for January: Thomas Chatterton, 1752–1770*. London: Menard, 1970.
Makonnen, Atesede. "'The Actual Sight of the Thing': Blackness and the White Gaze in Early Nineteenth-Century British Literature." *Symbiosis: A Journal of Transatlantic Literary and Cultural Relations* 23, no. 1 (Spring 2019): 21–42.
Malchow, H. L. *Gothic Images of Race in Nineteenth-Century Britain*. Stanford, CA: Stanford University Press, 1996.
Mallipeddi, Ramesh. *Spectacular Suffering: Witnessing Slavery in the Eighteenth-Century British Atlantic*. Charlottesville: University of Virginia Press, 2016.
Mani, Lata. *Contentious Traditions: The Debate on Sati in Colonial India*. Berkeley: University of California Press, 1998.
Marsh, Ian. *Suicide: Foucault, History and Truth*. New York: Cambridge University Press, 2010.
Marshall, David. *The Figure of Theatre: Shaftesbury, Defoe, Adam Smith and George Eliot*. New York: Columbia University Press, 1986.
———. *The Surprising Effects of Sympathy: Marivaux, Diderot, Rousseau, and Mary Shelley*. Chicago: University of Chicago Press, 1988.
Marshall, P. David. *Celebrity and Power: Fame in Contemporary Culture*. Minneapolis: University of Minnesota Press, 2014.
Marshall, Tim. *Murdering to Dissect: Graverobbing, Frankenstein, and the Anatomy of Literature*. Manchester, UK: Manchester University Press, 1996.
Martinez, Jenny S. "Antislavery Courts and the Dawn of International Human Rights Law." *Yale Law Journal* 118, no. 3 (2008): 550–641.
Massachusetts Coalition for Suicide Prevention. *Widening the Lens: Exploring the Role of Social Justice in Suicide Prevention—A Racial Equity Toolkit*, 2019. https://www.masspreventssuicide.org/wp-content/uploads/2019/09/WideningTheLensToolkit.pdf.
Massardier-Kenney, Francoise. "Duras, Racism, and Class." In *Translating Slavery: Gender and Race in French Women's Writing, 1783–1823*, edited by Doris Y. Kadish and Francoise Massardier-Kenney, 185–93. Kent, OH: Kent State University Press, 1994.
Matthew, Patricia A. "Here on the Margins: My Academic Home." *PMLA* 130, no. 5 (2015): 1510–14.

———. "Serving Tea for a Cause." *Lapham's Quarterly*, February 28, 2018. https://www.laphamsquarterly.org/roundtable/serving-tea-cause.
Mbembe, Achille Joseph. "Necropolitics." Translated by Libby Meintjes. *Public Culture* 15, no. 1 (Winter 2003): 11–40.
McBride, Dwight A. *Impossible Witnesses: Truth, Abolitionism, and Slave Testimony*. New York: New York University Press, 2001.
McGavran, James Holt, Jr. "Felicia Hemans's Feminist Poetry of the Mid 1820s." *Women's Writing* 21, no. 4 (2014): 540–58.
McGuire, Kelly. *Dying to be English: Suicide Narratives and National Identity*. London: Pickering and Chatto, 2012.
McKittrick, Katherine. *Demonic Grounds: Black Women and the Cartographies of Struggle*. Minneapolis: University of Minnesota Press, 2006.
McLane, Maureen. *My Poets*. New York: Farrar, Straus and Giroux, 2012.
———. *Romanticism and the Human Sciences*. New York: Cambridge University Press, 2000.
McNerthney, Casey, and Amy Clancy. "Seattle Police Re-Examine Cobain Suicide, Develop Scene Photos." *KIRO 7*, March 20, 2014. https://www.kiro7.com/news/only-kiro-7-seattle-police-re-investigate-kurt-cob/81808273.
Mellor, Anne. "'Am I Not A Woman and a Sister?' Slavery, Romanticism and Gender." In *Romanticism, Race, and Imperial Culture, 1780–1834*, edited by Alan Richardson and Sonia Hofkosh, 311–29. Bloomington: Indiana University Press, 1996.
———. "*Frankenstein*, Racial Science, and the Yellow Peril." *Nineteenth-Century Contexts* 23, no. 1 (2001): 1–28.
Metropolitan Museum of Art. "Alexander McQueen: Savage Beauty." Accessed February 28, 2015, http://blog.metmuseum.org/alexandermcqueen.
Miles, Tiya, and Sharon P. Holland, eds. *Crossing Waters, Crossing Worlds: The African Diaspora in Indian Country*. Durham, NC: Duke University Press, 2006.
Miller, Christopher. *Blank Darkness: Africanist Discourse in French*. Chicago: University of Chicago Press, 1985.
Mills, Charles W. *Black Rights/White Wrongs: The Critique of Racial Liberalism*. New York: Oxford University Press, 2017.
———. *The Racial Contract*. Ithaca, NY: Cornell University Press, 1999.
Minois, Georges. *History of Suicide: Voluntary Death in Western Culture*. Translated by Lydia G. Cochrane. Baltimore: Johns Hopkins University Press, 2001.
Mitchell, Robin. "'*Ourika* mania': Interrogating Race, Class, Space, and Place in Early Nineteenth-Century France." *Africa and Black Diaspora: An International Journal* 10, no. 1 (2017): 85–95.
Mitter, Siddhartha. "'What Does it Mean to Be Black and Look at This?' A Scholar Reflects on the Dana Schutz Controversy."

Hyperallergic, March 24, 2017. https://hyperallergic.com/368012/what-does-it-mean-to-be-black-and-look-at-this-a-scholar-reflects-on-the-dana-schutz-controversy/.

Mohdin, Aamna. "UK's First Black Female History Professor to Research Bristol's Slavery Links." *Guardian*, October 30, 2019. https://www.theguardian.com/education/2019/oct/30/olivette-otele-uk-first-black-female-history-professor-to-research-bristol-slavery-links.

Moody, Joycelyn. *Sentimental Confessions: Spiritual Narratives of Nineteenth-Century African American Women*. Athens: University of Georgia Press, 2001.

Morgan, Jennifer. *Laboring Women: Reproduction and Gender in New World Slavery*. Philadelphia: University of Pennsylvania Press, 2004.

Moretti, Franco. *The Way of the World: The Bildungsroman in European Culture*. London: Verso, 1987.

Morris, Steven. "Bristol Celebrates its Poet Genius Who Died at Just 17." *Guardian*. March 30, 2020. https://www.theguardian.com/uk-news/2020/mar/30/bristol-celebrates-poet-thomas-chatterton-who-died-at-17

Moten, Fred. "Black Op." In *Stolen Life*, 155–160. Durham, NC: Duke University Press, 2018.

———. "Chromatic Saturation." In *The Universal Machine*, 140–246. Durham, NC: Duke University Press, 2018.

———. "Erotics of Fugitivity." In *Stolen Life*, 241–68. Durham, NC: Duke University Press, 2018.

———. "Knowledge of Freedom." In *Stolen Life*, 1–95. Durham, NC: Duke University Press, 2018.

Mulvey-Roberts, Marie. *Dangerous Bodies: Historicizing the Gothic Corporeal*. Manchester, UK: Manchester University Press 2016.

Murray, Alexander. *Suicide in the Middle Ages*. New York: Oxford University Press, 2009.

Newsweek. "Kurt Cobain: Poet of Alienation—How *Newsweek* Grappled with the Musician's Suicide in 1994." *Newsweek*, April 5, 2018. https://www.newsweek.com/kurt-cobain-poet-alienation-how-newsweek-grappled-musicians-suicide-1994-873712.

Norris, John. "Denzel Curry on his New Album 'Ta13oo,' Why Kurt Cobain is Glorified for the Wrong Reasons & His Connection to Trayvon Martin." *Billboard*, August 8, 2018. https://www.billboard.com/articles/columns/hip-hop/8469090/denzel-curry-ta13oo-album-clout-cobain-interview.

O'Connell, David. "*Ourika*: Black Face, White Mask." *French Review* 47, no. 6 (Spring 1974): 47–56.

Old Elizabeth. *Memoir of Old Elizabeth, A Colored Woman*. Philadelphia: Collins Printer, 1863. https://docsouth.unc.edu/neh/eliza1/eliza1.html.

Painter, Nell Irvin. *The History of White People*. New York: W. W. Norton, 2010.

Parisot, Eric. "Suicide Notes and Popular Sensibility in the Eighteenth-Century British Press." *Eighteenth-Century Studies* 47, no. 3 (2014): 277–91.
Patterson, Orlando. *Slavery and Social Death: A Comparative Study*. Cambridge, MA: Harvard University Press, 1985.
Paxton, Barbara. "Mammy Water: New World Origins?" *Baessler-Archiv, Neue Folge* 31 (1983): 407–46.
Perry, Imani. *Vexy Thing: On Gender and Liberation*. Durham, NC: Duke University Press, 2018.
Phillips, David P. "The Influence of Suggestion on Suicide: Substantive and Theoretical Implications of the Werther effect." *American Sociological Review* 39 (1974): 340–54.
Pierson, William D. "White Cannibals, Black Martyrs: Fear, Depression, and Religious Faith as Causes of Suicide among New Slaves." *Journal of Negro History* 62, no. 2 (April 1977): 147–59.
Pollin, B. R. "Fanny Godwin's Suicide Re-examined." *Etudes anglaises* 18, no. 3 (1965): 258–68.
Poovey, Mary. *The Proper Lady and the Woman Writer*. Chicago: University of Chicago Press, 1984.
Powell, Timothy. "Summoning the Ancestors: The Flying Africans' Story and Its Enduring Legacy." In *African American Life in the Georgia Lowcountry: The Atlantic World and the Gullah Geechee*, edited by Philip Morgan, 253–80. Athens: University of Georgia Press, 2010.
Prasad, Pratima. *Colonialism, Race, and the French Romantic Imagination*. New York: Routledge, 2009.
Pratt, Samuel Jackson. *Harvest-Home*. London: Richard Phillips, 1805.
Pressly, William L. *The Artist as Original Genius: Shakespeare's "Fine Frenzy" in Late Eighteenth-Century British Art*. Newark: University of Delaware Press, 2007.
Prince, Mary. *The History of Mary Prince, a West Indian Slave*. London: F. Westley and A. H. Davis, 1831. https://docsouth.unc.edu/neh/prince/prince.html.
Radford, Andrew, and Mark Sandy. "Introduction: Romanticism and the Victorians." In *Romantic Echoes in the Victorian Period*, edited by Andrew Radford and Mark Sandy, 1–15. Burlington, VT: Ashgate, 2008.
Radin, Margaret Jane. "Property and Personhood." *Stanford Law Review* 34, no. 5 (May 1982): 957–1015.
Rediker, Marcus. *The Slave Ship: A Human History*. New York: Penguin, 2007.
Reznikoff, Charles. *Chatterton, The Black Death*. London: Forgotten, 2012.
Richardson, Robbie. *The Savage and Modern Self: North American Indians in Eighteenth Century British Literature and Culture*. Toronto: University of Toronto Press, 2018.

Rifkin, Mark. *Fictions of Land and Flesh: Blackness, Indigeneity, Speculation*. Durham, NC: Duke University Press, 2019.
Rivers, Bryan. "'Revolting Burial': A Victorian Commentary on the Harriet Shelley Inquest." *Notes and Queries* 52, no. 4 (December 2005): 478–80.
——. "'Tenderly' and 'With Care': Thomas Hood's 'The Bridge of Sighs' and the Suicide of Harriet Shelley." *Notes and Queries* 53, no. 3 (September 2006): 327–29.
Robinson, Mary Darby. *A Letter to the Women of England on the Injustice of Mental Subordination*. London: Longman, 1799. https://romantic-circles.org/editions/robinson/index.html.
——. "The Negro Girl." In *Mary Robinson: Selected Poems*, edited by Judith Pascoe, 234–39. Peterborough, ON: Broadview, 1999.
——. "The Storm." *Morning Post and Fashionable World*, February 3, 1796. http://spenserians.cath.vt.edu/TextRecord.php?textsid=38639.
Rosenbaum, Nancy. *Another Liberalism: Romanticism and the Reconstruction of Liberal Thought*. Cambridge, MA: Harvard University Press, 1987.
Ross, Marlon B. *The Contours of Masculine Desire: Romanticism and the Rise of Women's Poetry*. New York: Oxford University Press, 1989
——. "The Race of/in Romanticism: Notes Toward a Critical Race Theory." In *Race, Romanticism, and the Atlantic*, edited by Paul Youngquist, 25–58. Burlington, VT: Ashgate, 2013.
Rossetti, Dante Gabriel. *The Complete Poetical Works of Dante Gabriel Rossetti*, edited by William M. Rossetti. Boston: Little, Brown, and Company, 1899.
Rubin, David S. *It's Only Rock and Roll: Rock and Roll Undercurrents in Contemporary Art*. New York: Prestel, 1996.
Russell, Charles Edward. *Thomas Chatterton, The Marvellous Boy: The Story of a Strange Life, 1752–1770*. New York: Moffatt, Yard, 1908.
Sackville-West, Vita. *Chatterton: A Drama in Three Acts*. London: Through Leaves, 2002.
Sancho, Ignatius. *Letters of the Late Ignatius Sancho, an African*. London: J. Nichols, 1782. https://docsouth.unc.edu/neh/sancho1/sancho1.html.
Sanderson, Richard K. "'Glutting the Maw of Death': Suicide and Procreation in *Frankenstein*." *South Central Review* 9, no. 2 (Summer 1992): 49–64.
Schuller, Kyla. *The Biopolitics of Feeling: Race, Sex, and Science in the Nineteenth Century*. Durham, NC: Duke University Press, 2018.
Severn, Joseph. *Joseph Severn: Letters and Memoirs*, edited by Grant F. Scott. New York: Routledge, 2016.
Sexton, Jared. "Ante-Anti-Blackness." *Lateral: Journal of the Cultural Studies Association* 1 (2012). http://csalateral.org/section/theory/ante-anti-blackness-afterthoughts-sexton/.

———. "People-of-Color Blindness: Notes on the Afterlife of Slavery." *Social Text* 28, no. 2 (2010): 31–56.

———. "The Social Life of Social Death: On Afro-Pessimism and Black Optimism." *InTensions* 5 (2011): 1–47.

———. "Unbearable Blackness." *Cultural Critique* 90 no. 1 (2015): 159–78.

Sharpe, Christina. *In the Wake: On Blackness and Being*. Durham, NC: Duke University Press, 2016.

Shelley, Mary. *Frankenstein*, edited by J. Paul Hunter. New York: W. W. Norton, 1995.

———. Vol. 1 of *The Journals of Mary Shelley, 1814–1844*, edited by Paula R. Feldman and Diana Scott-Kilvert. Oxford: Clarendon, 1987.

———. *The Original Frankenstein*, edited by Charles E. Robinson. New York: Vintage Classics, 2009.

Shelley, Percy Bysshe. "A Defence of Poetry." In *Shelley's Poetry and Prose*, edited by Neil Fraistat and Donald H. Reiman, 509–39. New York: W. W. Norton, 2002.

———. "A Fragment on Miracles." In *Shelley's Prose*, edited by David Lee Clark, 143–44. Bel Air, CA: New Amsterdam, 1988.

———. "On Love." In *Shelley's Poetry and Prose*, edited by Neil Fraistat and Donald H. Reiman, 302–4. New York: W. W. Norton, 2002.

———. "On the Devil, and Devils." In *Shelley's Prose*, edited by David Lee Clark, 264–74. Bel Air, CA: New Amsterdam, 1988.

———. "A Refutation of Deism," in *Shelley's Prose*, edited by David Lee Clark, 138-40. Bel Air, CA: New Amsterdam Books, 1988.

———. "Speculations on Morals." In *The Prose Works of Percy Bysshe Shelley*, edited by Richard Herne Shepherd, 194–207. London: Chatto and Windus, 1906.

Singleton, Henry, and Edward Orme. *Death of Chatterton*. Stipple engraving, 1794. London: National Portrait Gallery. http://www.npg.org.uk/collections/search/portrait/mw135838/Death-of-Chatterton.

Soderburg, Brandon. "The Rap on Kurt: Hood Pass 4 Life." *SPIN*, July 18, 2011. https://www.spin.com/2011/07/rap-kurt-hood-pass-4-life/.

Smallwood, Stephanie. *Saltwater Slavery: A Middle Passage from Africa to American Diaspora*. Cambridge, MA: Harvard University Press, 2007.

Smith, Adam. *Theory of Moral Sentiments*, edited by Knud Haakonssen. New York: Cambridge University Press, 2002.

Smith, Alan Lloyd. "'This Thing of Darkness': Racial Discourse in Mary Shelley's *Frankenstein*." *Gothic Studies* 6, no. 2 (2004): 208–22.

Smith, Valerie. *Not Just Race, Not Just Gender: Black Feminist Readings*. New York: Routledge, 1998.

Snyder, Terri L. *The Power to Die: Suicide and Slavery in British North America*. Chicago: University of Chicago Press, 2015.

———. "Suicide, Slavery, and Memory in North America." *Journal of American History* 97, no. 1 (June 2010): 39–62.

Somerset v. Stewart, 1 *Lofft* (King's Bench, 1772), 499–509. Available at Commonwealth Legal Information Institute. http://www.commonlii.org/.

Southey, Robert. "Poems on the Slave Trade." In *The Poetry of Slavery: An Anglo-American Anthology, 1764–1865*, edited by Marcus Wood, 214–18. New York: Oxford University Press, 2003.

Spencer, Anne. "Dunbar." In *The Book of American Negro Poetry, With an Essay on the Negro's Creative Genius*, edited by James Weldon Johnson, 174. New York: Harcourt, Brace, 1922.

Spillers, Hortense. "Mama's Baby, Papa's Maybe: An American Grammar Book." *Diacritics* 17, no. 2 (Summer 1987): 65–81.

Stewart, Catherine A. *Long Past Slavery: Representing Race in the Federal Writers' Project*. Chapel Hill: University of North Carolina Press, 2016.

Stoler, Ann Laura. *Race and the Education of Desire: Foucault's History of Sexuality and the Colonial Order of Things*. Durham, NC: Duke University Press, 1995.

Strauss, Neil. "Kurt Cobain's Downward Spiral: The Last Days of Nirvana's Leader." *Rolling Stone*, June 2, 1994. https://www.rollingstone.com/music/music-news/kurt cobains-downward-spiral-the-last-days-of-nirvanas-leader-99797.

Swaminathan, Srividhya, and Adam R. Beach, eds. *Invoking Slavery in the Eighteenth-Century British Imagination*. Burlington, VT: Ashgate, 2013.

Sypher, Wylie. "The African Prince in London." *Journal of the History of Ideas* 2, no. 2 (1941): 237–47.

Taylor, Eric Robert. *If We Must Die: Shipboard Insurrections in the Era of the Atlantic Slave Trade*. Baton Rouge: Louisiana State University Press, 2006.

Todd, Janet. *Death and the Maidens: Fanny Wollstonecraft and the Shelley Circle*. Berkeley: Counterpoint, 2007.

———. *Gender, Art and Death*. Cambridge: Blackwell, 1993.

———. "Reason and Sensibility in Mary Wollstonecraft's *The Wrongs of Woman*." *Frontiers* 5, no. 3 (1981): 17–20.

———. *Sensibility: An Introduction*. London: Methuen, 1986.

———. "Suicide and Biography." *Comparative Criticism* 25 (2004): 57–66.

Thomas, Helen. *Romanticism and Slave Narratives: Transatlantic Testimonies*. New York: Cambridge University Press, 2000.

Thompson, Ayanna. "RaceB4Race." Accessed May 17, 2020. https://www.ayannathompson.com/raceb4race.

Thorson, Jan, and Per-Arne Öberg. "Was There a Suicide Epidemic After Goethe's *Werther*?" *Archives of Suicide Research* 7, no. 1 (2003): 69–72.

Turner, Sasha. *Contested Bodies: Pregnancy, Childrearing, and Slavery in Jamaica*. Philadelphia: University of Pennsylvania Press, 2017.

Van Sant, Gus, dir. *Last Days*. New York: HBO Films, 2005.
Vendler, Helen. *The Odes of John Keats*. Cambridge, MA: Harvard University Press, 1983.
Victoria and Albert Museum. "Alexander McQueen: Savage Beauty—About the Exhibition." Accessed September 28, 2018, http://www.vam.ac.uk/content/exhibitions/exhibition-alexander-mcqueen-savage-beauty/about-the-exhibition.
Viswanathan, Gauri. *Masks of Conquest: Literary Study and British Rule in India*. New York: Columbia University Press, 1989.
Wagner, Bryan. *Disturbing the Peace: Black Culture and the Police After Slavery*. Cambridge, MA: Harvard University Press, 2009.
Waldau, Paul. "Will the Heavens Fall? De-Radicalizing the Precedent Breaking Decision." *Animal Law* 7 (2001): 75–117.
Wall, Cheryl A. *Women of the Harlem Renaissance*. Bloomington: Indiana University Press, 1995.
Wallis, Henry. *The Death of Chatterton*. Painting, ca. 1856. Yale Center for British Art, Paul Mellon Collection. http://collections.britishart.yale.edu/vufind/Record/1665521.
Walker, Daniel E. "Suicidal Tendencies: African Transmigration in the History and Folklore of the Americas." *Griot* 18, no. 2 (Spring 1999): 10–18.
Ware, Vron. *Beyond the Pale: White Women, Racism, and History*. 2nd ed. London: Verso, 2015.
Washington, Mary Helen, ed. *Black-Eyed Susans and Midnight Birds: Stories By and About Black Women*. New York: Doubleday, 1989.
Watt, Jeffrey R. "Introduction." In *From Sin to Insanity: Suicide in Early Modern Culture*, edited by Jeffrey R. Watt, 1–9. Ithaca, NY: Cornell University Press, 2004.
Weaver, John, and David Wright. *Histories of Suicide: International Perspectives on Self Destruction in the Modern World*. Toronto: University of Toronto Press, 2009.
Weheliye, Alexander. *Habeas Viscus: Racializing Assemblages, Biopolitics, and Black Feminist Theories of the Human*. Durham, NC: Duke University Press, 2014.
Welchman, Jennifer. "Locke on Slavery and Inalienable Rights." *Canadian Journal of Philosophy* 25, no. 1 (March 1995): 67–81.
West, Elizabeth J. *African Spirituality in Black Women's Fiction: Threaded Visions of Memory, Community, Nature, and Being*. Lanham, MD: Lexington, 2011.
West, Raphael Lamar, and Francesco Bartolozzi. *Unknown Man Called Thomas Chatterton*. Engraving, 1801. National Portrait Gallery, London. http://www.npg.org.uk/collections/search/portrait/mw35507/The-Death-of-Chatterton.

Wert, Justin J. *Habeas Corpus in America: The Politics of Individual Right.* Lawrence, KS: University Press of Kansas, 2011.
Wheatley, Phillis. "On Imagination." In *The Collected Works of Phillis Wheatley*, edited by John C. Shields, 65–69. New York: Oxford University Press, 1989.
White, Jane Baber. *Lessons Learned from a Poet's Garden.* Hoboken, NJ: Blackwell, 2011.
White, R. S. *Natural Rights and the Birth of Romanticism in the 1790s.* New York: Palgrave Macmillan, 2005.
Whitehead, James. *Madness and the Romantic Poet.* New York: Oxford University Press, 2017.
Wilderson Frank B., III. *Afropessimism.* New York: W. W. Norton, 2020.
———. *Red, White, and Black: Cinema and the Structure of U.S. Antagonisms.* Durham, NC: Duke University Press, 2010.
Williams, Carolyn D. "'Inhumanly Brought Back to Life and Misery': Mary Wollstonecraft, *Frankenstein*, and the Royal Humane Society." *Women's Writing* 8, no. 2 (2001): 213–34.
———. "'The Luxury of Doing Good': Benevolence, Sensibility, and the Royal Humane Society." In *Pleasure in the Eighteenth Century*, edited by Roy Porter and Marie Mulvey Roberts, 77–107. Basingstoke, UK: Macmillan, 1996.
Williamson, Michael T. "Impure Affections: Felicia Hemans's Elegiac Poetry and Contaminated Grief." In *Felicia Hemans: Reimagining Poetry in the Nineteenth Century*, edited by Nanora Sweet and Julie Melnyk, 19–35. London: Palgrave Macmillan, 2001.
Wilson, Eric. *How to Make a Soul: The Wisdom of John Keats*, Evanston, IL: Northwestern University Press, 2015.
Wind, Astrid. "'Adieu to All': The Death of the American Indian at the Turn of the Eighteenth Century." *Symbiosis: A Journal of Anglo-American Literary Relations*, 2, no. 1 (April 1998): 39–55.
Wolfe, Patrick. *Traces of History: Elementary Structures of Race.* London: Verso, 2016.
Wolfson, Susan. *Borderlines: The Shifting of Gender in British Romanticism.* Stanford, CA: Stanford University Press, 2006.
Wollstonecraft, Mary. *Letters Written in Sweden, Norway, and Denmark.* New York: Oxford World's Classics, 2009.
———. *Mary, A Fiction and The Wrongs of Women, or Maria*, edited by Michelle Faubert. Peterborough, ON: Broadview, 2012.
———. *A Vindication of the Rights of Woman.* New York: Oxford World's Classics, 2008.
Wood, Marcus. *Blind Memory: Visual Representations of Slavery in England and America, 1780–1865.* New York: Routledge, 2000.

———. *The Horrible Gift of Freedom: Atlantic Slavery and the Representation of Emancipation*. Athens: University of Georgia Press, 2010.

———. *Slavery, Empathy, and Pornography*. New York: Oxford University Press, 2002.

Woolf, Jake. "The White Sunglasses You're Seeing Everywhere Now Have a New Name." *GQ*, July 25, 2017. https://www.gq.com/story/kurt-cobain-sunglasses-clout-coggles.

Wordsworth, William. "Resolution and Independence." In *The Major Works*, edited by Stephen Gill, 260–65. New York: Oxford World's Classics, 2008.

Wright, Tony. *Citizens and Subjects: An Essay on British Politics*. New York: Routledge, 2003.

Wu, Duncan. *30 Great Myths About the Romantics*. Chichester, UK: John Wiley, 2015.

Wynter, Sylvia. "On Disenchanting Discourse: 'Minority' Literary Criticism and Beyond." *Cultural Critique* 7 (Autumn 1987): 207–44.

———. "Unsettling the Coloniality of Being/Power/Truth/Freedom: Towards the Human, After Man, Its Overrepresentation—An Argument." *CR: The New Centennial Review* 3, no. 3 (Fall 2003): 257–337.

Young, Elizabeth. *Black Frankenstein: The Making of an American Metaphor*. New York: New York University Press, 2008.

Young, Jason R. "All God's Children Had Wings: The Flying African in History, Literature, and Lore." *Journal of Africana Religions* 5, no. 1 (2017): 50–70.

Youngquist, Paul. "The African Queen." In *Race, Romanticism, and the Atlantic*, edited by Paul Youngquist, 79–106. Burlington, VT: Ashgate, 2013.

———. "The Afro Futurism of DJ Vassa." *European Romantic Review* 16, no. 2 (2005): 181–92.

———. "Introduction." In *Race, Romanticism, and the Atlantic*, edited by Paul Youngquist, 1–24. Burlington, VT: Ashgate, 2013.

Youngquist, Paul, and Fran Botkin. "Black Romanticism: Romantic Circulations." In *Circulations: Romanticism and the Black Atlantic*, edited by Paul Youngquist and Fran Botkin. College Park, MD: Romantic Circles Praxis Series, 2011. http://www.rc.umd.edu/praxis/circulations/HTML/praxis.2011.youngquist.

Youngquist, Paul, and Joel Pace, eds. "Black Romanticism." Special issue, *Studies in Romanticism* 56.1 (Spring 2017): 3–123.

Zogbé, Mama (Vivien Hunter-Hindrew). *Mami Wata: Africa's Ancient God/dess, Unveiled*. Martinez, GA: Mami Wata Healers Society of North America, 2007.

Index

abolitionist movement and writings, 4–7, 11–14, 17, 19–20, 23–27; 38–40, 44, 48, 55–57, 62–64, 69, 71, 76–77, 81, 90, 115, 123. Duras on, 62–63; *The Dying Negro* and, 25; Equiano on, 77; iconography of, 144n68; Robinson and, 57; and suicide, 4
academia, western, romanticism and, 12
Adanson, Michel, 36
Adonais (Shelley), 119
Aesthetics of suicide, 15, 41, 75, 122
Africa, Equiano on, 91
Afropessimism, 4, 9–10, 19, 24, 38, 89, 97, 114–115; term, 137n69. *See also* Frank B. Wilderson III; Jared Sexton
afterlife: of slavery, 4, 40, 44, 128; literary afterlife, 21, 118–119; *The Dying Negro* on, 40, 42–45. *See also* literary immortality; posthumous
agency: Equiano on, 86, 90; *Frankenstein* on, 115; Jackson on, 71; Mami Wata and, 86; Robinson on, 58; versus social death, 43; strategies of, 39

Ahmed, Sara, 15, 54
alienation: Duras on, 60; natal, 70, 154n89
Allewaert, Monique, 84, 156n42
American Revolution, 16, 38.
Ann and Mary, 26.
analogy, ruse of, 9. *See also* Frank B. Wilderson III
Anderson, Amanda, 136n67
Andrews, Kehinde, 136n63
animals: Equiano on, 82–89; Keats on, 93–95; and personhood, 25; and suicide, 2. *See also* fish; birds
anthropomorphism, in epitaphs, 41–42
antiblackness, 11; suicide tropes and, 4–5
antiracist thought, 12, 159n85
apostrophe, 144n70; in epitaphs, 42
aristocratic heroine, Duras on, 59, 63
Ashanti, and suicide, 40
Atlantic Ocean: and blackness, 74–75; Equiano on, 76–89; Gilroy on, 76; Glissant on, 87–88
Augustine of Hippo, 142n47
autobiography, Jackson and, 69–71

193

Badiou, Alain, 89
Bailey, Benjamin, 158n70
Baker, Samuel, 75
Balzac, Honoré de, 1–2
Baraka, Amiri, 73, 75
Barthes, Roland, 166n22
Bartolozzi, Francesco, 120
Baucom, Ian, 75
Behn, Aphra, 5, 41, 139n5
Bennett, Andrew, 15, 118
Bernier, Celeste-Marie, 35–36
Bicknell, John, 20, 23–26, 33, 35–45, 58, 76. *See also* Thomas Day and *The Dying Negro*
birds, Keats on, 93–95
Birk, Sandow, 124, 127. See also *The Death of Kurt Cobain*
Black Atlantic, 76, 88. *See also* Paul Gilroy and Olaudah Equiano
black life, 10, 82; Equiano on, 77, 86–87, 91; Moten on, 89
blackness, 5, 17, 102; and Atlantic Ocean, 74–75; and criminality, 145n79; and death, 4, 9–10, 42–43; Duras on, 60; *The Dying Negro* and, 41; Equiano on, 76–82, 91; fungibility of, 103; humanity and, 8; liberalism and, 113–16; romanticism and, 96; term, 137n69, 154n11; Wagner on, 76; Wilderson on, 4, 9–10, 37
black optimism, 10, 19; and Equiano, 89–92; term, 137n69. *See also* Fred Moten
black radical tradition, 137n67
Blackstone, William, 48, 145n79
black studies, 16–19
black women, 47–49, 53, 59–64, 69–76; and suicide, 47–71, 153n84
Blake, William, 122
Botkin, Fran, 16
bourgeoisie, 4–5, 14, 21–22, 51–53, 63, 67, 71, 118, 122–23;

bourgeois white male individualism, 5, 21–22, 122; myth of romantic suicide and, 118; and romanticism, 14–15. *See also* bourgeoisie
"Bridge of Sighs, The" (Hood), 99
"Bride of the Greek Isle, The" (Hemans), 67–68, 153n82
Bristol, 128, 167n41
Bristow, Joseph, 122
British and suicide, 2, 6, 78, 100, 132n16
British romantics: and Chatterton, 119–23; cultural context of, 5–11; and racism, 12–14, 18; and sympathy, 103; and water imagery, 75. *See also* romanticism
Brown, Charles, 92
Brown, Ron, 121
Brown, Vincent, 43
Brown, William Wells, 5, 73–76, 153n84
Byron, George Gordon, lord, 1–2, 114, 132n16

Cachexia Africana, 78. *See also* George Davidson
Cambrian, The, 101
canonical romanticism, 4, 12, 14, 16, 93, 118–19, 122. *See also* British romantics; romanticism
Carby, Hazel V., 53
Carey, Brycchan, 26, 143n63
celebration, black thought and, 89
Chander, Manu Samriti, 12, 14, 103
Charles I, king of England, 28
Chatterton, Thomas, 5–6, 15–16, 21–23, 45, 117–28, 167n41
Chatterton's suicide, 119, 121–122. *See also* Thomas Chatterton
Cheyne, George, 6, 78
Christianity, 6–7; Duras on, 60–61, 63; *The Dying Negro* on, 33, 35–37, 40, 142n50, 143n63; Equiano on,

90–91; and suicide, 133n22, 142n47
class: Duras on, 59, 62–63; myths and, 166n22; Robinson on, 54–56; and romanticism, 14; Wollstonecraft on, 51–52
Clotel; or the President's Daughter (Brown), 5, 73–76, 153n84
"Clout Cobain" (Curry), 125–28. *See also* Kurt Cobain
Cobain, Kurt, 21, 119, 124–28
Coëtnempren, Guy de, 63
Coleman, Bonnie Watson, 168n42
Coleridge, Samuel Taylor, 94, 98, 119, 122
collective suicide, 80. *See also* Igbo Landing
colonialism, 8, 17, 27, 36, 52, 55–56, 60, 69, 86, 106; and romanticism, 12–14
Commander, Michelle D., 86
Congressional Black Caucus (US), 128
contracts, Locke on, 31
Cooper, James Fenimore, 65
corporations, and personhood, 25
coverture, laws of, 48
criminality, and blackness, 145n79
Cross, Charles, 124–25, 166n26
Cugoano, Ottobah, 156n32
culture: and resurrection, 100; and suicide, 2–3, 5–11, 39
Curry, Denzel, 125–28
Curtis, Ian, 119

Davidson, George, 78
Davis, Henry George, 99
Day, Iyko, 10
Day, Thomas, 20, 23–26, 33, 35–45, 58, 76. *See also* John Bicknell and *The Dying Negro*
Deans, Zev, 125–26
death, 10–11; and blackness, 4, 9–10, 42–43; Equiano on, 76; Hemans on, 64–68; Moten on, 31–32; Native Americans and, 66; and water tropes, 92. *See also* social death
Death of Chatterton, The (Wallis), 124
Death of Kurt Cobain, The (Birk), 124, 127
Delamayne, Thomas Hallie, 30
Deneen, Patrick, 134n46
Destroyer (LaValle), 21, 97–98, 114–16
Diaby, Bakary, 12–13, 16
Dicey, A. V., 28
Drescher, Seymour, 35
Drewal, Henry John, 157n51
Duras, Claire de, 20, 49, 54, 59–64, 67, 71; background of, 63
Durkheim, Émile, 133n20
Drug use, 125–27. *See also* Kurt Cobain; War on Drugs
Dying Negro, The (Day and Bicknell), 20, 23–45, 48, 58, 76; influence of, 25, 44–45
Dykes, Eva Beatrice, 12–13

Eagleton, Terry, 14
Eau de Werther, 2. *See also The Sorrows of Young Werther*
ecology: Equiano on, 82–89, 91; term, 88
economic issues: Locke on, 29; Robinson on, 55; Shelley (Mary) on, 99
Eden, William, 146n79
Education: Duras on, 59; *Frankenstein* on, 105–6, 109–10; literary, and control, 13–14, 109; Robinson on, 56–57; Wollstonecraft on, 50
Elegiac Sonnets (Charlotte Smith), 94
Ellis, Cristin, 159n85

Ellis, Markham, 148n7
Ellison, Ralph, 137n67
emotions: Chatterton and Werther and, 5; Duras on, 60; Equiano on, 76; *Frankenstein* on, 111; Jackson on, 70
Endymion (John Keats), 119
English Malady, The (Cheyne), 6, 78. See also methods of suicide
enlightenment: and suicide, 6; term, 137n69
enslavement: England and, 26–27; *Frankenstein* on, 113–14; Hemans on, 153n82; Locke on, 31–32, 34–35, 141n33; versus marriage, 48–49; Moten on, 31–32; Robinson on, 55; Wollstonecraft on, 52–53. See also trade in enslaved Africans; Middle Passage
epistemology: Glissant on, 88; Weheliye on, 44
epitaphs, 41–42; *The Dying Negro* as, 144n69; of Keats, 73, 92; of Shelley, 92
Equiano, Olaudah, 75–89
Estwick, Samuel, 30–31
exclusion: *Frankenstein* on, 107, 115; LaValle on, 114–15; myth of romantic suicide and, 118

Fanon, Frantz, 60, 115
fashion: Goethe and, 2; McQueen and, 2–3
Faubert, Michelle, 48, 53, 119–20
Feder, Rachel, 101
Federal Writers' Project, 80. See also Floyd White; Igbo Landing; St. Simon's Island
Feldman, Paula R., 98
felony, term, 145n79
Ferguson, Moira, 52
Festa, Lynn, 40
Filmer, Robert, 31

fish, Equiano on, 83–85
Five English Poets (Rossetti), 122
Flaxman, John, 121–22
flesh: Spillers on, 44, 81; Weheliye on, 44, 81–82
flight: Equiano on, 85; African folktales on, 80, 86, 156n32; Keats on, 95
Fordyce, James, 52–53
forfeiture, 99, 145n79
Frankenstein (Shelley), 21, 97–116
Franklin, Benjamin, 100
freedom, 5; black imagination and, 95–96; *The Dying Negro* and, 33–38; Equiano on, 81, 87; Hume on, 9; Locke on, 32, 34–35; Moten on, 31–32; Wood on, 34
free will, Hume on, 7
French identity, Duras on, 59–64
French revolution, 62–63
Friedrich, Caspar David, 2–3
friendship, *Frankenstein* on, 107–12
futurity, Equiano on, 81

Galvani, Luigi, 100
Gates, Henry Louis, Jr., 8
gender: and romantic writers, 12, 14; and suicide, 47–71, 130n5, 146n1; and whiteness, 15
genius, suicide myth and, 3, 15–16, 117–23
geophagy, 78. See also George Davidson; *Cachexia Africana*
Georgics (Virgil), 93–94
Ghana, 86
Giaour, The (Byron), 1
gift, term, Wood on, 34
Gilroy, Paul, 76, 88. See also Black Atlantic
Girard, René, 123
Glissant, Édouard, 87–88
Gloster, Marcus, 125

Index

Godwin, William, 50, 98
Goethe, Johann Wolfgang von, 2, 5–6, 106, 124
Gorton, John, 5
Goslee, Nancy Moore, 152n76
Greeson, Jennifer Rae, 31, 141n33
Gronniosaw, James Albert Ukawsaw, 153n86
Groom, Nick, 122
Grossman, Allen, 93–94
Gutzman, Kevin, 28

habeas corpus, 23–45; history of, 27; term, 29
Habeas Corpus Act of 1679, 27–29
habeas viscus, term, 24–25, 44
Haitian revolution, 6, 16, 38, 62–66
Halliday, Paul, 24
Harney, Stefano, 135n46
Hartman, Saidiya, 11, 17–18, 39, 103, 113
Hazlitt, William, 117
Hemans, Felicia, 20, 49, 64–68, 71
Hernani (Hugo), 119
Hessell, Nikki, 138n75
Hickman, Jared, 16, 114
Higonnet, Margaret, 48, 56, 132n18, 152n76
hip-hop, and Cobain, 125–28
Holland, Sharon Patricia, 35, 44, 82–83
Hood, Thomas, 99
hooks, bell, 137n67
Hugo, Victor, 16, 119
humanity, 5; Allewaert on, 84; blackness and, 8; Brown on, 73–74; *The Dying Negro* on, 36; Equiano on, 82–89, 92; *Frankenstein* on, 115; Keats on, 95; LaValle on, 115; Orpheus and, 93; personhood and, 26; Robinson on, 57; Snyder on, 80; Weheliye on, 44; Wilderson on, 4, 9–10

Hume, David, 7–11, 97–98, 100, 102–4, 113, 161n25
Hunter, John, 100

Igbo, 78
Igbo Landing, 80. *See also* St. Simon's Island
imagination: of alternatives, 44, 96; black, 95–96; and Chatterton's death, 120; Shelley (Percy) on, 104
Imlay, Fanny, 100–101, 160n16. *See also* suicide notes
Immerwahr, John, 8
Incesticide (Nirvana), 124. *See also* Kurt Cobain, Nirvana
"Indian Woman's Death Song" (Hemans), 65–67
individualism, 4–5; 14, 45, 76, 98, 113, 123; *The Dying Negro* on, 33; *Frankenstein* on, 107–12; Glissant on, 87–88; habeas corpus and, 28; Locke on, 32–33; myth of romantic suicide and, 5. *See also* bourgeois white male individualism
individual rights, Hume on, 7, 9
inhabitants of the deep, 93; Equiano on, 80–82, 85, 92
interdisciplinary studies, and romanticism, 16–17
Interesting Narrative of the Life of Olaudah Equiano, The (Equiano), 20–21 71, 75–77, 79, 81–82, 84, 89–90
interracial relationships: Duras on, 61–62; *The Dying Negro* on, 40
invisibility, 15, 137n67; Wollstonecraft and, 52–53
isolation, 21, 111–12

Jackson, Mattie J., 49, 69–71, 100
Jamaica, 8, 26
Jay-Z, 125
Jefferson, Thomas, 73–74

Johnson, Barbara, 41–42, 144n70
Jones, Shelley, 56

Keating, William, 65
Keats, John, 1–2, 21, 73, 76, 92–96, 117–22, 158n70; and Chatterton, 119; Spencer on, 117
Kelly, Gary, 64
Kesselring, K. J., 145n79
Knowles, John, 26
Koh, Adeline, 60–61
Kool Keith, 125
Kramnick, Isaac, 29
Kweli, Talib, 125

labor, Locke on, 28
Lamar, Kendrick, 125
Last Days (Van Sant), 124
"Last Song of Sappho, The" (Hemans), 67–68
LaValle, Victor, 21, 97–98, 114–16
Lee, Debbie, 114
legal issues: felony, 145n79; and gender, 48–49; personhood, 25; *Somerset v. Stewart*, 23–45; writ, 93
Letter to the Women of England on the Injustice of Mental Subordination (Robinson), 54–55
liberal, term, 134n46
liberal arts, 134n46
Liberal subjectivity, 3, 21, 25, 31–44, 98, 102, 109, 111, 125. *See also* bourgeois white male individualism; individualism; "Man"
liberalism, 3–5, 7, 11–12, 16–22, 24–25, 29, 33, 37, 41–42, 44, 55, 59, 63–63, 66, 68–69, 74–76, 81–82, 87, 89, 91, 96–97, 101–2, 109, 113, 115–16, 123, 126; Anderson on, 136n67; blackness and, 113–16; *Frankenstein* on, 106–7; Locke and, 29; myth of romantic suicide and, 118; romanticism and, 17–18; social life and, 44–45; suicide and, 102; women writers and, 47–71
liberty, 23–45
life. *See* black life; social life
Lil Peep, 125
Lincoln, Abraham, 27
Lincoln, Bruce, 164n4
literary genius, 3, 5, 15–16, 19, 21, 92, 118–19, 122–23, 128
literary immortality, 15, 117
Locke, John, 20, 25, 28–34, 141n33; influence of, 29
Lootens, Tricia, 49, 53, 130n5, 153n82
love, Shelley (Percy) on, 107–8
Love, Courtney, 166n26
Lyrical Tales (Robinson), 55

MacDonald, Michael, 39
Magna Carta, 30
Makonnen, Atesede, 16
Malchow, H. L., 114
Mami Wata, 85–86, 93, 157n50–51
"Man," 17, 26; *The Dying Negro* on, 36; Equiano on, 90; Hume on, 10; Locke on, 28; sacrifice and, 123; Wynter on, 8
marginality, 137n67
marriage: Duras on, 60–61; Wollstonecraft on, 51–53; analogy to slavery, 48–49
Marshall, David, 103
Marshall, Rebecca N., 122
Marshall, Tim, 100
martyrdom: Chatterton and, 122–23; *The Dying Negro* on, 35–37; Equiano on, 77
Matthew, Patricia A., 16
Mbembe, Achille, 77
McBride, Dwight, 16
McDonald, Michael, 6
McGuire, Kelly, 6, 48
McLane, Maureen, 107

McQueen, Alexander, 2–3, 119
mental illness, 6–7, 18
Meredith, George, 120
Metamorphoses (Ovid), 93
Methodism, and suicide, 133n22
methodology, 11–19
Middle Passage, 75–76, 85, 96; Baraka on, 73, 75; Equiano on, 79–80; Wilderson on, 11. *See also* Black Atlantic; slave trade; Zong Massacre
Mills, Charles W., 18
Mitchell, Robin, 59
modernity. *See* liberalism
"Monody on the Death of Thomas Chatterton" (Coleridge), 119
Moody, Joycelyn, 69
Morgan, C. Lloyd, 2
Moten, Fred, 10, 17, 31–32, 42, 89, 95, 135n46, 137n69, 154n11. *See also* black optimism
MTV Video Music Awards, 126
Mulvey-Roberts, Marie, 114
Murphy, Terrance R., 6
Murray, William, 27. See also *Somerset v. Stewart*
myth(s): ideological functions of, 3, 123, 164n4, 166n22; term, 119
myth of romantic suicide, 2, 5, 15–16, 18–19, 21; Chatterton and, 117–23; Cobain and, 124–28; Curry on, 128; ideological functions of, 5, 118–23; McQueen and, 2–3, 118

natal alienation, 70; and social death, 154n89
Native Americans: Hemans on, 65–66; Wilderson on, 9–10
"Negro Girl, The" (Robinson), 55–59
Nevermind (Nirvana), 125. *See also* Kurt Cobain, Nirvana
nightingale, Keats on, 93–94

"Nightingale, The: A Conversation Poem" (Coleridge), 94
Nirvana, 124–26. *See also* Kurt Cobain

ocean. *See* Atlantic Ocean
"Ode to a Nightingale" (Keats), 1, 93–96
"Of National Characters" (Hume), 8
Old Elizabeth, 153n86
"On Love" (Percy Shelley), 21, 102, 107–9, 113
On Suicide (Hume) 7–11, 97, 113–14
ontological blackness, 4, 9, 24–25, 41–44, 48, 76, 81–82, 86–87, 97, 114. *See also* Afropessimism, Frank B. Wilderson III, Fred Moten, black optimism
optimism. *See* black optimism
Orme, Edward, 120
Oroonoko (Behn), 5, 41
Orpheus, 93–94
Otele, Olivette, 167n41
Ourika (Duras), 59–64, 71
Ourika, Charlotte Catherine Benezet, 59
Ovid, 93–94

Pace, Joel, 16
paintings: of Chatterton's death, 120–22; of Cobain's death, 124; by Turner, 75
parahuman, Allewaert on, 84, 156n42
Parisot, Eric, 39
patriarchy, 15; Hemans and, 68; Robinson on, 59; and white supremacy, 54–64
Patrickson, Proctor, 98–99. *See also* William Godwin
Patterson, Orlando, 43, 70

personhood, 4, 18, 20–21, 29–33, 140n24; *The Dying Negro* on, 37–42; and epitaphs, 42–45; legal issues in, 24–26. *See also* Afropessimism; black optimism; John Locke
personification, in epitaphs, 41–42
Phillips, David, 132n15
Philomela, 93–94
photographs, of Cobain death scene, 127
Pitt, William, 27
Plath, Sylvia, 130n5
poetry: Brown and, 74; Chatterton and, 117–18; *The Dying Negro*, 23–45; epitaphs, 41–42; Equiano and, 89–92; *Frankenstein* on, 109; Hemans and, 64–68; Jackson and, 70–71; Keats and, 92–96; Robinson and, 54–59; Wheatley and, 96
politics: *The Dying Negro* on, 33–38, 41; sentimentalism and, 39; suicide and, 3–4, 6, 16, 23–45
posthumanism, 159n85
posthumous: fame, 16, 76, 92, 118–119, 124; haunting, 75. *See also* afterlife; literary immortality
Prasad, Pratima, 61
Pratt, Samuel Jackson, 100
Pressly, William L., 120
Prince, Mary, 47, 153n86
property: Estwick on, 31; Locke on, 28–33; marriage laws and, 48; personhood and, 25; types of, 30; Wollstonecraft on, 51
"Properzia Rossi" (Hemans), 67–68
prosopopoeia, in epitaphs, 42

race: and gender, 47–71; Hemans on, 65–68. *See also under* black; white
racialization, definition of, 25–26
racism: Curry on, 126; Duras on, 60; Hume and, 8; romantic writers and, 12–14, 18; Shelley (Percy) and, 103; and suicide, 128
Radford, Andrew, 120, 122
Radin, Margaret Jane, 140n24
Rankin, John, 39
rationality: Duras on, 59–60, 62; in epitaphs, 42; Hume on, 7; and personhood, 25; Robinson on, 54, 56–58; and suicide, 6, 24; Wollstonecraft on, 50–52
reader: *Frankenstein* on, 106; Keats and, 94–95
reading: *Frankenstein* on, 109–10; Shelley (Percy) on, 104
reason. *See* rationality
Rediker, Marcus, 81
relation, ethic of, Equiano and, 82–83, 87
religion: Duras on, 60–61, 63; *The Dying Negro* on, 33, 35–37, 40; Equiano on, 90–91; Hume on, 7; Mami Wata, 85–86; and suicide, 6, 133n22, 142n47
reputation, 93; Chatterton and, 117–23; Cobain and, 124–28; Keats and, 92–96
residence time, 83
resistance, Equiano on, 81, 86
revenge, *The Dying Negro* on, 37
Rifkin, Mark, 10
Robinson, Mary, 20, 49, 54–59, 63, 67, 71
romanticism: blackness and, 96; Equiano and, 76–82; interdisciplinary studies and, 16–17; term, 14, 137n69. *See also* British romantics
romantic suicide. *See* myth of romantic suicide
Ross, Marlon, 12, 16
Rossetti, Dante Gabriel, 122
Royal Humane Society, 99–100, 110

sacrifice, Chatterton as, 123
Sancho, Ignatius, 153n86
Sanderson, Richard K., 160n17
Sandler, Matt, 16
Sandy, Mark, 120, 122
Sappho, 67–68
Schiller, Friedrich, 65
Schneider, Rebecca, 16
Schöning, Maria Elonora, 98–99
Schuller, Kyla, 148n7
science, Shelley (Mary) and, 100, 105
Scott-Kilvert, Diana, 98
self-consciousness: Duras on, 60; and personhood, 25
sensibility, 39; Duras on, 59, 61; Jackson on, 69–71; Robinson on, 57–58; term, 50, 148n7; Wollstonecraft on, 49–54
sentimentalism, 39; Jackson on, 70; term, 148n7
Severn, Joseph, 92, 158n70
Sexton, Jared, 10, 44, 88–89. *See also* Afropessimism; black optimism
Shakespeare, William, 92
Sharp, Granville, 26
Sharpe, Christina, 10–11, 83, 114–15, 134n45
Shelley, Harriet, 99–100
Shelley, Mary, 21, 97–116, 161n25
Shelley, Percy, 92, 98, 117, 119, 161n25; on sympathy, 102–8
"Sicilian Captive, The" (Hemans), 67–68
Singleton, Henry, 120–22
slavery. *See* enslavement; trade in enslaved Africans
Smith, Adam, 98, 102–5
Smith, Alan Lloyd, 114
Smith, Charlotte, 94
Snyder, Terri L., 40–41, 78, 80
social death, 32, 35; *The Dying Negro* on, 40, 42–45; *Destroyer* on, 115–116; Equiano on, 75, 87, 89; *Frankenstein* on, 101, 106; gender and, 64; Moten on, 10; natal alienation and, 154n89; Sexton on, 44; Wilderson on, 4, 10. *See also* Orlando Patterson
social life, 24–25, 32; Equiano on, 77, 86; *Frankenstein* on, 106; white women writers and, 67
Somerset, James, 23–24, 26, 142n50
Somerset v. Stewart, 20, 23–24, 26–27, 30, 33–36
Sorrows of Young Werther The (Goethe), 2, 5–6, 23, 45, 50, 106, 124
Southey, Robert, 23
sovereignty: Hume on, 7; Locke on, 31–33; Mbembe on, 77; Wilderson on, 9–10
"Speculations on Morals" (Percy Shelley), 21, 102–4, 107
Spelman, Elizabeth, 53
Spencer, Anne, 117–18
Spillers, Hortense, 44, 81, 147n4
St. Simon's Island, GA, 80. *See also* Igbo Landing
Staël, Germaine de, 132n16
Stewart, Charles, 26. See also *Somerset v. Stewart*
Stoler, Ann Laura, 65
"Storm, The" (Robinson), 55–59
Story of Mattie J. Jackson, The (Jackson), 20, 49, 69–71
suffering of others, 39, 53, 64, 75; Brown on, 73–74
suicidal genius. See myth of romantic suicide
suicidal slave figure, 4–5, 11, 37, 44–45; term, 131n11
suicide, 1–22; African American youth and, 128, 168n42; Brown on, 73–76; Chatterton and, 117–23; Cobain and, 124–28;

suicide *(continued)*, culture and beliefs on, 5–11, 39; Duras on, 60; Durkheim on, 133n20; *The Dying Negro* on, 33–38; Equiano on, 77–78, 84, 90; Hemans on, 64–68; Keats and, 158n70; Locke on, 28–33; methods of, Africans and, 78, 81; prevention of, 99–100, 166n26; Robinson on, 55–59; Shelley (Mary) and, 97–116; Wollstonecraft on, 47–71, 100. See also myth of romantic suicide

suicide notes, 37–42; by Chatterton, 119–20; by Cobain, 124; by Imlay, 101; publication of, 2, 38–39

Sunbury, Jonah, 80

sympathy, 97–116; Brown on, 73–74; *The Dying Negro* on, 40; *Frankenstein* on, 113; Shelley (Percy) on, 102–8; and suicide notes, 39

texts: anxieties about, 162n41; Shelley (Percy) on, 104. See also Werther effect

"Tiber, Niles, and Thames" (Rossetti), 122

Thomas Chatterton Taking the Bowl of Poison from the Spirit of Despair (Flaxman), 121

Thompson, Ayanna, 135n48

Thompson, L. S., 69

Todd, Janet, 51

trade in enslaved Africans: Bristol and, 167n41; Glissant on, 87–88; Robinson on, 55; Zong Massacre, 74–75. See also enslavement; Middle Passage

transmigration, 41, 68; Equiano on, 77–78, 90. See also Mami Wata; Igbo Landing

Trippie Redd, 125

Turner, Ellen, 69–70

Turner, J. M. W., 75

Turner, Sasha, 147n4

Van Sant, Gus, 124

Vendler, Helen, 95

Vigny, Alfred de, 119

Vindication of the Rights of Woman, A (Wollstonecraft), 50–54

Viswanathan, Guari, 14

Wagner, Bryan, 76, 154n11

Wagner, Roy, 157n51

Wallis, Henry, 120–21, 121*f*, 122

Wanderer Above the Sea of Fog, The (Friedrich), 3

War on Drugs, 127. See also Denzel Curry; drug use; Kurt Cobain

Washington, Mary Helen, 153n84

water imagery, 73–96; Equiano on, 76–82; Keats and, 92–96

Wedgwood, Josiah, 144n68

Weheliye, Alexander, 17, 24–26, 44, 8

Werther effect, 5–6, 124, 132n15, 162n41

West, Raphael Lamar, 120–22

the west, 17, 76; term, 137n69

West African peoples, and suicide, 40

Westbrook family, 99. See also Harriet Shelley

Westmacott, Richard the younger, 67

Wheatley, Phillis, 56, 90, 95–96

White, Floyd, 80

white male individualism, 5, 14, 113, 123. See also bourgeois white male individualism

whiteness, 18; Andrews on, 136n63; Duras on, 59–60; *The Dying Negro* on, 42–43; *Frankenstein* on, 115; Hemans and, 64–68; Hume and, 8; romanticism and, 13–14; term, 14–15

white supremacy: and liberal feminism, 47–59, 69, 147n4, 149n42; and patriarchy, 54–64

white women: and patriarchy, 49,

53–54; and rights, 6–7, 18, 20, 48–69, 71, 78; and sensibility, 50; and white supremacy, 47–69. *See also* Duras; Hemans; Robinson; Wollstonecraft
Wilde, Oscar, 122
Wilderson, Frank B., III, 4, 9–11, 24, 37, 64, 82, 115–16, 128, 137n69. *See also* Afropessimism
Williams, Carolyn, 100
Williams, Robin, 119
Wind, Astrid, 66
Wolfson, Susan, 64
Wollstonecraft, Mary, 21, 47–71, 99–100, 110

women. *See* black women; gender; white women
Wood, Marcus, 34–35, 37
Wordsworth, William, 119
Wrongs of Woman, or Maria, The (Wollstonecraft), 50–51
Wynter, Sylvia, 8

Yoruba, and suicide, 40
Young, Elizabeth, 114
Young, Jason R., 156n32
Youngquist, Paul, 14, 16, 76

Zong Massacre, 74–75
Žižek, Slavoj, 89

www.ingramcontent.com/pod-product-compliance
Lightning Source LLC
Chambersburg PA
CBHW020332240426
43665CB00043B/451